The Legal Guide
for Canadian Churches

The Legal Guide
for Canadian Churches

DAVID BLAIKIE AND DIANA GINN

NOVALIS

Cover design and layout: Dominique Pelland
Cover images: Jupiter Images (photos.com)

Business Offices:
Novalis Publishing Inc.
10 Lower Spadina Avenue, Suite 400
Toronto, Ontario, Canada
M5V 2Z2

Novalis Publishing Inc.
4475 Frontenac Street
Montréal, Québec, Canada
H2H 2S2

Phone: 1-800-387-7164
Fax: 1-800-204-4140
E-mail: books@novalis.ca
www.novalis.ca

Library and Archives Canada Cataloguing in Publication
Blaikie, David
    The legal guide for Canadian churches / David Blaikie and
Diana Ginn.

Includes bibliographical references and index.
ISBN-13: 978-2-89507-798-5
ISBN-10: 2-89507-798-3

    1. Clergy–Legal status, laws, etc–Canada. 2. Church management–
Law and legislation–Canada. I. Ginn, Diana Edith II. Title.

KE4502.B58 2006   340.02'42   C2006-904534-8

This book is not intended to replace legal advice.

Printed in Canada.

We acknowledge the financial support of the Government of Canada through the Book Publishing Industry Development Program (BPIDP) for our publishing activities.

5   4   3   2   1   10   09   08   07   06

For my daughters, Laura and Kathryn,

and in memory of their grandfather, Rev. L. E. Blaikie

D. L. B.

For my husband, Malcolm Boyle,

and our children, Katherine, John and Rachel

D. G.

Contents

Foreword

What do Canadian churches need to know about the law? Plenty, because churches are functioning in a commercial society, doing business, entering into contracts, managing property and, through their employees, engaging in all sorts of interpersonal relationships that are rife with potential civil liability.

This book does not purport to hold all of the answers. The authors expressly advise the reader to consult a lawyer skilled in the applicable area of the law when a real problem unfolds for a church.

The authors provide an excellent primer on the impact of the law on religious denominations – their members and employees – in the common-law provinces of Canada. It is an explanation of the civil law as it has developed through court decisions, as modified and supplemented by statutory laws. *The Legal Guide for Canadian Churches* is not a survey of the ecclesiastical courts of the various denominations, but rather an explanation of how church courts must meet the requirements of human rights codes and administrative law requiring due process and fairness.

In the process of providing guidance to Canadian churches on legal matters, David Blaikie and Diana Ginn have necessarily cast a broad overview of the legal system as it functions in common-law jurisdictions. The review is stated in clear, compact language that accurately sets forth the main elements of the law. It will hold the interest of the reader whether he or she is concerned about the impact of the law on churches, or is simply curious about the legal system in general.

The text of this book is not, however, exclusively about the law. For example, the chapter on risk assessment is a practical guide for any organization or corporation – church or otherwise – with some commonsense suggestions for protecting against a variety of potential risks or purchasing insurance for that purpose.

There is also a chapter dealing with alternative dispute resolution, or ADR. Some disputes are best resolved through intelligent negotiation of a settlement, or by mediation or arbitration. Common sense tells us to explore these possibilities as alternatives to the cost and time of litigating a dispute through the courts.

Whether ADR becomes the chosen path may depend in large measure on the soundness of the claim, or the validity of the defence, as the case may be. The authors provide a brisk and accurate outline of the law of contract, tort, and trust law, which will help the potential plaintiff or defendant make an interim assessment of the potential litigation – until a qualified legal advisor affirms that assessment.

Not every issue is neatly packaged. The chapter dealing with employee–employer relationships deals with (among other matters) the vexing question of whether a priest or minister is an employee, or whether the appointment is of a spiritual nature, excluding it from the ambit of secular law. The question remains unresolved, for it would seem that for certain purposes the cleric will be regarded as an employee, while in other circumstances the answer will be different.

The basic theme, however, is that common sense prevails. Under close examination, the law itself – the combination of federal, provincial and territorial statutes coupled with the development of case law in the areas ungoverned by statutory rules – makes a great deal of common sense. Church corporations, congregations and employees will avoid legal entanglements by exercising that same common sense in their day-to-day activities.

The Honourable Mr. Justice Charles R. Huband
Winnipeg, Manitoba
August 2006

Preface

The precepts of the law are these: to live honourably,
not to injure another, to give each his due.
—Justinian, Emperor of Rome, 527–565, *Institutes*

This book provides an overview of a number of legal issues that may be of interest to those working in churches – clergy, lay people or volunteers. There is a wealth of legal writing on the various topics that we discuss here, but very little of it, at least in a Canadian context, is written with a lay (i.e. non-lawyer) audience in mind.[1]

We hope that a grounding in some basic legal concepts, and in their practical implications, will help church decision makers avoid potential pitfalls and also ensure they fulfill their legal duties and responsibilities. Thus, for example, an awareness of what the duty of fairness encompasses may enable church committees, boards and courts to structure their decision-making processes so as to avoid allegations of procedural irregularity (see Chapter 3). A working knowledge of the law on vicarious liability may provide church decision makers with an appreciation of their potential liability for the actions of employees or volunteers, and lead to the drafting of appropriate policies (see Chapters 5 and 9). An introduction to the case law on wrongful dismissal may help churches deal more effectively with problem employees, and also give employees an awareness of their rights (see Chapter 15).

If this book helps prevent legal issues from turning into legal problems, we will have achieved our primary purpose. However, we know that even with the best planning and intentions, things can go awry. Therefore, a theme that runs throughout each chapter (sometimes explicitly, sometimes implicitly) is the wisdom of seeking legal advice early, before issues become problems or disputes. When issues do arise, it is usually less costly in the long run, in terms of both financial and human resources, to consult a lawyer promptly to get a clear view of the situation, rather than wandering unaware into a legal quagmire.

As lawyers trained in the common-law tradition, we have limited our focus to the common-law jurisdictions within Canada; this encompasses all the provinces and territories except Quebec. An attempt to include the law of Quebec could make some chapters unwieldy and is, in any event, a task better undertaken by an author trained in the civil law. (For further discussion on what is meant by common-law jurisdictions or civil law, see Chapter 22.)

While the legal principles that we discuss in this book are also relevant to other religions, we have limited our discussion of the application of those principles to the Christian church, since this is the context with which we are familiar. David Blaikie is a member of the Presbyterian Church in Canada;

Diana Ginn is a member of the United Church of Canada. Perhaps others will adopt our approach and apply it to other faith traditions.

We are grateful to colleagues, friends and family who gave generously of their time to read all or portions of various drafts of this book and who provided helpful comments and insights, including Judge Jamie S. Campbell of the Nova Scotia Provincial Court; professors Dawn Russell, QC, and A. Wayne MacKay, CM, of Dalhousie Law School; the Rev. Dr. Susan McAlpine-Gillis, minister of the United Church of Canada; the Rev. Douglas E. Blaikie, minister of the Presbyterian Church in Canada; Cynthia Gunn, legal counsel to the United Church of Canada; Malcolm Boyle, partner in the law firm of McInnes Cooper; and Alan C. MacLean, partner in the law firm of Patterson Law.

We would like to thank four law students who did diligent research tracking down material and providing helpful assistance in a variety of ways: Cory Binderup, Sharon French, Chris MacIntyre and Andrew Sowerby. Each was a pleasure to work with, and we wish them well in their legal careers. We also gratefully acknowledge research funding provided by Dalhousie Law School, and the secretarial assistance of Tiffany Coolen-Jewers.

We make the point throughout the book that the demands of the secular law can be met with the right mix of common sense, reasonable care and appropriate planning and, where necessary, consultation with a lawyer. It may also be helpful to consider that the overarching goal of the secular law coincides with the aim and mission of the Christian church. Both seek to realize the vision of a just society, a society in which all citizens live in harmony, peace and joy.[2] While Canadian law is not based on Christian principles or teachings, those teachings have, to some extent, informed our society's view of what is just, fair and reasonable.[3] Acting in accordance with Christian principles, such as respect and concern for others, will take a church a long way toward complying with the secular law and reaching the shared vision of a just society.

David Blaikie and Diana Ginn
Halifax, Nova Scotia
July 2006

Notes

[1]   Our intention here is to provide an overview, coupled with practical advice. Those who wish to delve into issues of churches and the law in greater depth can find excellent discussion and analysis in a number of Canadian works. Pre-eminent among these are the writings of Professor M. H. Ogilvie and Terrance S. Carter, many of which are referenced throughout this book.

[2]   This important insight was drawn to our attention by one of the book's reviewers, Judge Jamie S. Campbell.

[3]   See the writings of Harold J. Berman, including *Faith and Order: The Reconciliation of Law and Religion* (Atlanta: Scholars Press, 1993); *Law and Revolution: The Formation of the Western Legal Tradition* (Cambridge: Harvard University Press, 1983).

Introduction:

How to Use This Book

It is hard to say whether the doctors of law or of divinity
have made greater advances in the lucrative business of mystery.
—attributed to Samuel Goldwyn,
American movie producer, 1882–1974

L awyers are often criticized for their lack of clarity (the
law has its own jargon and lawyers make subtle and
seemingly odd arguments), although Mr. Goldwyn puts
us in good company on that point. Lawyers are also renowned
for their perceived inability to give an unqualified and firm answer to a question. A lawyer's response to a question about the
law is often "it depends," and what "it depends on" is usually
the facts. It is impossible to state the law accurately without
knowing all the relevant facts of a particular issue or problem.
Moreover, to do so would be professional negligence, and so
lawyers, when they do not have a command of all the facts,
seek refuge in generalities, much to the frustration of clients.

We have tried to address these challenges in several ways. In most parts of the book, the connection between the law and the practical steps required to ensure compliance is made explicit. Some chapters, such as those on negligence (Chapter 11) or defamation (Chapter 12), although general in scope, impart important practical information. Just understanding, for example, the broad outlines of the tort of defamation will suggest practical ways for a church to order its affairs to avoid liability. In other chapters – those on church decision making (Chapter 3) and human rights (Chapter 16), to name two – we provide more detailed advice and practical steps that churches may take to help ensure that they meet the requirements of the secular law. Throughout the book, we illustrate legal principles by describing, whenever possible, real cases in which the principles were applied. As well, each chapter ends with a series of questions and answers. We thought this might be useful in at least two ways. It gives the reader a quick overview of most of the material the chapter covers, and the question-and-answer format provides an opportunity for us to give answers that are as clear, simple and concrete as possible.

It remains true, nevertheless, that neither this book nor any book on the law can provide ready-made answers to particular, fact-specific problems and issues. It is never as simple as looking up "the answer." What this book can do, and we hope it does, is provide a framework for recognizing and understanding legal issues generally and give some direction about matters a church should consider as it works to order its affairs in compliance with the law.

Books on the law are rarely read cover to cover by anyone (at least at one sitting). Most readers, we expect, will consult this book with specific questions in mind or to gain needed background in a particular area. That said, most of the chapters are brief, so it will not take long to read large portions of the book at one time.

The book is divided into five parts: Governance and Decision Making, Civil Liability, Employment, Property, and Canadian Law Background.

Part I, Governance and Decision Making, describes the implications of church structure for decision making, liability, and the ownership and control of property. It then outlines the duties of those involved in church decision making, whatever the organizational structure. Also discussed is how to resolve disputes, an integral part of governance. An important duty of church leaders is to establish policies and procedures, and the final chapter in Part I gives some guidance about the content and drafting of same.

Part II, Civil Liability, begins with an overview of the different areas of potential liability, a description of the court structure and the process of a lawsuit. The main focus of the remaining chapters is on specific areas of potential liability, such as negligence and defamation. It concludes with a discussion of religious communication privilege, an issue that arises in the context of a lawsuit.

Part III, Employment, discusses employment issues that may arise within a church setting and suggests ways to avoid potential difficulties. In addition, the law on human rights and its implications for employers and employees are discussed. Part III ends with an exploration of privacy and confidentiality, two issues that are prominent in the employment context.

Part IV, Property, gives an overview of some of the property-related issues in the life of a church and deals with such matters as the law of trusts, trespass and copyright. It concludes with a discussion of two property-related torts, occupiers' liability and nuisance.

Part V, Canadian Law Background, provides the reader with an introduction to the sources of Canadian law: the Constitution, legislation and the common law. Some readers may choose to begin with this section; others may turn to it as needed to understand earlier parts of the book.

At the back of the book, the reader will find a glossary of legal terms, a guide to understanding legal citation and finding cases, a selected bibliography and, last but not least, an index.

A note about a few of the terms used in the book. We have tried to find terms that apply across denominations; for this reason, we use the words *clergy* and *cleric*. Also, when we use the word *court*, we are always referring to a secular court rather than a church court. When we refer to a church court, we make that explicit.

Part I:

Governance and Decision Making

Part I encompasses chapters on church structure, governance and decision making, alternative dispute resolution, and the development of church policies and procedures aimed at preventing harm and reducing risk. These chapters are connected by a focus on how churches go about the work of governing themselves and ordering their affairs.

Chapter 1, on church structure, asks the fundamental question of who has decision-making authority within the church. To answer this question, we outline three structural models (episcopal, presbyterian and congregational) that churches use to allocate the authority to make decisions. Chapter 1 also looks at the difference between a corporation and an unincorporated association. There is a great deal that we do not touch on in terms of the nuts and bolts of structuring a church as a corporation. For instance, we do not, except in the briefest of ways, set out the process to follow to form a corporation. We do not discuss the law on operational requirements such as corporate or association by-laws; requirements for record keeping; financial reporting and holding of meetings; the rights of members to vote, attend meetings and receive information; or taxation. There are excellent resources available for those who wish to delve into these areas.[1] These matters are sufficiently complex that when specific issues arise, church decision makers will probably need advice from a lawyer, accountant or other qualified professional.

Lastly, Chapter 1 introduces the concept of trusts. When church property is held in trust (and this is frequently the case), decisions regarding the use of that property must abide by the terms of the trust. Thus, the existence of a trust may affect the kinds of decisions that can be made with regard to a particular piece of church property.

Chapter 2, on governance, builds on the concepts introduced in Chapter 1 and outlines the duties of those involved in the governance of the church. Two key duties (the duty of care and the duty of loyalty) apply, whatever the structure of the church, whether the church is incorporated or not, and whether or not property is held in trust. This chapter also discusses the extent to which the members of a governing body may be held personally liable for decisions taken by the governing body. The chapter closes by setting out the key tasks of effective governance.

While Chapters 1 and 2 focus on the authority and responsibilities of decision makers within the church, Chapter 3 looks at *how* decisions should be made. This chapter explores the following questions: What kinds of procedures should church boards, committees and courts follow in order to be seen as acting fairly? When a person affected by a church decision thinks that the church failed to follow the proper process or thinks that the outcome itself is wrong, can he or she challenge the decision in the courts?

Chapter 4, on alternative dispute resolution, recognizes that, even within the church, conflicts will sometimes arise. This chapter outlines three methods (negotiation, mediation and arbitration) by which disputes may be resolved without resort to litigation. These approaches to dispute resolution may help those within a church to find creative ways to resolve disputes and to repair relationships that have been ruptured by conflict.

Part I concludes with Chapter 5, which discusses various policies and procedures that churches should have in place. This chapter's focus on preventing harm and reducing risk ties to the earlier discussion on governance, since one of the key duties of church leaders is to establish and implement policies and procedures that identify and control risks and so reduce the possibility of causing harm. Having such policies and procedures in place also reduces the likelihood of conflict within a church and in a church's relationship with others. Chapter 5 also discusses a few methods of transferring risk, the most common being insurance. It concludes with advice on how to choose a lawyer, one of several experts who can help a church deal with risk.

Notes

[1]   In particular, see the writings of Donald J. Bourgeois and Terrance S. Carter. The list of topics set out in this paragraph is derived from the table of contents in Donald J. Bourgeois, *The Law of Charitable and Not-for-Profit Organizations*, 3rd ed. (Markham, Ont.: Butterworths, 2002).

1

Church Structure

By wisdom a house is built,
and by understanding it is established.
—Proverbs 24:3 (NRSV)

Sometimes when a church is involved in decision making, it isn't just a question of asking, "What is the best course of action?" Sometimes it may also be necessary to ask, "What body within the church has the authority to make this particular decision?" "Who would bear legal responsibility if the decision led to harmful consequences?" And, if the decision relates to property, "Are there limits on the kinds of decisions we can make regarding this particular piece of property?" Suppose that, in response to falling numbers, a congregation decides to amalgamate with a neighbouring congregation and sell its current church building. Even though the congregation knows what course of action it wishes to take, it may still have to ask, "Do we have the authority to make these decisions, or do we have to go to some higher body within the church?" "Is the church building held by way of trust, the terms of which limit how the property can be dealt with?" "What if, as a result of layoffs arising from the amalgamation, an employee alleged wrongful dismissal? Who within the church could be sued?" These are the kind of questions that we address in this chapter, since the way in which a church is structured reflects who, within the church, has decision-making authority and who bears liability.

This chapter opens by outlining three models of church structure: episcopal, presbyterian and congregational.[1] Next, it describes the differences between a corporation and an unincorporated association – a distinction that determines who will be held liable for decisions that cause harm to others. Third, this chapter introduces the concept of property being held by way of a trust. Trust property must be dealt with in certain ways, which places limits on the kinds of decisions that can be made regarding such property. This chapter and Chapter 2 are very much companion pieces and should be read together.

Decision-making structure

The term *church governance* (or *church polity*) is used to describe the way a church is organized and its decision-making structure. At its most basic level, church governance centres on who holds decision-making authority. Many denominations have a handbook or manual that sets out the authority of various bodies or offices within their church.[2] Also, some denominations have developed excellent websites that provide information on a range of topics, including the way the denomination is structured. What follows here is a brief overview of three forms of church governance:

- episcopal (government by bishops);

- presbyterian (government by representative courts); and

- congregational (government by independent congregations).

Episcopal

In simplest terms, an episcopalian church is a church that has bishops; for example, the Roman Catholic, Anglican and Orthodox churches.

The Roman Catholic Church is divided into geographical and jurisdictional units called dioceses. Each diocese is administered by a bishop, who is also responsible for its religious welfare and pastoral governance. Thus, authority for matters relating to the diocese resides not in an assembly or council, but in "the single personality" of the person appointed to the office of bishop.[3] Roman Catholic bishops are "appointed for the government of one portion of the faithful of the Church," under the direction of the Bishop of Rome (the Pope), who is the Supreme Head of the Church.[4] The Pope has "jurisdiction over the faithful, and ... supreme authority to define in all questions of faith and morals."[5] The exercise of papal primacy does not occur in a vacuum; for instance, the Pope may consult with bishops through synods, which are "ecclesiastical gatherings ... for the discussion and decision of matters relating to faith, morals or discipline."[6]

The Anglican Church is also organized around dioceses, headed by bishops. In the Anglican Church of Canada, the levels of organization are the parish, diocese, provincial synod and General Synod. The General Synod of the Anglican Church of Canada is comprised of bishops, priests and laity from each of the 30 dioceses in Canada.

Presbyterian

Presbyterian church structure is characterized by a hierarchy of church courts moving from the congregational to the national level. Authority resides in these courts, which are made up of lay and ordained representatives, rather than in a particular office or in the individual congregations.

This form of church government was first used by the Church of Scotland. The two main examples of presbyterianism in Canada are the Presbyterian Church in Canada and the United Church of Canada.

The governance structure of the Presbyterian Church in Canada is set out in the *Book of Forms*. Individual congregations are governed by session, which is made up of the minister or ministers and the elders of that congregation. Lay and ordained representatives from each congregation form the presbytery, the next level of church court. Presbytery deals with regional matters, as well as issues relating to preaching, the administration of the sacraments and the use of church property. Groups of presbyteries are organized into synods, which deal with matters coming from session and presbytery. The highest church court is the General Assembly of the Presbyterian Church in Canada.

The structure of the United Church of Canada is very similar, although different names are assigned to the two highest courts. In the United Church, these are referred to as Conference and General Council. Each of the courts of the United Church of Canada is made up of equal numbers of lay and ordained members.

Congregational

With congregational church structure, each congregation is an independent, autonomous body. Congregationalist churches developed from the theory that a congregation should be able to make its own decisions "without pope, prelate, presbytery, prince or parliament."[7] Congregationalism is the least hierarchical of the three church structures described here.

Congregationalist churches may choose to associate with other like-minded congregations; however, in a truly congregationalist system, these associations do not have binding decision-making authority. Even when the association has the power to pass resolutions, these are not binding on the individual congregations.

In Canada, the Baptist Church is an example of this kind of church structure. Each congregation makes its own decisions about church membership, whom to call as a pastor and all other matters relating to the congregation. Most local churches do associate with other Baptist congregations to work toward common goals.

The effect of incorporation

A church can exist as either an unincorporated association or a corporation. If a group of individuals come together to worship and carry on other church-related activities, the group will exist as an unincorporated association unless the members take steps to incorporate. What follows is a general introduction to the difference between a corporation and an unincorporated association, particularly regarding who would be held liable if the church were sued. A lawyer should certainly be consulted when a congregation is in the process of deciding whether to incorporate, or when a congregation needs detailed information about how its current structure affects such things as decision making, liability and property ownership.

Incorporation

A corporation is defined as follows:

> A legal entity, allowed by legislation, which permits a group of people, as shareholders (for-profit companies) or members (non-profit companies), to create an organization, which can then focus on pursuing set objectives, and empowered with legal rights which are usually only reserved for individuals, such as to sue and be sued, own property, hire employees or loan and borrow money.[8]

The law allows an individual or group of individuals to incorporate. A church might be incorporated under a number of different kinds of statutes:

- Incorporation by way of letters patent under a statute dealing with corporations generally. The individuals who wish to incorporate must submit the requisite documents and meet the prescribed criteria, as set out in the legislation. If the application is successful, letters patent will be issued. (Letters patent is a general term for a government document that grants a right or privilege; in the context of incorporation, the letters patent grant the applicants the right to incorporate.)

- Incorporation under a statute dealing with religious or charitable corporations. Some provinces and territories have legislation that provides for the incorporation of charitable corporations generally, or religious corporations specifically. An example of this is the Alberta *Religious Societies' Land Act*.

- Incorporation by way of a special statute whose sole purpose is the creation of a particular church corporation.

Different entities within a church may be incorporated for different purposes. For instance, in the Anglican and Roman Catholic churches, it is common to have statutes that incorporate the office of the bishop and the diocese, and vest the corporation with title to church property within the diocese. It is also possible to have incorporation occur at the congregational or community level. For instance, individual congregations within the Evangelical Lutheran Church are usually incorporated, and in the Mennonite and Amish traditions, a "colony corporation" may be formed to hold land communally.[9] In some situations, a church may form additional corporations for particular purposes, such as to hold and direct the use of money for a building fund, to own property to be used for a convent, or to deal with funds set aside to compensate residential school claimants.

The most important thing to remember about a corporation is that, in the eyes of the law, it is a legal person, separate from the directors, officers and members. To give an example, let us imagine that Mary Smith wishes to open a corner store. She could choose to do this without incorporating, in which case Mary herself would rent or own the store premises, own the inventory and be the employer of anyone hired to work in the store. On the other hand, Mary could decide to incorporate a company called Fine Foods Ltd. Once the corporation is formed, then Fine Foods Ltd., not Mary, is recognized in law as the entity that rents or owns the premises, owns the inventory, and employs anyone working in the store. Similarly, when a new church is established, the members may decide to exist as an unincorporated association (discussed below), or they may decide to incorporate. When a corporation is formed, then the corporation, not the individual members of the congregation, owns the church building and employs the staff. Furthermore, the church corporation continues to exist, even as the membership of the congregation changes.

The separate identity of a corporation has significant legal consequences. As a legal person, a corporation can enter into contracts, buy and sell land, have its own bank accounts, and sue and be sued in its own name. When an individual feels that he or she has been wronged by the corporation (for instance, the corporation has broken a contract or has acted in a negligent way that caused harm), in most cases that individual may sue only the corporation itself, not the individual officers or directors of the corporation. If the individual is successful in the lawsuit and the corporation is ordered to pay damages (i.e. money), the general rule is that the corporation pays these damages out of its assets; in other words, the officers and directors are not required to pay out of their personal assets.

This is the principle of limited liability, which is one of the key characteristics of a corporation. In this way, a corporation provides significant protection from personal liability. Directors of a church corporation will not be held personally liable for anything the corporation does, unless the directors breach their duties of loyalty and care or fail to ensure corporate compliance with certain laws (see Chapter 2). It is rare for directors of a corporation to be found personally liable.

As a separate legal entity, a corporation may even be found criminally liable. When a criminal offence is committed by an individual within a corporation who can be described as the "directing mind" (that is, a senior officer or employee who has a significant say in the policy or operations of the corporation), the corporation itself may be found guilty of a criminal offence.

Unincorporated association

The term *unincorporated association* is used to describe a group of individuals who have entered into an agreement "which articulates their common purpose, establishes an organization to achieve that common purpose and sets out how that organization is to be operated to achieve that purpose"[10] but who have not formed a corporation. Examples of unincorporated associations include sports organizations, social clubs, trade unions, employer organizations, community service organizations, charitable organizations and churches. Of course, groups such as these could decide to incorporate, but if they have not done so, they exist as unincorporated associations.

The chief difference between a corporation and an unincorporated association is that the latter is not seen as a separate legal entity, and so the members of an unincorporated association do not enjoy the protection of limited liability. One expert in church law has noted the following:

> Although many churches within the mainline denominations, such as the United Church of Canada, the Anglican Church, and the Catholic Church, already work within the established corporate structure, there are in excess of 3,000 independent churches (source: Canadian Council of Christian Charities) which are autonomous from the direct control of a central denomination and have existed for years, if not decades, as unincorporated associations of individuals subject to all the inherent risks that are associated with that form of organization.[11]

When an unincorporated association is formed, this creates a legal relationship among its members, rather than creating a separate legal entity, as is the case with a corporation. Because an unincorporated association has no legal existence apart from its directors and members, the association itself may not hold property, enter into contracts or sue. These things must be done by individuals on behalf of the association. Directors and members may be held personally liable for the acts of the unincorporated association. Their liability is not limited. For example, directors of an unincorporated association who sign a contract may be personally liable when it is breached. A member of an unincorporated association who takes part in decision making may also be found personally liable for the outcomes of those decisions. If a director or member is found personally liable, he or she would be required to pay, out of his or her own personal assets, any damages ordered by the court.[12]

Trust

A trust is not, strictly speaking, an organizational structure. It is instead one way to hold property (see also Chapter 19). It is not unusual, however, to see trusts discussed in the context of organizational and decision-making structure, because the existence of a trust can have a significant impact on decisions made by an organization. Whether a church is episcopal, presbyterian or congregational in structure, and whether or not the church is incorporated, the duties of the trustee and the requirement to adhere to the terms of the trust remain the same. These duties and requirements will limit the kinds of decisions that can be made regarding property held by way of trust.

Trust law is large and complex; in its simplest form, how-ever, a trust exists when one person (or a group of people) holds property for the benefit of others. The person in whose name the property is held is called the trustee. The people who are entitled to benefit from the property are called the beneficiaries. To use an everyday example of a trust, parents might state in their wills that if they both die while their chil-dren are young, any property left by the parents is to be held by a family member in trust for the children until they reach a given age. If the will came into effect, the family member would hold the property as a trustee, for the benefit of the children (the beneficiaries).

In order for a trust to be created, the intention to do so must be clear; the property that is to be covered by the trust must be clearly identified; and the beneficiaries must be "readily apparent or ascertainable by name or class description."[13] Trusts are usually created by way of written documents. It is not unusual to see a trust set out in a will, but it is also possible to create a trust during one's lifetime.

When the trust is a charitable one, the trust simply sets out the charitable purposes for which the property is to be used, rather than identifying the beneficiaries. For instance, someone might, in their will, leave money to a university, stating that it is to be used to provide scholarships for students from a particular province, based on a combination of academic merit and financial need. Or, in the church context, a member of the congregation might, by will, leave money to be held in trust and used for "Christian camping."

Trusts are frequently used in the church setting. Even when a congregation or other church entity has incorporated, and so can own property in its own right, it may still use trusts to hold money for some specific purpose. Where a congregation operates as an unincorporated association, it is usual for trustees to be appointed to hold all church property on behalf of the congregation. Nova Scotia, Ontario, Manitoba, Saskatchewan, Alberta, British Columbia, Northwest Territories and Nunavut have legislation that allows trustees of unincorporated religious bodies to hold land. One of the advantages conferred by such legislation is that the trustees are deemed to have perpetual succession – that is, when some individuals cease to be trustees and new ones are appointed, the church property does not have to be conveyed from one set of trustees to the next. Without such legislation, trustees of an unincorporated congregation could still hold property, but the congregation would not have the benefit of perpetual succession.

Although, in law, the trustee is seen as an owner of the property, it is a very particular type of ownership, bound by strict rules. Some of the fundamental rules of trust law include the following:

- The trustee must at all times be diligent and honest in dealing with the trust property;

- The trustee must be aware of, and strictly adhere to, any terms expressly or impliedly set out in the document creating the trust (see Chapter 19 for further discussion of express and implied trusts); and

- The trustee must deal with the property so that it benefits the beneficiary, not the trustee, and must avoid any conflict of interest. In a church setting, a congregation may select trustees to manage church property for the benefit of the congregation. Since the trustees are themselves members of the congregation, they receive the same benefits as any other member, but they must not deal with the property in ways intended to give themselves greater personal benefit. (Chapter 13 discusses fiduciaries, who must also act in the best interests of others. Fiduciary is a broader term than trustee, and fiduciary duties can exist in relationships where there is no property being held on behalf of others.)

Liability for the improper use of trust property depends on who has decision-making authority. If the trustees have the authority to act independently, the trustees will be held liable for any misuse of trust property. If the trustees only act under the direction of others within the church, then the individuals giving the direction bear the legal responsibility.

Conclusion

This chapter addresses decision-making authority and liability within the church by looking at church structure (who holds decision-making authority within the church); the effect of incorporation (how liability is allocated in corporations and in unincorporated associations); and trusts (how the existence of a trust may affect the kinds of decisions that can be made regarding trust property). This chapter should be read in conjunction with Chapter 2, which focuses on the duties of a church's governing body.

Church Structure: Questions and Answers

Q. What do the terms *church structure, church governance* or *church polity* mean?

A. These terms refer to the form of church government.

Q. What does the term *incorporation* mean?

A. Incorporation happens when an organization or group becomes a separate, artificial "person" under the law. It is as if the organization becomes a living, breathing person for the purposes of owning property, entering into contracts and assuming liability, among other things.

Q. **How does a church incorporate?**

A. A church may incorporate in a number of ways, including under legislation dealing generally with corporations, under legislation pertaining to charitable or religious organizations, or under legislation whose sole purpose is to create a particular religious corporation.

Q. **When a church is incorporated, are the officers and directors of the corporation held personally liable for the actions of the corporation?**

A. No. In law, a corporation is seen as a separate person, distinct from its officers or directors. Therefore, damages ordered by a court are paid out of the corporation's assets, not the personal assets of the officers and directors. There are, however, some very limited exceptions to this rule that are discussed in Chapter 2.

Q. **What is an unincorporated association?**

A. An unincorporated association is an organization of people who have a common purpose and who are seen to have entered into an agreement about the way that purpose is to be achieved. Examples include sports organizations, social clubs and community service organizations, as well as some churches.

Q. May the members of an unincorporated association be held liable for the acts of the association?

A. Yes, members who are involved in directing the operations of an association may be held liable when the association acts negligently or breaches a contract, and they may be required to pay damages out of their own personal assets.

Q. What is a trust?

A. A trust is not an organizational structure, but rather a way of holding property. Church property may be held in a trust, which is overseen by one or more trustees. Trustees must follow the terms of the trust and look after the property for the benefit of the beneficiary, not for their own benefit.

Q. What is required to create a trust?

A. To create a trust, the intention to do so must be clear, the property covered by the trust must be clearly identified, and the beneficiaries must be readily apparent or ascertainable. Trusts are usually created in written documents.

Notes

[1]   Churches are sometimes described as being part of the voluntary sector, a category that includes non-profit and charitable organizations. A recent report describes the key characteristics of a voluntary sector organization: the work of the organization provides a public benefit, it relies on volunteers in its governance structure, it receives financial support from individuals and the government has little direct influence on it, except with regard to tax status. Churches are also described as non-profit organizations; this is a very broad term, including

> almost every type of voluntary organization, charity, church, trade and professional association and advocacy organizations. ...

> Non-profit organizations enjoy special tax exemptions, which they gain by fulfilling the requirements of the *Income Tax Act*. They enjoy this status unless and until Revenue Canada determines that they are not non-profit in nature according to the terms of the *Act*. ...

> A subset of non-profits, the charitable sector, is the narrowest concept. It usually refers to those organizations that are registered under the *Income Tax Act* as meeting a set of criteria, which exempts them from income taxes and permits them to provide receipts for donations that can be claimed as tax credits.

See Panel on Accountability and Governance in the Voluntary Sector, *Building on Strength: Improving Governance and Accountability in Canada's Voluntary Sector* (www.vsr-trsb.net/pagvs/Book.pdf), pp. 7–8.

[2]   For instance, see the following, available through the denominations' websites:
*   Anglican Church of Canada (www.anglican.ca):
    Handbook of the General Synod of the Anglican Church of Canada;
*   Fellowship of Evangelical Baptist Churches in Canada
    (www.fellowship.ca): *The Board Chairman's Handbook*, 2005;
*   Presbyterian Church in Canada (www.presbyterian.ca):
    Book of Forms;
*   Roman Catholic Church (www.cccb.ca):
    The Codes of Canon Law;

- United Church of Canada (www.united-church.ca):
  The Manual.

3   *Catholic Encyclopedia,* s.v. "bishop" (www.newadvent.org).

4   *Ibid.*

5   *Ibid.,* s.v. "Pope."

6   *Ibid.,* s.v. "synod."

7   *Ibid.,* s.v. "congregationalism."

8   *Duhaime's Online Legal Dictionary,* s.v. "company"
    (www.duhaime.org).

9   Alvin Esau, *Law and Property: The Establishment and Preservation of
    Mennonite Semi-Communalism and Hutterite Communalism in North
    America: 1870–1925* (www.colonialpropertycolloq.law.uvic.ca).

10 Donald J. Bourgeois, *The Law of Charitable and Not-for-Profit Organiza-
    tions,* 3rd ed. (Markham, Ont.: Butterworths, 2002), p. 40 [*Bourgeois*].

11 Terrance S. Carter, "To Be or Not to Be: Incorporation Issues for Chari-
    ties with an Emphasis on Autonomous Churches" in *Fit to be Tithed:
    Risks and Rewards for Charities and Churches* (Toronto: Law Society of
    Upper Canada, 1994), p. A-1.

12 See generally *Bourgeois,* note 10, and Robert Flannigan, "The Liability
    Structure of Nonprofit Associations: Tort and Fiduciary Liability
    Assignments" (1998) 77 *Canadian Bar Review* 73, p. 75.

13 *Bourgeois,* note 10, p. 39. What does "ascertainable by name or class
    description" mean? In the example given above of the parents' wills,
    the wills may say, "All the property that I possess when I die is to be
    held by great-aunt Myrtle in trust for my children Anna, Bob and
    Clara." In that case, the beneficiaries are ascertainable by name, and
    only Anna, Bob and Clara may benefit from the trust. However, to
    provide for the eventuality of more children being born after the will
    was made, the parent may simply state, "All the property that I possess
    when I die is to be held by great-aunt Myrtle in trust for my children."
    In that case, no beneficiaries have been identified by name, but they
    are identified by a class: "my children."

2

Governance

The art of governing consists simply of being honest,
exercising common sense, following principle,
and doing what is right and just.
—Thomas Jefferson, third American president,
1743–1826, *Rights of British North America*

Every church, incorporated or unincorporated, local
church or national body, should be concerned about
and committed to good governance. An important
and valuable report, *Building on Strength: Improving Gover-*
nance and Accountability in Canada's Voluntary Sector, noted
the following:

> Effective governance and accountability begin
> at home: in one's own organization, no matter
> how large or small. Voluntary organizations are
> first and foremost self-governing. An organiza-

tion's leadership has a moral, legal and fiduciary responsibility to its members, constituencies, users and beneficiaries, staff and volunteers, as well as the general public. Specifically, it is responsible for effective governance of the organization.[1]

Whether a particular church has an episcopal, presbyterian or congregationalist structure, and whether the church is incorporated or operates as an unincorporated association (see Chapter 1), each church has a governing body, variously named the board of trustees, board of directors, board of elders or parish council. It is the responsibility of this governing body "to oversee the conduct of the organization's affairs, ensure that an effective team is in place to carry out day-to-day activities, account for its financial and other resources, and ensure that no issue falls between the cracks in steering the organization toward the fulfillment of its mission."[2] In short, the governing body is responsible for managing the affairs of the organization.

A director is a person who is a member of a church's governing body. Directors may also be officers, holding, for example, the position of secretary or treasurer.

Directors and officers owe two basic duties to the church organization, church members, employees, volunteers and the general public who may be affected by their decisions: the duty of care and the duty of loyalty. The duty of care requires directors to act with the competence of a reasonable person and to be diligent in preparing for, attending and participating in meetings of the governing body. The duty of loyalty requires directors to act honestly and in good faith when pursuing the best interests of the organization. Directors may be held personally liable for their failure to fulfill these duties. There are also various statutes that impose personal liability on directors and officers.[3]

This chapter briefly describes the duty of care and the duty of loyalty, the responsibilities imposed by statutes, and the relationship between church structure and the potential personal liability of directors. The chapter ends by setting out eight key tasks that comprise effective board governance.

Duty of care

Directors of a church's governing body are expected to perform their duties with the care, skill and diligence of a reasonably competent or prudent person, with similar education, experience and skills. It is by this standard that their performance is judged. A director is not held to the standard of an expert. However, when a director has expert skills in certain areas, such as law or accounting, he or she may be held to a higher standard. An accountant would be expected to bring to bear a higher level of skill and knowledge with respect to financial matters, for example.

The duty of care requires a director to ensure that appropriate policies and procedures are in place, and to make reasonable enquiries about the day-to-day management of the church.

To fulfill the duty of care, a director must attend meetings of the governing body diligently and be informed about the issues under consideration. When a director does not understand, for example, the financial statements under review, he or she should ask questions and seek additional information.

Asking questions and requiring answers are key elements of the duty of care. A director should not, on any issue, simply defer to the opinion of another director.

Duty of loyalty

The duty of loyalty requires a director to act honestly and in good faith, solely in the interests of the organization. The duty of loyalty is sometimes referred to as a fiduciary duty because it requires that a director subordinate his or her personal interests to the interests of the organization and act solely in the organization's interests. (A fiduciary is a person who, like a trustee discussed in the previous chapter, is obligated to act solely for the benefit and in the interest of another. See Chapter 13.)

The central aspect of the duty of loyalty is the requirement to avoid conflicts of interest. A conflict of interest is any situation in which a person's private interest differs from his or her duties as a director. For example, a church's governing body may be considering hiring an accounting firm. When a director is a member of that accounting firm, he or she will be in a conflict of interest. Or a church board may be considering entering into a contract with a construction company partly owned by a director. A director who has a conflict of interest must disclose the conflict and abstain from participating in the discussion and voting on the issue.

Confidentiality is another aspect of the duty of loyalty. The general rule is that directors must keep confidential all matters discussed at meetings of the church's governing body and any information learned through membership. The governing body must take steps to ensure that appropriate safeguards are in place regarding storing confidential documents. It is also important to establish a clear policy on confidentiality that directors know about and understand. In certain situations, a duty to disclose confidential information arises (see Chapter 18). See also Chapter 17 regarding privacy and personal information.

Personal liability of directors

Directors who breach the duty of care or the duty of loyalty may be personally liable for any harm caused. In other words, in certain situations, directors could be sued as individuals and be obligated to pay an award of damages from their own assets. For example, a director who fails to disclose an interest in a construction contract awarded by the church to his or her company (in breach of the duty of loyalty) may be liable to account to the church organization. Members of a governing body who fail to implement procedures for screening and monitoring staff (in breach of the duty of care) might be sued personally by someone harmed as a result.

Numerous federal and provincial statutes impose personal liability on directors for a failure by an organization to comply with the law.[4] The three most important areas that these laws cover are employment, taxation and the environment.[5]

For example, under provincial employment legislation, directors may be held personally liable for unpaid employee wages and vacation pay. Directors may also be held personally liable for a failure by the organization to remit to the Receiver General for Canada employer and employee contributions to the Canada Pension Plan and Employment Insurance. Provincial health and safety legislation, such as Ontario's *Occupational Health and Safety Act*, requires that directors take all reasonable care to ensure that the organization complies with the *Act* by maintaining a safe workplace. Section 217.1 of the *Criminal Code* imposes criminal liability for serious health and safety violations. It establishes a duty on "[e]very one who undertakes, or has the authority, to direct how another person does work or performs a task … to take reasonable care to prevent bodily harm to that person, or any other person, arising from that work or task" and imposes significant fines, and even imprisonment, upon conviction.

Almost all of these laws provide a due diligence defence (one notable exception is director liability for unpaid employee wages). A defence of due diligence requires showing that a director took reasonable care in the circumstances, which generally involves showing that a system was in place to ensure compliance with the law and that reasonable steps were taken to ensure the system operated effectively. A director who exercised due diligence will not be held personally liable for an organization's failure to comply with a law.

It is important here to underscore the relationship between church structure and the potential personal liability of directors.

As noted in the previous chapter, a church or a unit within a church may be incorporated or may exist as an unincorporated association. A church corporation is a legal entity that exists separate and distinct from its directors and members. Directors of a church corporation will not be held personally liable for any act of the corporation unless they breach their duties of loyalty and care, or fail to ensure corporate compliance with certain laws.[6]

An unincorporated association has no legal existence apart from its directors and members. It may not hold property, enter into contracts, sue or be sued. Directors and members may be held personally liable for the acts of the unincorporated association. Their liability is not limited. For example, directors of an unincorporated association who sign a contract may be personally liable when it is breached.[7] Directors of an unincorporated association may also be held personally liable when they breach their duties of loyalty and care or fail to ensure compliance with certain statutes.

Putting the risk of liability in perspective

The level of risk to directors is often misunderstood. It is becoming difficult to find people to serve as directors, because of a fear of personal liability. We have described a potential risk. Understandably, a reader might conclude that there is a significant risk of personal liability. However, such a conclusion would be incorrect. As a matter of fact, it is rare for directors of a non-profit organization such as a church to be held personally liable. The actual risk of personal liability to directors can be described as very low and should not deter anyone from serving on a church board. The key to eliminating the potential risk of liability is good governance (see also Chapter 5 for other risk-avoidance methods).

The Panel on Accountability and Governance in the Voluntary Sector set out eight tasks of effective board governance:

- steering toward the mission and guiding strategic planning;

- being transparent, which includes communicating to members, stakeholders and the public and making information available upon request;

- developing appropriate structures, such as nominating and audit committees;

- ensuring the board understands its role and avoids conflicts of interest;

- maintaining fiscal responsibility;

- ensuring that an effective management team is in place and overseeing its activities;

- implementing assessment and control systems, which includes a code of ethical conduct and a method to evaluate the board's performance; and

- planning for the succession and diversity of the board.[8]

Conclusion

Churches have significant legal, fiduciary and moral duties to ensure that their "governance mechanisms are up to the task and that accountability is both effective and seen to be effective."[9] Although of great significance, the duties are not onerous. Directors of a church board fulfill their basic duties by exercising the care and diligence of a reasonably competent person and by acting honestly and in good faith, solely in the interests of the church.

Governance: Questions and Answers

Q. What is the role of a church's governing body, variously named the board of directors, board of elders or parish council?

A. It is the responsibility of this governing body to oversee the conduct of the church's affairs.

Q. What is a director?

A. A director is a member of a church's governing body. Directors may also be officers; for example, a treasurer.

Q. What are the two basic duties of a director?

A. Directors have a duty of care and a duty of loyalty. The duty of care requires directors to act with the competence of a reasonable person. The duty of loyalty requires directors to act honestly and in good faith in pursuing the best interests of the church.

Q. What are the key tasks of effective governance?

A. Key tasks include developing appropriate structures, avoiding conflicts of interest and maintaining fiscal responsibility.

Notes

¹ Panel on Accountability and Governance in the Voluntary Sector, *Building on Strength: Improving Governance and Accountability in Canada's Voluntary Sector* (www.vsr-trsb.net/pagvs/book.pdf) [*Building on Strength*].

² *Ibid.*, p. 41.

³ The applicable law regarding a director's duties is found in church rules and by-laws, incorporating legislation, various statutes, and court decisions. See generally, Peter Broder et al., *Primer for Directors of Not-for-Profit Corporations (Rights, Duties and Practices)* (Industry Canada, 2002) [*Broder*]. A pdf version of this book is available at http://strategis.ic.gc.ca. See also, Donald J. Bourgeois, *The Law of Charitable and Not-for Profit Organizations*, 3rd ed. (Markham, Ont.: Butterworths, 2002) [*Bourgeois*]. The standard to which a director is held can vary. For example, directors of a charitable corporation are held to a standard similar to that of a trustee. "Problems arise because the standards vary in different provinces, depending on whether common or statutory law provisions apply, and are different in application to charitable corporations and trusts, and quite unclear for unincorporated associations. Under different statutes higher standards have been applied to the application of care for the fiduciaries of trusts than for those of nonprofit or for-profit corporations." *Building on Strength*, note 1, p. 76. See also *Bourgeois*, pp. 210 and following.

⁴ Most of these statutes apply only to the directors of a corporation.

⁵ See generally, Gowling LaFleur Henderson LLP, *A Study of the Liabilities Facing Directors and Officers of Nonprofit Corporations in Canada* (2001) (http://strategis.ic.gc.ca); *Broder*, note 3, pp. 36 and following; *Bourgeois*, note 3, pp. 238 and following.

⁶ Directors of a corporation are only held personally liable in tort when they "have engaged in some conduct that gives rise to an independent tort on the part of the director. Typically, he or she must have taken some action beyond taking part in decisions made by the board of directors." Carol Hansell, *What Directors Need to Know: Corporate Governance* (Toronto: Carswell, 2003), p. 152. Personal liability in contract could only arise in rare situations, such as when a director of a corporation enters into a contract without proper authorization. See Chapter 6 for a discussion of the basic meaning of contract and tort. In Nova Scotia, legislation called the *Volunteer Protection Act*,

S.N.S. 2002, c. 14, limits the personal liability of volunteers working for non-profit corporations. It states in section 3(1) that no volunteer (which would include a director or officer) doing work on behalf of a non-profit corporation "is liable for damage caused by an act or omission of the volunteer." There are some exceptions, such as when the loss is caused by a volunteer driving a motor vehicle.

[7]   "According to the original English jurisprudence, and subsequent Canadian and American authorities, those members who participate in controlling the affairs of the association [the directors] will be held responsible as principals for contractual obligations. In practice, this usually means that the committee members [the directors] will be liable. However, it is clear that ordinary members will be characterized as principals if they possess rights to participate in managing the undertaking." Robert Flannigan, "The Liability Structure of Nonprofit Associations: Tort and Fiduciary Liability Assignments" (1998) 77 *Canadian Bar Review* 73, p. 75.

[8]   *Building on Strength*, note 1, p. 24. There are good sources of advice and guidance on governance issues. See generally, *Bourgeois*, note 3; *Broder*, note 3; The People's Law School, *Volunteers and the Law: A Guide for Volunteers, Organizations and Boards*, 3rd ed. (www.publiclegaled.bc.ca). Useful articles by Terrance S. Carter and others appear at www.carters. ca; see, for example, Terrance S. Carter, *Due Diligence in Avoiding Risks for Directors of Charities and Not-for-Profits* and *Risk Protection* (2002). Useful resources are also available at Volunteer Canada (www. volunteer.ca).

[9]   *Building on Strength*, note 1, p. ii.

3

Church Decision Making

Common sense often makes good law.
—Justice William Douglas,
Supreme Court of the United States,
Peak v. United States (1957)

I f you spend any time at all in church circles, it is likely that you sit on a committee, board or court within the church. If you do, then of course you want to carry out your duties as fairly and reasonably as you can. Reasonable decisions, fairly arrived at, are more likely to be accepted by the church community. Furthermore, when church decisions are made unfairly or appear to be unreasonable, it is possible that courts may intervene.[1]

This chapter is divided into two parts. The first part focuses on procedures. In this part, we consider the processes that church committees, boards and courts should follow in order to meet the requirements of the secular law regarding fairness in decision making. A person who feels that fair procedures have not been followed may decide to challenge the decision in the courts. Or, to put it another way, that person might seek judicial review on procedural grounds. Judicial review is the term used when a court reviews a decision made by a body such as a tribunal, board or committee. The courts have made it quite clear that they are willing to review the decision-making procedures of voluntary organizations such as churches, in order to ensure that proper process has been followed.

The second part of this chapter focuses on the substantive aspects of decision making. If a person is unhappy with the outcome of a church decision (as opposed to the procedures followed to reach that decision), he or she may try to challenge it in the courts. This is referred to as seeking judicial review on substantive grounds. While courts are more reluctant to overturn the decisions of voluntary organizations on substantive grounds, sometimes they will intervene.

The law on decision making can seem nebulous and complex, but the core advice to follow is quite simple: when you are involved in making decisions that will have a significant impact on others, make sure that a fair process is followed and that you do your best to reach a sensible decision, based on the relevant facts and law. Otherwise, the courts might intervene.

This chapter can be read as a stand-alone piece for a general overview on how to go about implementing fair procedures and reaching reasonable decisions. It can also be read in conjunction with the chapters on employment (Chapter 15) and property (Chapter 19), since the principles discussed here are relevant to decisions about disciplining or dismissing employees and decisions about the acquisition, use and disposal of property.

Procedure: Following fair procedures

Procedural fairness focuses on the processes followed by the church committee, board or court, rather than on the actual outcome. The question being asked is "What process should the committee, board or court follow when making decisions?" One way for church decision makers to think about procedural fairness is to ask, "If somebody did challenge our decision-making process in a court, would the court think that we had acted fairly?"

Before answering this question, it is important to note that the law does not become involved in every kind of church decision. Decisions about whether to hold the church lobster dinner in May instead of June, or which hymns will be sung on a particular Sunday, are not in danger of being set aside by the courts. Courts do not become involved in reviewing the procedures followed by a church committee, board or court unless the decision being challenged has a significant impact on the rights or interests of the individual who wants to have the decision reviewed. Furthermore, when there are several stages to the decision-making process, the courts will not become involved at the preliminary stages. The decision must be a final one, and all internal avenues of appeal must have been used before the courts will review for procedural fairness.[2]

Fair procedures

Church committees, boards or courts sometimes do make decisions that have significant consequences for individuals' rights and interests. In these situations, thought must be given to ensuring that fair procedures are followed. When a court reviews the procedure followed by a decision-making body, the court will ask the following three questions, each of which is examined in more detail below.

- Did the decision maker follow the procedures required by statute?

- Did the decision maker follow the procedures required by its internal rules?

- Did the decision maker meet its common-law duty of fairness? (Older case law sometimes uses the term *natural justice* instead of *duty of fairness*.)

Statutory procedural requirements

Church decision makers need to be aware of any procedural requirements set out in statutes. For instance, the Alberta *Religious Societies' Lands Act* states:

> 17(1) A meeting of an incorporated congregation to consider any proposed dealing with its property shall be called by giving not less than 2 weeks' notice, including 2 Sundays, before the date of the meeting.

(2) The notice

(a) shall state the time, place and particular object for which the meeting is called,

(b) shall be posted at the church or meeting house of the congregation, and

(c) shall be read at all intervening services held in the church or meeting house.[3]

Sometimes it may be necessary to obtain legal advice in order to ensure that all relevant statutory requirements have been taken into account. The basic rule is that statutory requirements must be followed and that failure to do so may result in the decision being overturned.

The need for careful adherence to statutory requirements is illustrated in the case of *Hong v. Young Kwang Presbyterian Church of Vancouver*.[4] The church had been incorporated as a society under the British Columbia *Society Act* and so had to follow the procedures set out in the *Act*. The *Society Act* required that at least fourteen days' notice be given for a congregational meeting; insufficient notice was given for a congregational meeting held to approve the hiring of a new pastor. The vote confirming the new pastor was challenged. Because the church had not adhered to the procedures required by the *Society Act*, the court set the vote aside.

Internal rules

Similarly, when a church has, by valid internal processes, created rules or by-laws governing the procedures to be followed in particular situations, it may be possible to have a decision set aside when it was made without following those procedures.

This is reflected in the case of *Jeon v. Presbytery of Northwest America Korean American Presbyterian Church.*[5] Two factions within a congregation of the Korean American Presbyterian Church in British Columbia were in dispute over whether a senior pastor had been properly appointed. Two congregational meetings had been held. At one, the minister in question was confirmed as the senior pastor; at the other he was not. Each of the opposing groups alleged procedural irregularities at the congregational meetings and asked a court to intervene. The by-laws of the church required that fourteen days' notice be given for congregational meetings; however, only seven days' notice had been given for each of the congregational meetings. Therefore, the decisions taken at both congregational meetings were set aside by the court.

So, just as it is important for members of church committees, boards and courts to know about requirements set out in statutes, they also need to be familiar with, and follow, the church's internal procedural rules.

Duty of fairness

In addition to any procedural requirements set out in statutes or internal rules, decision makers are also bound by what is called the duty of fairness. Exactly what procedures will be required in order to fulfill the duty of fairness will vary significantly, depending on context. Sometimes a church decision maker may need to consult a lawyer about what the duty of fairness requires in a particular situation.

There are three key questions that a court will ask to determine whether a decision that significantly affects a person's interests or rights was made in accordance with the duty of fairness.

- Did the person know the case against him or her?

- Was the person given an opportunity to respond?

- Were the decision makers impartial?

Let us consider these three aspects of the duty of fairness in the context of an employment-related decision. Suppose that difficulties have arisen between a congregation and its cleric.[6] The congregation has asked the appropriate body within the church to impose some sort of training as a condition of the cleric remaining in a pastoral relationship with that congregation. Clearly, this decision would significantly affect the interests of the cleric. The relevant church committee, board or court knows the relevant procedural requirements imposed by statute or by the rules of the congregation, and intends to follow those rules. By doing so, the first two requirements for procedural fairness will be met: adherence to statutes and adherence to internal rules. The next step is to determine whether the duty of fairness requires anything further in the way of procedure. To answer this, the decision maker must look to the questions set out above: does the cleric know the case against him or her; will he or she be given a chance to respond; and will the requirement of impartiality be met?

Ensuring the individual knows the case against him or her

The cleric would need to be provided with information about the kinds of allegations or complaints that had been made by the congregation, and told that the congregation had made a request for the imposition of training as a term of the cleric remaining in this pastoral relationship.

The cleric would have to be given sufficient particulars to be able to respond to the congregation's complaints or allegations. It would not be sufficient simply to say, "Everybody thinks that you are really terrible at pastoral care." This is so vague and subjective that it would be almost impossible to defend against. Instead, the cleric should be given specifics; for instance, "You spent only an average of one hour per month visiting congregants in hospital during the past six months. You visited only three people (Mrs. Brown, Ms. Smith and Mr. Jones) out of eighteen people on the shut-in list during this time, although the minister's job description indicates that 20 per cent of your time is to be spent on pastoral care." This makes clear exactly what is being alleged, and, when the allegations are inaccurate, allows the cleric to provide accurate information.

Providing an opportunity to respond

Any person who will be significantly affected by a decision must be given an opportunity to be heard on the issue; thus, in the example above, the cleric must be given an opportunity to respond to the allegations. The opportunity to respond involves several components, as set out below.

The decision-making body must give notice of when the matter is to be decided and what process is to be followed (for instance, is there to be an oral hearing? If so, where and when? Before whom?). Such notice must be given sufficiently ahead of time to allow the individual reasonable time to prepare. In our example, preparation might include finding and reviewing documents, speaking with others to confirm the cleric's own memory of events, taking advice from others, perhaps finding witnesses who can confirm the cleric's position and, in some circumstances, consulting a lawyer. Furthermore, the person against whom allegations have been made may not be in a position simply to drop all other responsibilities and focus on responding to the allegations. Obviously, too, the more complex the matter, or the more serious the consequences, the more time will be required to prepare. All these factors must be taken into account in order to make a realistic assessment of the time needed to prepare. Clearly, a day or two's notice is highly unlikely to be sufficient. Several weeks or longer may well be appropriate.

In situations in which the requirements of fairness must be weighed against the protection of other individuals (for instance, where someone within the church has been accused of abusing a child), it may be necessary to take some sort of action right away, such as relieving the individual of duties immediately, pending an investigation and hearing to take place as soon as possible. In such a serious case, legal counsel should be involved from the beginning.

While church committees, boards and courts must give the person involved sufficient time to prepare a response, they must, on the other hand, avoid unnecessary delay. When it is known within the congregation or community that allegations have been made, this will be very stressful for the cleric who wants an opportunity to clear his or her name as soon as possible. In such a situation, unnecessary delays and adjournments on the part of the church committee, board or court will undermine the cleric's sense of being dealt with fairly.

The hearing does not have to be as formal as proceedings in a court, but it must involve an opportunity for each side to be heard and to respond to the other side. Not all decisions by church bodies require that an oral hearing be held; sometimes it may be sufficient simply to allow all parties to provide written submissions, perhaps coupled with an opportunity for each side to make written comment on the other's submissions. Sometimes, however, the only fair way to proceed is to hold an oral hearing. This is more likely to be the case when issues of credibility are at stake.

Whether an opportunity for actual cross-examination is required, and whether parties must be given an opportunity to bring legal counsel, depends on the situation. For instance, on the issue of counsel, a court would look at various factors, including the complexity of the issues raised, the seriousness of the possible outcome, and the ability of the particular individual to speak for himself or herself.

It is important that both sides are treated in a similar manner. In our example, if those making complaints about the cleric were given several hours to make their allegations, and if their lawyers were allowed to cross-examine the cleric, it would clearly be unfair if the cleric was not permitted to cross-examine the complainants and was told, "You have ten minutes to make your case."

Avoiding a reasonable apprehension of bias

On the issue of impartiality, a court does not ask itself, "Was the decision maker, in fact, partial or impartial?" Instead, the court asks whether a "reasonable apprehension of bias" existed. Thus, instead of trying to second-guess the actual thought processes and attitudes of those who made the decision, the court asks, "Would a reasonable person, who has been reasonably informed of the situation, perceive this decision maker to be biased?" When the answer to that question is yes, then the individual affected is entitled to have the decision set aside and the matter reheard by others who would not raise a reasonable apprehension of bias.

Exactly what circumstances will give rise to an apprehension of bias depends on the situation. In some cases, before an allegation comes to a hearing, there is a preliminary investigation to see whether the matter has any merit or whether it should be dismissed without going any further. It might raise an apprehension of bias if the same person who did the initial investigation (and concluded that the allegation had sufficient merit to go on to a hearing) then became the decision maker at the hearing. To use an analogy from criminal law, this would be seen as allowing the same person to act as prosecutor and judge.

Other examples might include these: the decision maker has made derogatory comments about or otherwise shown hostility toward the individual about whom the decision is being made; the decision maker seems to have made up his or her mind before the process begins; or the decision maker is closely related to or affiliated with one party. It is difficult to give hard and fast rules about what will be seen as a close relationship or affiliation, particularly within a church community in which most people know each other, and may have worshipped and served on committees together for decades. In that context, the duty of fairness does not demand that the decision maker be a stranger to the parties. However, continuing to use our example of allegations against a cleric, the decision-making body should not include people who are immediate family members of the chief complainants. Furthermore, when there are groups within the congregation who are perceived as being for or against the cleric, individuals from those groups should not be on the decision-making committee, board or court. It may be helpful for members of the decision-making body to ask, "If I was in the shoes of the person being complained about, would I be likely to see this committee, board or court as impartial?"

Impact of a finding of procedural irregularity

When an individual is dissatisfied with the decision of a church body, he or she may decide to challenge it within the church by asking for an informal reconsideration or by making a formal appeal to a higher church body. Once the individual has exhausted all internal appeals that are available within the church, he or she may ask a court to intervene. A finding that a statutory requirement has not been met, that an internal rule has not been followed or that the duty of fairness has been breached cannot be answered by arguing that the actual decision is reasonable or that greater procedural fairness would not have changed the outcome. If the court finds that the decision in question significantly affects the rights or interests of the person bringing the challenge, and if the decision-making process is found to have been flawed, it is very likely that the decision will be set aside.

An example of this willingness to intervene is the case of *Davis v. United Church of Canada*. This case involved two ministers against whom sexual harassment complaints had been made. The ministers sought judicial review of the way the church handled the complaints, arguing that the procedures used in investigating the allegations had not been fair. The court made it clear that it had jurisdiction to review the procedures followed by the church. The court stated:

> Even if one goes back to the very early reported cases involving Church Ministers … our courts have taken the position that if the rules of natural justice [i.e. the duty of fairness] have been breached, the court will step in and rule on the matter.[7]

As an expert on judicial review has noted, "There is a long history of the courts imposing procedural obligations – commonly known as the rules of natural justice or procedural fairness – on clubs, trade organizations, and even religious organizations, particularly when these groups are dealing with rights pertaining to membership."[8] Similarly, in a review of cases involving discipline of clergy, Professor M. H. Ogilvie concludes that "… courts have repeatedly intervened when ecclesiastical rules of procedure or church courts have not complied with the principles of natural justice …."[9]

If a decision is overturned by the courts, it is, however, open to the decision maker to rehear the matter and arrive at the same decision, so long as proper procedure is followed. Professor Alvin Esau describes one such situation in his study of judicial review of disputes relating to church property:

> … the Supreme Court judicially reviewed the expulsion of a number of Hutterites on the ground of insubordination at …[a] Manitoba

colony. The court asserted that when voluntary associations expel members, the court may judicially review the process to ensure that the association has first followed its own internal rules, whether customary or written, and then secondly that the process complies with the basic principles of natural justice in terms of notice and fair opportunity to be heard by an unbiased tribunal. The court voided the expulsion of the Hutterites because they allegedly had not been given adequate notice that their expulsions would be considered at a meeting of members. Following this decision the colony in question simply returned to the drawing board, gave proper notice and then proceeded to expel the members again. A Manitoba court upheld these expulsions ....[10]

Summary on procedure

In summary, then, when a church committee, board or court makes decisions that may have a serious impact on an individual's rights or interests, the church body must follow fair procedures, or risk having the decision set aside if it is reviewed by a court. Procedural fairness requires that decision makers adhere to any processes stipulated by relevant legislation or in internal church rules and that they meet the duty of fairness. The scope of this duty depends on the particular situation, but the court will want to be assured that the individual whose rights or interests are at stake knew the case against him or her and had an opportunity to participate and respond. Fairness also requires that the decision was made by an impartial decision maker.

While case law proceeds from the perspective of asking, after the fact, whether a decision should be set aside because of flawed procedure, obviously the practical approach for decision makers is to determine ahead of time what procedures are required in order to meet the duty of fairness in a particular situation. As Professor M. H. Ogilvie has noted, church manuals and handbooks for church decision making should be reviewed regularly to ensure that they reflect the current law on procedural fairness and that they are written in clear, understandable language.[11] Ogilvie also emphasizes that church decision makers should be provided with training on procedural requirements.

Following this advice should enhance procedural fairness and reduce the likelihood that church decisions will be challenged on procedural grounds. In some instances, it may be necessary to consult with a lawyer who is familiar with both the church context and the secular law on decision making, in order to determine what procedures should be implemented.

Substance: Making reasonable decisions

Substantive review by a court focuses on the actual decision that was made, not on the procedures that were followed in making it. In substantive review, the person challenging the decision is saying, "Even if all the right procedures were followed, the outcome is so unreasonable that it should be set aside."

Availability of substantive review

In the past, courts have been reluctant to become involved in the substantive review of internal decisions of voluntary organizations such as churches. *Ash v. Methodist Church*, decided in 1900, involving a challenge to a disciplinary decision of the Conference of the Methodist Church, provides an example of this reluctance. In *Ash*, the Supreme Court of Canada stated that it had "no right to interfere in a matter clearly within the powers of a domestic forum and in which they have taken action."[12] One writer has suggested that the courts see individuals who join voluntary organizations as having entered into a contract with each other. By doing so, they have "effectively elected to have the substantive issue in any dispute adjudicated internally, and, by implication, [they have] agreed to displace the courts of law as the primary forum."[13]

Despite this reluctance, a few cases suggest that substantive review of decisions made by voluntary associations such as churches may be available. In a 1975 decision, *Christensen v. Bodner et al.*, a minister servant of the Society of Jehovah's Witnesses was accused of apostasy and expelled from the Society.[14] He started a court action, asking for a declaration that he was a member in good standing of the Society of Jehovah's Witnesses. The Jehovah's Witnesses asked the court to dismiss the action before it went to trial, on the ground that "the removal of the plaintiff from this voluntary religious association does not give rise to any civil right which would justify a civil [i.e. secular] Court interfering with internal practices of such religious association."[15] The court refused to dismiss the action without a trial, stating, "… today courts are prepared to grant much more comprehensive remedies to members of voluntary associations."[16]

A 2003 decision, *McGarrigle v. Canadian Interuniversity Sport*, also underscores the possibility of substantive review of internal decisions made by voluntary associations. This case involved an appeal board of Canadian Interuniversity Sport (CIS). The CIS was described as follows: "Its function is to regulate interuniversity sports in Canada. It does so, not by virtue of any statutory authority, but by virtue of the authority given to it by its members."[17] On the issue of whether it had jurisdiction to review the decision of the CIS panel, the court in *McGarrigle* stated that decisions of bodies such as this are "subject to review by the court for errors of law, acting in excess of jurisdiction and failure to comply with the principles of natural justice."[18]

The first two grounds referred to by the court – error of law and excess of jurisdiction – are substantive errors. So, in *McGarrigle* we see a court engaging in substantive review of a board created by a voluntary organization; that is, reviewing the decision itself and not just the process by which the outcome was reached. Although this case involved a sports organization, the court's reasoning would apply equally to church decision makers. Because there is not a great deal of case law in this area, we cannot state with certainty when a court would or would not hear an application for substantive review of a church decision-making body, but such a review is a possibility.

As with procedural review, a court is unlikely to enter into substantive review unless all internal avenues of review or appeal have been exhausted.

Deference

If a court does review the merits of an internal church decision (i.e. engages in substantive review) and concludes that it would have reached a different outcome, this might cause the court to overturn the decision; however, this is not automatically the case. Whether the original decision is overturned would depend on whether the court felt that it should treat the church decision with deference. In some circumstances, the court might say, "We would have reached a different outcome, but we don't see the church's decision as completely unreasonable. Given that the issue being decided here falls squarely within the expertise of the church, we should defer to the church decision maker, and allow this decision to stand."

A court engaged in substantive review may choose from one of three levels of deference:

- The court could be very deferential. Here, a court will set aside the decision only when it is persuaded that the decision is so grossly unreasonable that it cannot be allowed to stand.

- The court could be somewhat deferential. Here, a court will intervene to set aside the decision when it is persuaded that the decision is unreasonable. It is sometimes difficult to distinguish between moderate deference (the decision will stand so long as it is reasonable) and high deference (the decision will stand so long as it is not grossly unreasonable). The very deferential approach leaves the original decision maker with more leeway – out of all the possible decisions it could reach, it must only avoid the grossly unreasonable ones. When the test is moderate deference, the decision maker must avoid not only those decisions that are grossly unreasonable, but also those decisions that are simply unreasonable.

- The court could decide to show no deference at all. Here, the court will determine how it would have decided the matter, and then overturn any decision that does not accord fully with that outcome.

When a court is deciding the issue of deference, it will usually put significant emphasis on the expertise of the body whose decision is being reviewed. The court will ask itself whether that body is more expert than the court performing judicial review. If so, then the court is likely to be quite deferential and step in only when the decision is egregiously wrong. On the other hand, if the court has more expertise on the issues, it will apply the least deferential standard and set aside any decision that the court considers to be wrong.

To use examples outside the church context, courts are usually willing to acknowledge that labour boards have particular expertise regarding the relationship between, and the interests of, unions and management. Therefore, a court will not be quick to overturn decisions of labour boards. On the other hand, when the decision of a human rights tribunal is challenged, courts frequently take the position that understanding and adjudicating on fundamental human rights lies at the core of their own expertise; therefore, they tend to be less deferential when reviewing the decisions of human rights tribunals.

Turning to decision making by churches, when decisions have a clear spiritual or ecclesiastical aspect, it is likely that courts would see an internal church decision maker as having expertise in the area. In that case, a court would be quite deferential in any review of the merits of a decision.

On the other hand, one of the grounds for judicial review cited by the court in *McGarrigle* (referred to above) was "error of law." Quite a number of judicial review cases make it clear that when the issue before a committee or board turns on the interpretation of secular law, courts see this as falling squarely within their own special expertise and so do not show deference. Thus we cannot state categorically that courts will always be deferential when they undertake substantive review of a decision made by a church committee, board or court.

Reaching reasonable outcomes

Given the possibility of substantive review of church decision making, church committees, boards and courts need to do their best to ensure that they are making reasonable decisions. Substantive review by a court is a backward-looking exercise; the court will ask whether the church committee, board or court made a sufficiently bad decision that the courts should intervene. To avoid such intervention, church decision makers should be forward-looking, striving to avoid the kinds of errors that would lead a court to strike down a decision.

Church decision makers should ask themselves:

- Are we straight on the facts? Going back to the example of the allegation that a cleric is not providing good pastoral care, it would be important to know whether there is a job description that sets out the expectations regarding pastoral care and, if so, what those expectations are. It would also be important to find out, as accurately as possible, just how much time the cleric does spend on pastoral care.

- Does this issue require an interpretation or application of the law? If so, are we sure that we understand the law? Do we need to seek advice on this?

- Is this a situation in which the decision maker can choose from a range of options? If so, have we been careful to exercise our discretion based on relevant considerations and for proper purposes? For instance, assume that the cleric is found to have been lax in providing pastoral care. Let us also assume that the relevant church rules allow a fair bit of discretion as to what penalty, if any, should be imposed. The decision-making body is considering bypassing options such as simply talking to the cleric to stress the importance of pastoral care or asking the Ministry and Personnel Committee to meet more regularly with the cleric to support him or her in carrying out pastoral care duties. Instead, the church committee, board or court in question is considering requiring the cleric to take a fairly rigorous refresher course on pastoral care. Is it imposing this for proper reasons? ("Pastoral care is an extremely important part of church life; Rev. Smith seems to want to get it right, but really doesn't have a clue what good pastoral care means. Furthermore, we've heard good reports about this particular course.") Or is the decision-making body requiring the refresher course for improper reasons? ("Rev. Smith is far too independent minded – look at how our suggestions for alternative worship services were rejected. Let's really make Rev. Smith sweat through this course – that will show who's in charge around here!")

There is no way to ensure that church decision making is completely immune from substantive review by courts; however, the likelihood of a successful challenge on the decision itself (as separate from the procedures) will be greatly reduced if church committees, boards and courts are attentive to the need to make decisions based on pertinent facts and on an understanding of the relevant law, and are careful to exercise their discretion based on proper considerations. Even more important, using this approach is more likely to result in decisions that are wise and just!

Conclusion

This chapter has focused on two aspects of church decision making. First, when will a court review a church decision on procedural grounds, and how can a church ensure that its procedures are fair? Second, when will a court review a church decision on substantive grounds, and how can a church ensure that its decisions are reasonable?

On the first issue, when a church committee, board or court is making decisions that have a significant impact on individuals' rights and interests, its procedures should be reviewed periodically. It may be necessary to get legal advice as part of this review. Church decision makers must adhere to any requirements set out in legislation or in church rules, and must also meet their duty of fairness. This duty of fairness requires that the individual being affected by the decision must "know the case" and have an opportunity to respond. Also, decision makers must not only be impartial, but must be seen to be impartial. If the church decision maker fails to meet these requirements, a challenge in the courts is likely to be successful.

While the availability of procedural review is clear, the law on substantive review of internal decisions made by voluntary organizations such as churches is less settled. However, it seems likely that, in some circumstances at least, a court would undertake substantive review of a church decision. In other words, on an application for judicial review, the court may sometimes be willing to inquire into whether the decision reached by a church committee, board or court was correct, or at least not too unreasonable (depending on how deferential the court felt it should be). Decision making is a difficult process, particularly when there are a number of interests to be balanced. However, the more that church committees, boards and courts ensure that they are basing their decisions on the relevant facts and law, and exercising their discretion based on relevant considerations, the more likely it is that those within the church community will be willing to live with the decision, and the less likely it is that the outcome could be successfully challenged in the courts.

Although the law on decision making can become complex at times, much of it can be boiled down to questions that should be familiar to all churchgoers: When we are making decisions, have we treated the person affected in the way that we would like to be treated? Even when difficult or contentious decisions have to be made, have we been careful to listen respectfully to all sides, and have we tried to base our decision on the appropriate considerations?

Church Decision Making: Questions and Answers

Q. What types of bodies make decisions within churches?

A. Church committees, boards and courts make decisions with respect to various aspects of church governance and administration.

Q. When an individual feels that the process followed by a church decision maker was flawed, may he or she ask a court to review the decision-making process?

A. Yes, judicial review of procedures by the courts is available when:

- the decision is final (i.e. it is not simply a preliminary decision taken at the first stage of a multi-stage decision-making process);

- the individual has exhausted all internal avenues of appeal within the church; and

- the rights or interests of that individual have been directly affected by the decision.

Q. **What kinds of things will a court consider when it undertakes procedural review of a church's decision-making procedures?**

A. The court will ask whether the church committee, board or court

- followed any procedures required by statute;

- followed the procedures required by the internal rules of that church; and

- met the duty of fairness.

Q. **What is meant by the duty of fairness?**

A. Exactly what this term encompasses will depend on the situation, but in general terms it means that the person affected by the decision must

- know the case against them;

- have an opportunity to respond; and

- have the matter decided by an unbiased decision maker.

Q. **What will happen when a court determines that a church committee, board or court did not follow fair procedures?**

A. The decision will be set aside; that is, the decision will no longer be valid.

Q. **What if a person wants to have a court review the actual outcome of a church decision; that is, to review the decision itself and not just the process used to reach the decision? Is that kind of review available in the courts?**

A. Here the answer is less clear cut. Traditionally, courts have been reluctant to engage in substantive review of the decisions of voluntary organizations such as churches. However, a few cases do suggest that this kind of review is sometimes available, if all internal avenues of appeal have been exhausted.

Q. **What if a court does undertake substantive review of an internal church decision, and concludes that it would have reached a different decision? Will the church's decision be set aside?**

A. This is not automatically the outcome. The court must ask itself whether it should show deference to the original decision – perhaps because the decision involves spiritual matters on which the church committee, board or court is more expert than the court. When the court decides that it will be deferential, it will allow the decision to stand unless it is unreasonable or even (if the court is being highly deferential) unless the decision is grossly unreasonable. However, when the court decides that no deference is due, it will set aside any decision that does not accord with its determination of the correct answer.

Q. What should church decision makers do in order to make reasonable decisions?

A. Church decision makers should ask themselves:

- Are we straight on the facts?

- Do we understand the relevant law and how to apply it? and

- If we are exercising discretion, have we done so on the basis of relevant considerations and for proper purposes?

Notes

[1] Throughout this book, when we use the word *court*, we are referring to secular courts, unless we state explicitly that we are discussing church courts.

[2] "Canadian courts have expressed the view that they will hear only appeals from the highest tribunal of the religious institution concerned." M. H. Ogilvie, "Christian Clergy and the Law of Employment: Office-holders, employees or outlaws" (1999) 3 *Journal of the Church Law Association of Canada* 2, p. 20.

[3] *Religious Societies' Lands Act*, R.S.A. 1980, c. R-14, s. 17.

[4] *Hong v. Young Kwang Presbyterian Church of Vancouver*, 2002 BCSC 1503.

[5] *Jeon v. Presbytery of Northwest America Korean American Presbyterian Church*, 2000 BCSC 1218.

[6] We would like to thank Cynthia Gunn, legal counsel to the United Church of Canada, for providing this example.

[7] *Davis v. United Church of Canada* (1991), 8 O.R. (3d) 75 (Ct. J. (Gen. Div.)), para. 47.

[8] David Mullan, *Administrative Law* (Toronto: Irwin Law, 2001), p. 4.

[9] M. H. Ogilvie, "Ecclesiastical Law – Jurisdiction of Civil Courts – Status of Clergy: *McCaw v. United Church of Canada*" (1992) 71 *Canadian Bar Review* 597, p. 605.

[10] Alvin Esau, "The Judicial Resolution of Church Property Disputes: Canadian and American Models" (2003) 40 *Alberta Law Review* 767, p. 768.

[11] M. H. Ogilvie, "Church Discipline: Doing What Comes Naturally," *The Presbyterian Record* (January 1994) 27, p. 29.

[12] *Ash v. Methodist Church* (1900), 27 O.A.R. 602 (C.A.), para. 1, affirmed 31 S.C.R. 497.

[13] Robert K. Forbes, "Judicial Review of the Private Decision Maker: The Domestic Tribunal" (1976) 15 *University of Western Ontario Law Review* 123, p. 128. Forbes does, however, indicate that substantive judicial review would be available when a decision is made in bad faith or when the decision maker is acting outside its jurisdiction.

14 The *Encyclopedia Britannica* defines apostasy as "the total rejection of Christianity by a baptized person who, having at one time professed the faith, publicly rejects it" (www.britannica.com).

15 *Christensen v. Bodner et al.* (1975), 65 D.L.R. (3d) 549 (Man. Q.B.), para. 4.

16 *Ibid.*, para. 9.

17 *McGarrigle v. Canadian Interuniversity Sport*, 2003 CanLII 17862 (Ont. S.C.) (CanLII), para. 22.

18 *Ibid.*, para. 23.

4

Alternative
Dispute Resolution

Discourage litigation. Persuade your neighbors to compromise
whenever you can. Point out to them how the nominal winner
is often a real loser – in fees, expenses, and waste of time.
As a peacemaker the lawyer has a superior opportunity
of being a good man. There will still be business enough.
—Abraham Lincoln,
sixteenth American president, 1809–1865,
The Collected Works of Abraham Lincoln,
Volume II, "Notes for a Law Lecture"

Alternative dispute resolution (ADR) is sometimes also referred to as conflict management or conflict resolution. These are umbrella terms that encompass a variety of processes, all of which share one characteristic: the desire to resolve disputes without necessarily resorting to the adversarial approach typified by litigation. Thus, the word *alternative* in ADR refers to an alternative to the courts.[1] (This is not to suggest that there is always a clear-cut dichotomy between litigation and alternatives such as negotiation or mediation; after all, most lawsuits, once initiated, are ultimately resolved through some form of settlement between the parties before the matter goes to court.)

This chapter describes several of the processes of dispute resolution that fall under the umbrella term ADR and examines some of the potential benefits and pitfalls of each. While the term ADR encompasses a range of approaches (and could, in fact, be used to describe everything except a dispute decided by a court), for the purposes of this chapter, we will focus primarily on negotiation, mediation and arbitration, with a brief reference to restorative justice.

The idea of alternative dispute resolution is, of course, not a new one; for as long as there have been formal processes established for the resolution of disputes, some disputes and disagreements have been dealt with outside those processes. However, ADR has become significantly more recognized and talked about in the last several decades.

Benefits of an ADR approach

The ADR movement has grown out of a desire to find better, more consensual, less costly and less time-consuming ways to deal with conflict. Some proponents assert that ADR is not just about saving time and money, or even just about resolving specific disputes, but is also about rebuilding and transforming relationships.

This need for reconciliation is reflected in a number of passages in the Christian scriptures,[2] and so it is hardly surprising that many churches are interested in the idea of ADR. One commentator suggests that "Christians should be predisposed to support methods of conflict resolution that emphasize non-violence, forgiveness and connectedness between persons."[3]

There are many contexts in which churches or individual congregations might be involved in conflict resolution, including the following:

- helping members of a fractious church committee find meaningful ways to work together;

- mediating a dispute between two individuals or factions within a congregation;

- responding to conflict between the cleric and the congregation, or between the cleric and another church employee; and

- responding to claims from those outside the church community.

Some denominations have already developed a core of trained and experienced mediators who are available to congregations trying to deal with difficult and divisive situations. (Mediators are sometimes called facilitators. For simplicity's sake, we use just the one term – mediator – to refer to any neutral individual who helps parties work through a dispute or problem.) Therefore, if your congregation feels itself in need of such assistance, a first step would be to check whether this resource is available within your church.[4] Increasing numbers of lawyers are also trained in mediation, and some provinces have networks or associations of trained mediators; these, too, may be useful sources.

When ADR may not be appropriate

We do not suggest that, in every situation, ADR will offer a panacea. Arguably, there are times when having a conflict resolved or a wrong adjudicated by the courts is the most appropriate route. Thus, there may be times when the principle at stake, or the right needing to be vindicated, is of such importance that there should be a public affirmation of public values. In that situation, as a society we should not be willing for the parties to settle for whatever they can agree to.[5] This sense of societal judgment and affirmation is difficult to achieve through negotiation, mediation or arbitration, for at least two reasons.

First, there is generally no state involvement in ADR, since parties simply negotiate between themselves or decide on who to appoint as mediator or arbitrator. When the issue at stake is sufficiently significant, however, we want to see the state – through the legal system – take a position on the matter. Such issues might include the denunciation of wrongs (such as sexual abuse of children) or the affirmation of fundamental societal values (such as equality rights or non-discrimination).

Second, one party might insist, as a condition of agreeing to ADR, that the terms of any settlement be kept confidential. The court process, on the other hand, is by and large a public one, and reported decisions of judges are available to the public. Therefore, where it matters that the facts and outcomes of a dispute be part of the public record, then ADR may not be the right approach.

It is contexts such as these that have led some writers to emphasize that ADR is not appropriate in all situations. Thus, as eloquently stated by Owen Fiss,

> [W]hen one sees injustices that cry out for correction … the agony of judgment becomes a necessity. Someone has to confront the betrayal of our deepest ideals and be prepared to turn the world upside down to bring it to fruition.[6]

That said, this chapter is written in the belief that alternative approaches to dispute resolution do have much to offer in many situations. Conflict should not simply be allowed to fester until it disrupts relationships, and "see you in court" is not always an appropriate response. Not only is litigation adversarial, based on notions of winning and losing, but it is also quite simply not an option for those who lack the resources to fund litigation or for those whose claims and needs have not yet been recognized by the law. As one textbook notes, "Interest in North America in alternatives to litigation is at a new high. There is a growing sense – in government, in commerce, and in the courts – that it is time to consider a spectrum of dispute resolution alternatives."[7]

Seeking legal advice

Even when alternative dispute resolution seems appropriate for a particular conflict, it may still be wise to seek legal advice, depending on the issues at stake and the possible consequences. In fact, such advice may be useful in making the initial determination of whether litigation or ADR is the best approach. When the conflict involves legal rights, it might also be necessary to consult a lawyer before deciding whether to agree to a particular settlement. To evaluate a proffered settlement, a party needs to be able to weigh the costs and benefits of the settlement against the likely outcome of going to court.[8]

Negotiation

As one text on ADR notes, "Negotiation pervades everyday life."[9] We have probably all negotiated with our children about how many bedtime stories we will read or what time the lights are to go out. Many of us may have negotiated informally in the workplace over questions such as who will take vacation when, or how certain tasks will be allocated. Negotiations occur not only between individuals, but also between entities such as management and unions, between different levels of government, and between nations. Negotiations can involve just two parties or be multi-party. Parties to a negotiation may do the negotiating themselves, or may be represented by a lawyer or other individual skilled in negotiation. In negotiation, there is no third party involved who has the authority to make a decision. The key element of negotiation is that there are at least two entities who hold differing views on an issue and who are prepared to enter into discussions with each other to see whether they can reach an agreement.

So long as a willingness to enter into negotiations exists, this approach to dispute resolution can be useful in many situations. For instance, imagine that two employees in a church office would like to take summer vacation during the same weeks. While both recognize that at least one of them must be in the office at any time, one employee feels that she should get the first choice of vacation times because she has been working for the church longer; the other employee feels that he should receive first choice because he has to co-ordinate his vacation time with childcare responsibilities once his children are out of school. The employees know that if they take this issue to the church board, either they will be told to "work it out yourselves" or the board may come up with something that does not work for either employee. On the other hand, the dispute cannot simply be shelved or no one will get vacation time. The two employees might decide to sit down together and brainstorm about possible solutions, in the hopes of finding a way to meet at least some of the needs of both employees. In doing so, they would be engaging in a form of negotiation called interest-based negotiation.

Interest-based negotiation

Obviously, it is possible to negotiate in ways that are quite destructive; for instance, by making outrageous demands, refusing to budge from one's initial position, or trying to use coercion or lies to force the other side to change its position. However, it is also possible to engage in constructive negotiation. One such approach, frequently called interest-based negotiation, is founded on five principles.[10]

1. *Separating the people from the problem.* The focus here is on finding ways to recognize and deal with conflict without destroying the underlying relationship. To use the example above, negotiations are more likely to be successful if the two employees can focus on the need to allocate vacation times fairly, rather than thinking "there now – isn't that just like Bob! No consideration at all for other people!"

2. *Focusing on interests rather than on positions.* Skilled negotiators will try to identify – both for themselves and for the other parties – what is really important, what the underlying motivation is, and what each party is hoping to achieve from the negotiations. This requires uncovering the interests that lie beneath the stated positions of the parties. For instance, if a union takes the position during collective bargaining that its members will "only accept $X an hour and not a cent less," the interests underlying this position (for instance, the workers' desire for financial security and for recognition of the value of their work) might be achieved in another way. Perhaps a smaller pay raise with increased benefits would meet the interests equally well.

3. *Generating a range of options before deciding on a solution.* As interests are uncovered, and a range of creative solutions suggested, it may be possible to discover opportunities for mutual gain; in other words, it may be possible to meet some interests of each side in ways that do not detract from the other side's interests. A simple example that is sometimes used to explain the idea of mutual gain is as follows: two children are arguing over who will get the last orange in the fridge. One solution might be to give each child half the orange; however, it may turn out that one child wants to eat the orange, while the other wants to use the rind in baking. If one child gets the fruit inside, and the other child gets the rind, each will have had their interest met – a situation of mutual gain.[11]

4. *Having a commitment to seeking solutions based on objective standards.* When interests do conflict, a principled negotiator will try to find objective standards against which to measure each side's proposals. Let us assume that a church secretary is negotiating with the church board about a pay raise. To find objective standards against which to measure the percentage raise proposed by each side, it would be logical to seek information about pay rates and percentage raises among other churches and non-profit organizations of a similar size with similar budgets.

5. *Know your BATNA* (Best Alternative to a Negotiated Agreement). To be able to assess what offer to put forward, how strongly to argue, and how to respond to any offer put forward by the other side, you need to know what your best (realistic) alternative is, should a negotiated agreement not be reached. Is it to continue in the current situation, which you find intolerable? If so, even a negotiated agreement that does not meet all your interests, but which provides some improvements, is well worth pursuing. On the other hand, if you know that failure to reach a negotiated settlement will lead to the matter going to the church board for a decision, and you have a realistic expectation that the board will decide in your favour, then you are unlikely to agree to a settlement unless it goes a long way toward answering the concerns that brought you to negotiations in the first place. Knowing your BATNA does not mean that you should become spineless (in the first scenario) or that you should aggressively steamroller the other party's interests (in the second scenario). On the other

hand, if parties do reach a negotiated settlement, it is much more likely to be an enduring settlement if, at the time of agreement, both sides had a pragmatic understanding of what their other options were.

Interest-based versus positional negotiation

Interest-based negotiation (referred to in the quotation below as integrative negotiation) can be contrasted to positional bargaining:

> Integrative bargaining is important because it usually produces more satisfactory outcomes for the parties involved than does positional bargaining. Positional bargaining is based on fixed, opposing viewpoints (positions) and tends to result in compromise or no agreement at all. Oftentimes, compromises do not efficiently satisfy the true interests of the disputants. Instead, compromises simply split the difference between the two positions, giving each side half of what they want. Creative, integrative solutions, on the other hand, can potentially give everyone all of what they want.[12]

The following chart illustrates some of the differences between interest-based negotiation and positional bargaining.[13]

Positional Negotiation	Interest-based Negotiation
disputants are adversaries	disputants are joint problem solvers
goal is victory	goal is wise decision
demand concessions	work together to determine who gets what
dig into position	focus on interests, not positions
mislead, use tricks	be open about interests, use fair principles
insist on your position	insist on objective criteria; consider multiple answers
apply pressure	use reason; yield to principle, not pressure
look for win for you alone	look for win-win opportunities

Benefits of interest-based negotiation

The benefits of interest-based negotiation include the following:

- There is no need to wait for a judge or arbitrator; the parties can start negotiating as soon as they are ready;

- No decision will be imposed "from on high"; any concessions or gains will be made by the parties themselves. Because it may be possible for parties to reach a settlement that is customized to their particular situation, there may be "increased satisfaction and compliance" with the settlement;[14]

- Because of the focus on interests rather than positions, it may be possible to find solutions that respond very effectively to the parties' needs and concerns;

- The focus on each other's interests may also allow the parties to see things from the other's viewpoint, thus allowing them to move to reconciliation; and

- Even if a settlement is not reached, the very process of negotiation might help to clear the air and build understanding.

Despite these benefits, we are not suggesting that interest-based negotiation is always an easy approach to use, particularly when the other person seems to be engaging in positional bargaining. When that happens, you may need to stop and put yourself in the other person's shoes to try to understand why he or she is behaving in this way. Then, you may need to deal with the issue directly, perhaps by courteously asking questions such as "How do you see that proposal as moving us toward a solution that could work for everyone?"[15]

Issues of difference and inequality

When deciding whether or how to negotiate, parties need to be aware of issues relating to both difference and inequality of bargaining power. With regard to difference, some research suggests that characteristics such as gender, race and culture could affect how a person negotiates and how he or she is viewed by the other party in negotiations.[16] For instance, one author suggests that culture can influence communication (particularly non-verbal communication), perceptions of time and willingness to undertake risks – all of which could have a bearing on negotiations.[17] Obviously, this does not mean that individuals can negotiate only with others of the same gender, race or culture, but it does mean that commitment to the process of negotiation may require sensitivity to others' perceptions.

Thought may also need to be given to real or perceived inequality of bargaining power. Significant disparities in what the parties have at stake, or in the ability of the parties to articulate their interests and priorities, or in their resources to hire others to do so may affect the likelihood of reaching a lasting agreement. A party who feels vulnerable to being taken advantage of by the other side may be very reluctant to enter into negotiations. Conversely, a party who feels that he or she has little to lose by refusing to negotiate may not be motivated to explore options and consider creative solutions. An enduring settlement is likely to occur only when both sides are committed to reaching a negotiated settlement, or at least are willing to acknowledge that a negotiated settlement will come closer to meeting their needs than the other alternatives available, which could range from going to court to simply walking away from the problem and perhaps the relationship.

An imbalance in bargaining power is not necessarily an insurmountable obstacle to negotiation, and the approach of interest-based, rather than positional, negotiating can go some way toward responding to this problem. That said, however, there may be situations where the bargaining power of the parties is so unequal, or when one party is so vulnerable to the other, that encouraging the dispute to be settled by negotiation would be not only inappropriate but also unethical. Thus, encouraging a victim of sexual abuse to enter into negotiations with the alleged abuser would be highly unlikely to produce anything like an equitable settlement and could, in fact, amount to further abuse of the victim.

Although the case of B.(V.) v. Cairns does not deal with a conventional negotiation, the facts are similar enough to be instructive here.[18] The plaintiff and her family were Jehovah's Witnesses. When the plaintiff was nineteen, she told an elder in her church that her father had sexually abused her as a younger teenager. After consulting with the Jehovah's Witness head office, an elder told the plaintiff that a passage in the New Testament (Matthew 18:15) applied to her situation and that she must therefore confront her father about the abuse.[19] The plaintiff was highly distressed at the prospect, but felt that she had no choice, so the meeting went ahead in the presence of two elders. Some time later, she sued the Jehovah's Witness church, and the elders who were involved.

The court in *Cairns* accepted the testimony of a church elder that "Matthew 18 applies to private disputes between people, such as disputes over financial matters, and cannot be applied to a serious sin against God's laws, such as child abuse."[20] The court also accepted that the confrontation was "difficult and traumatic"[21] for the plaintiff, and that the retraumatization resulting from the experience contributed to her current psychological difficulties, although it was certainly not the only factor. The church was held responsible for the actions of the elder who instructed the plaintiff to confront her father. The plaintiff was awarded damages of $5,000. This case suggests an important lesson: while ADR has much to offer, it is not always appropriate. Careful thought must be given as to whether ADR is likely to help resolve the conflict, or risk making the situation worse, particularly where vulnerable individuals are involved.

Mediation

Mediation involves a neutral third person who works with parties who are negotiating a dispute. For this reason, mediation is sometimes called assisted negotiation. Since the mediator does not have the authority to decide the outcome, he or she is seen as controlling the process but not the result. As with negotiation, a mediated settlement is crafted by the parties themselves.

Mediation can take place with just two individuals or among several parties. Whether mediation occurs with two parties or within a larger group, the key aspect is the presence of an additional person – one who is not involved in the conflict.

Benefits of mediation

Sitting down with a neutral third party to try to find solutions could be useful in a whole range of situations. For instance, perhaps a congregation is finding its numbers dwindling, to the point that it is hard pressed to maintain its activities and pay its bills. Everyone agrees that something must be done, but the question is what? Some within the congregation believe that there is potential for increasing the size of the congregation by making contact with those in the community who are not affiliated with a particular congregation and by reassessing program offerings to appeal to new members. Others believe that it will be very difficult to attract new people and that the best choice is amalgamation with a neighbouring congregation. Before such a significant decision is made, it is important that options are thought through clearly and that everyone in the congregation feels they have had an opportunity to be heard. The congregation might decide to have a series of meetings to talk through the issues, and might feel that the meetings are more likely to be constructive if they can be assisted by a neutral third party who has no stake in the decision. This person would not impose a solution, but would help the congregation work through issues and reach a decision.

The five principles of interest-based negotiation, described above, also apply to mediation. A mediator versed in the principles underlying interest-based negotiation can help the parties to use these principles:

> ... the mediator can identify and help in the narrowing of the issues; help identify and crystallize each side's underlying interests and concerns; carry less-subtle messages and infor-

mation between the parties; explore bases for agreement and the consequences of not settling; develop a co-operative, problem solving approach. ... the mediator can often identify options beyond the parties' original conception. The common denominator to all these efforts is the enhancement of communications between the parties in conflict.[22]

Specific benefits that may accrue from the involvement of a mediator include the following:

- Mediation may be constructive in a situation in which one or both parties feel the need to express their emotions. The presence of a mediator may help to ensure that this is done in a positive way;

- The mediator should be attuned to imbalances in the negotiating power of the parties and take steps to reduce the impact of that imbalance on the mediation process. For instance, the mediator can ensure that each person has the same amount of uninterrupted time to tell his or her story, can set and enforce ground rules for discussion (such as no interrupting, no name calling, no swearing) and can call a break when the mediation becomes too heated or one party is distraught;

- A skilled mediator will be sensitive to the ways in which characteristics such as culture and gender may affect a party's approach to negotiation, and may be able to help the parties be aware of and respond appropriately to such differences;

- Mediation can offer the parties privacy and confidentiality;

- Mediation will almost always be faster and less expensive than going to court; and

- Mediation allows the parties to maintain control and allows for creative, mutually acceptable outcomes.

Inequality of bargaining power

As noted above, a mediator may be able to help an otherwise vulnerable party become empowered. There can be situations, however, in which the imbalance of power between the parties or the vulnerability of one party is so great that a mediator cannot provide sufficient protection. There is an ethical imperative on anyone planning to act as a mediator, or urging mediation on disputants, to consider whether this is an appropriate process in the context.

Training for mediators

When individuals within the church find themselves called upon to mediate disputes, they should take training.[23] A number of centres across the country now offer training in conflict management. Both shorter, more introductory sessions and longer, more advanced courses are available. Some training centres might be willing to tailor their modules to the church setting and to offer a training session specifically for those who work or volunteer within a church. Although some of the attributes of a good mediator – including fairness, open-mindedness, sensitivity, listening skills and common sense – cannot easily be taught, such courses can provide a wealth of practical skills.

Arbitration

Arbitration is defined as

> The reference of a dispute to an impartial (third) person chosen by the parties to the dispute who agree in advance to abide by the arbitrator's award issued after a hearing at which both parties have an opportunity to be heard.[24]

Unlike a mediator who controls the process but does not decide on the outcome, an arbitrator actually decides the outcome.

In some situations, parties to an agreement may indicate that any disputes arising from the agreement will be dealt with in the first instance by arbitration. Thus, in unionized workplaces, it is usual for the collective agreement to state that grievances arising under the collective agreement will be heard by an arbitrator. A term stipulating that any disputes arising out of the contract are to be dealt with through arbitration is also frequently used in construction contracts and international commercial contracts.[25] In other situations, it may only be after a disagreement has arisen that those involved agree to submit the matter to arbitration.

However parties come to arbitration, the key element is that the issue will be decided by a third party and the decision will be binding on the parties, subject to any rights of appeal or judicial review (see Chapter 3). It is this characteristic – a third party having the authority to decide the issue – that distinguishes arbitration from negotiation and mediation.

Benefits of arbitration

As with negotiation and mediation, arbitration could prove useful in a variety of situations. Let us go back to the earlier example of two church employees wanting the same vacation weeks during the summer. The employees agree to sit down and negotiate, but are unable to find a satisfactory resolution. They are not interested in mediation because they feel it is unlikely that they can work things out, even with the help of a mediator. They realize they need someone else simply to make the decision, but have little faith that the church board will come up with a wise solution. However, both employees have great respect for a cleric who was with the congregation several years ago. Now retired, perhaps he would be willing to listen to both employees explain why they need to take vacation at a particular time in the summer, and then make a decision. Because he knows this congregation, he will have a good sense of the staffing needs over the summer, and since both employees trust him, they are willing to abide by whatever decision he makes. If the retired cleric agrees to this, he will be acting as an arbitrator.

Advantages of referring a church-related dispute to an arbitrator might include the following:

- Arbitration may allow the dispute to be settled more quickly or less expensively than would be the case with litigation;

- With arbitration, the parties choose the decision maker (thus, one would hope, increasing the likelihood of having the issues decided by an expert in the area who is sensitive to the church context);

- Arbitration allows the parties to retain their privacy, since, unlike courts, arbitrators are not required to make their decisions available to the public;

- Arbitration can dispense, at least to some degree, with the formality of court proceedings and with formal rules regarding evidence;

- Arbitration allows the parties to avoid litigation, while providing an opportunity for objective findings of fact. It may be that the parties are completely at odds as to what actually happened in a given situation, and may not be able to move to a resolution because of this. Having a third-party decision maker may be necessary when determining "what actually happened" is required. A neutral third-party decision maker can hear from each side, make a determination of the facts, and then rule on the appropriate outcome, given those facts; and

- Arbitration allows the parties to avoid litigation while still responding to a situation in which one or more of the parties feel the need to have a neutral third party justify their position. If, to be able to move beyond a particular conflict, one person needs to hear an objective third party say, "Yes, you were wronged" or "Yes, you were right to insist on X," then he or she may not be satisfied with negotiation or mediation.

Possible limitations of arbitration

Although arbitration can offer greater flexibility, it still encompasses some of the characteristics of litigation. Thus, although the decision is rendered by an arbitrator rather than a judge, arbitration still involves an adversarial approach and a decision imposed by a third party rather than created by the disputants themselves. Whether this is an advantage or a drawback depends on the situation.

Further, delay and expense may not be completely avoided. Established arbitrators with a proven track record may be booked well in advance, and their services may be expensive. Also, depending on the circumstances, it may not always be a straightforward matter for the parties to agree on an arbitrator. The parties should think carefully about what knowledge and attributes the arbitrator should have, and unless an arbitrator has an established reputation in dealing with the kinds of disputes at issue, the parties may need to do some initial investigation before deciding on a name or names to put forward. There is an added complication when, in a church context, the parties ask the cleric to act as the decision maker. Clergy need to consider how relationships within the congregation might be fostered or ruptured by their involvement.[26]

Depending on the seriousness of the issue and the potential ramifications, one or both parties may feel the need to be represented by counsel at the arbitration. If a church or congregation is involved in an arbitration, it should consult with its lawyers about the possible outcomes and whether the cost of being represented by a lawyer at the arbitration would be justified in the circumstances.

Despite some loosening of procedure, arbitrators will still need to ensure that the duty of fairness is met (see Chapter 3) and may, on occasion, turn for guidance to rules developed in the context of litigation – for instance, in order to decide how much weight to give certain kinds of evidence. Therefore, it would be unrealistic to assume that arbitration can always avoid the kinds of "technicalities" associated with litigation in the courts.

Restorative justice

There is a growing body of literature on restorative justice.[27] What these conceptions of restorative justice have in common is a focus on responding to wrongdoing (in most cases, criminal behaviour) in a way that reflects accountability and healing, rather than retribution and punishment. Restorative justice has been defined as "an approach to crime that focuses on healing relationships and repairing the damage crime causes to individuals and communities"[28] and as

> ... an approach to accountability for crime based on the restoration of balanced social relations and reparation of criminal harms that is rooted in the values of equality, mutual respect and concern and that uses deliberative processes involving crime victims, offenders, their respective supporters and representatives of the broader community under the guidance of authorized and skilled facilitators.[29]

Restorative justice is seen by many who work and write in the field as quite different from ADR. Restorative justice is not simply about helping parties reach a settlement that reflects their interests. Instead, restorative justice involves a recognition that a wrong has been done, both to an individual and to the whole community, and requires an acknowledgement of responsibility by the wrongdoer.

Restorative justice is a complex process that is likely to take place within an established framework; for instance, within the criminal justice system or within carefully formulated responses by an entire denomination to abuse claims by residential school survivors. Therefore, unlike negotiation, mediation and arbitration, which could be used fairly frequently and even informally, it seems improbable that a congregation would engage in individual or sporadic attempts at restorative justice, unsupported by the kinds of frameworks referred to above. Any church that is contemplating creating a process for restorative justice to respond to a specific issue would be well-advised to seek expert assistance in thinking through the relevant issues and developing any such process. We introduce the topic here only to give readers a sense of what restorative justice encompasses and how it differs from ADR processes such as negotiation, mediation and arbitration.

Conclusion

As with any other organization, congregations and other entities within the church carry within them the potential for conflict. There may be times when the only appropriate response to such conflict is litigation. At the other end of the spectrum, there may be times when the individuals or groups involved decide that it is best simply to "live with it" and get on with other aspects of church life. However, there will also be instances when those who are in conflict within the church want to seek a resolution but do not see recourse to the courts as the best approach.

While alternative dispute resolution is not a panacea for all situations, and while it is necessary to think carefully about the appropriateness of using a particular ADR approach in a particular situation, ADR does have the potential to offer cre-ative and effective ways of managing conflict. When conflict arises within a church, or in a church's relations with others, it is well worth considering whether processes such as negotia-tion, mediation or arbitration can offer solutions and create opportunities for growth and reconciliation.

Alternative Dispute Resolution: Questions and Answers

Q. What is alternative dispute resolution?

A. Alternative dispute resolution (ADR) is an umbrella term that refers to the various processes that may be used to resolve conflicts without resort to litigation in the courts. ADR includes negotiation, mediation and arbitration.

Q. In what sort of church contexts might ADR prove useful?

A. ADR may prove useful in helping members of church committees work together, mediating disputes between individuals or groups within congregations, resolving differences between clergy and other employees or church members, and responding to claims from those outside the church community.

Q. What are some of the benefits of ADR, as opposed to litigation?

A. First, there is the possibility that parties may be able to find creative solutions that meet at least some of the interests of all the parties involved. This is in contrast to litigation, which most often results in one party winning and the other losing. Second, the processes of ADR may be kept confidential, whereas the court process is a very public one. Third, ADR may help avoid the substantial costs of litigation.

Q. What is negotiation?

A. Negotiation is discussion between parties with opposing views aimed at achieving a settlement of their differences. Sometimes lawyers or professional negotiators work on behalf of the parties, but there is no neutral third party involved.

Q. What is mediation?

A. Mediation differs from negotiation in that a third-party mediator who is objective and independent from the parties becomes involved to help the parties reach a resolution. The mediator does not have any power to impose a resolution. Mediation may be useful in situations in which the parties have attempted negotiation but have been unsuccessful in reaching a settlement.

Q. What is arbitration?

A. Arbitration is similar to mediation in that it involves a third party, but differs in that the arbitrator has the power to impose a resolution on the parties. As a result, arbitration bears more resemblance to litigation than do the other forms of ADR.

Q. What is restorative justice, and how does it differ from the various forms of alternative dispute resolution?

A. Restorative justice responds to wrongdoing by seeking to heal relationships between the individuals and communities involved. Restorative justice is not simply about helping parties reach a settlement that reflects their interests; instead, it recognizes that a wrong has been done, both to an individual and to the whole community, and requires an acknowledgement of responsibility by the wrongdoer. Any church that is contemplating creating a process for restorative justice in order to respond to a specific issue should seek expert assistance in thinking through the relevant issues and developing any such process.

Notes

[1]   Throughout this book, when we use the word *court*, we are referring to secular courts, unless we state explicitly that we are discussing church courts.

[2]   These passages include Matthew 18:15, 2 Corinthians 5:18 and 1 Corinthians 12:24-27. (Our thanks to Cynthia Gunn, counsel to the United Church of Canada, for identifying these passages.) Matthew 18 is made up of a series of parables and exhortations about how to live in a right relationship with others and therefore with God. Between the well-known parables of the lost sheep and the unmerciful servant is this teaching: "If your brother sins against you, go and show him his fault, just between the two of you. If he listens to you, you have won your brother over." In 2 Corinthians 5, after declarations about what it means to be controlled by Christ's love (verse 14) and to be in a new creation in Christ (verse 17), Paul states, "All this is from God, who through Christ reconciled us to himself and gave us the ministry of reconcilia-tion." The need for harmonious relationships – and the consequences of discord – are set out in 1 Corinthians 12: 24-27, using the well-known metaphor of the body for the community of believers:

> 24: But God has so composed the body, giving the greater honour to the inferior part, 25: that there may be no discord in the body, but that the members may have the same care for one another. 26: If one member suffers, all suffer together; if one member is honored, all rejoice together. 27: Now you are the body of Christ and individually members of it.

[3]   Joseph Allegretti, "A Christian Perspective on Alternative Dispute Resolution" (2001) 28 *Fordham Urban Law Journal* 997, p. 998. (Note: in using this quotation, we are not suggesting that only Christians should feel this predisposition, but that Christians, among others, certainly should.)

[4]   Thanks to the Rev. Dr. Susan McAlpine-Gillis for this practical suggestion.

[5]   D. Misteravich, "The Limits of Alternative Dispute Resolution: Pre-serving the Judicial Function" (1992-93) 70 *University of Detroit Mercy Law Review* 37.

6   Owen Fiss, "Against Settlement" (1984) 93 *Yale Law Journal* 1073, pp. 1086–87.

7   Julie Macfarlane, *Dispute Resolution: Readings and Case Studies*, 2nd ed. (Toronto: Emond Montgomery, 2003), p. xvii [*Macfarlane*].

8   For instance, let us assume that a church employee has been fired and is alleging that she or he has been wrongly dismissed. Let us also assume that this former employee has entered into negotiations with the church about pay in lieu of notice. (For a discussion of wrongful dismissal and pay in lieu of notice, see Chapter 15.) The former employee would be operating in a vacuum if he or she did not know roughly what a court would see as reasonable pay in lieu of notice in the context. If the employee would be likely to receive a year's pay through the courts, then he or she might well settle for seven or eight months' pay, in order to avoid the costs and delay. On the other hand, the employee probably would not see one month as an attractive offer; however, without a sense of the legal rights involved, the employee would have no way of evaluating whether or not one month's pay was a reasonable offer.

9   John Manwaring, "Negotiation," in *Macfarlane*, note 7, p. 109.

10 The concept of interest-based negotiation and the five principles set out here are taken from a classic text on ADR: Roger Fisher and William Ury, *Getting to Yes: Negotiating Agreement Without Giving In*, 2nd ed. by Bruce Patton (Boston: Houghton Mifflin Company, 1991) [*Getting to Yes*]. This is an eminently readable book that provides an excellent introduction to interest-based negotiation. Since these principles are applicable to mediation, it is also an excellent resource for those training to become mediators. Interest-based negotiation goes by other names as well, such as integrative or principled negotiation.

11 This example is from *Getting to Yes, ibid.*

12 Brad Spangler, *Integrative or Interest-Based Bargaining* (2003) (www.beyondintractability.org).

13 *Ibid.*

14 Hon. Mr. Justice George Adams and Naomi Bussin, "Alternative Dispute Resolution and Canadian Courts: A Time for Change" (1995) 17 *Advocates' Quarterly* 133 [*A Time for Change*].

15 Two very useful sources for ideas on how to deal with positional bargainers are William L. Ury, *Getting Past No: Negotiating with Difficult*

People (New York: Bantam Books, 1991) and Douglas Stone et al., *Difficult Conversations: How to Discuss What Matters Most* (New York: Penguin Books, 2000).

[16]   Manwaring, "Negotiation" in *Macfarlane*, note 7, p. 180.

[17]   *Ibid.*, p. 205.

[18]   B.(V.) v. *Cairns* (2003), 65 O.R. (3d) 343 (Ont. (Sup. Ct. Jus.)) [*Cairns*]. *Cairns* is also discussed in Chapter 11.

[19]   See note 2.

[20]   *Cairns*, note 18, para. 62.

[21]   *Ibid.*, para. 178.

[22]   *A Time for Change*, note 14, p. 137.

[23]   When a cleric is asked to act as mediator between two individuals or elements within a congregation, it is necessary to consider whether this is likely to heal or further rupture relationships within the congregation. This may be slightly less of a concern than if the cleric is asked to act as arbitrator because, as mediator, he or she will be only guiding the process, not deciding upon the outcome. However, it is still a relevant issue to consider.

[24]   *Black's Law Dictionary*, 5th ed., s.v. "arbitration."

[25]   Such a term might read: "Any dispute arising out of or in connection with this contract, including any question regarding its existence, validity or termination, shall be referred to and finally resolved by arbitration .... The award of the arbitrator shall be final and binding and judgment thereon may be entered in any court of competent jurisdiction." See *Model Clauses* (www.arbiter.net).

[26]   Lee Tarte, "Clergy Arbitrator Liability: A Potential Pitfall of Alternative Dispute Resolution in the Church" (1988) 32 *Catholic Lawyer* 310.

[27]   Two of the best-known writers in this field are colleagues of ours at Dalhousie Law School: Professor Bruce Archibald and Professor Jennifer Llewellyn.

[28]   Department of Justice Canada, *Restorative Justice in Canada: A Consultation Paper* (www.justice.gc.ca).

[29]   Bruce Archibald, "Why Restorative Justice Is Not Compulsory Compassion" (2005) 42 *Alberta Law Review* 941.

5

Preventing Harm and Reducing Risk

The risk reasonably to be perceived
defines the duty to be obeyed.
—Justice Benjamin Cardozo, New York Court of Appeals
and later Justice of the Supreme Court of the United States,
Palsgraf v. Long Island R. Co. (1928)

Risk, defined as the possibility of loss or injury, is an inevitable part of most, if not all, activities in life. A church, as with any careful person or organization, must take reasonable measures to either eliminate or reduce risk. It is also prudent to consider and implement ways to transfer liability for risk through such means as insurance.

This chapter addresses the issue of risk by putting forward the key elements of risk management. It then provides advice on drafting policies and procedures, an important aspect of risk management. It also briefly describes a few common ways to transfer liability for risk, and concludes with some thoughts on how to go about choosing a lawyer, one of many professionals who can help avoid or minimize risk.

Risk management

A valuable book on risk management, *Better Safe… Risk Management in Volunteer Programs & Community Service*, defines risk management as being "about dealing with uncertainties. It is about the potential for, and the forecasting of, risks, and doing everything reasonable to control them."[1] It further notes that "risk management need not be expensive or highly technical. In fact, managing most risks requires little more than healthy doses of common sense, deliberate foresight, and good planning. *In most circumstances, good risk management is simply good management.*"[2]

The author describes a three-step approach to risk management:

1. Identify the Risks – Potential risks include accidents, theft, breach of confidentiality, sexual abuse, loss of standing within the community, etc.[3] To help generate a master list of potential and actual risks, Graff suggests consulting and reviewing a broad range of persons and records, including staff, supervisors, directors, safety records, existing policies and procedures, etc.[4]

2. Evaluate the Risks – Categorize risks according to their probability of occurrence and degree of potential harm. Prioritize and act on the most significant risks first.

3. Control Risks – Some risks can be eliminated by stopping the risky activity. Others can be reduced by taking appropriate action, which might involve repairing a stairway or providing better training to staff and volunteers. The liability for some risks can sometimes be transferred by various methods, including insurance and waiver of liability agreements.

Everyone on a church's governing board has an obligation to ensure that risks are assessed and controlled. Indeed, this should be every director's primary concern. Of course, risk management is not something that is accomplished all at once and then put aside. It is an ongoing commitment and concern of every prudent organization.

Policies and procedures

Policies and procedures are an essential aspect of risk management. The overall goal and purpose of most policies and procedures is to eliminate or reduce risks that cause harm. They serve as a focus for addressing risk-management issues.[5] To be of value, however, a church must be committed not only to drafting good policies and procedures, but also to ensuring that they are known and followed.

Churches are wise to develop policies with respect to a variety of risks and concerns, including such matters as confidentiality, privacy and personal information, conflicts of interest, internal financial management, volunteers, health and safety, sexual abuse and sexual harassment, to name several. The main purpose of this part of the chapter is to identify some of the key elements that churches might consider including in the development of their own individual policies on health and safety, sexual abuse and harassment. The approach we take is meant to provide a very basic introduction to the task of drafting a policy. The general components we suggest have been drawn from general advisory literature on the kinds of things to include, as well as from a comparison of specific church policy statements. This is certainly not meant to be a comprehensive list, and churches that are drafting policies should include other components important in their own particular circumstances.

Health and safety policy

Health and safety is clearly not as pressing an issue for a church as it is in an industrial setting or a workplace where considerable hazards exist. However, just because the potential health and safety concerns are neither as immediately obvious nor as serious does not mean they do not exist or are undeserving of attention. Attentiveness to health and safety considerations will undoubtedly have positive effects for church employees as well as those who attend services and utilize the facilities for other events.

Many churches have recognized this fact and have voluntarily implemented a health and safety policy. It is important to note that many provincial governments have enacted occupational health and safety legislation that places a legal duty on employers with a certain number of employees to develop such a policy.[6] Since churches typically employ at least a small number of staff, they should be aware that the creation of a health and safety policy may be legally mandated.

Policy components

The following chart contains some suggested elements that might be useful to include in a health and safety policy.[7]

Statement of Purpose	As a preliminary step, it is useful to identify the purpose of the health and safety policy that is being developed, paying particular attention to the context of the church that is developing it. This provides a structure and sets the tone for the actual policies that will be developed. → Example: The church is committed to ensuring that its premises are at all times safe and free from risks and hazards that could adversely impact on human health and safety.
Risk Assessment	In this section, the various health and safety issues and risks are identified, specific to the church involved. → Example: The church maintains a small quantity of gasoline on the premises used to power a lawnmower. This material is highly flammable and should therefore be stored away from heat sources and open flame. It is of potentially greatest risk to the custodian, who uses the gasoline when cutting the grass, as well as other employees on the premises.

Responsibilities of Stakeholders	It is necessary to identify the particular responsibilities of those who are stakeholders in the policy; this might include the administration, employees, members and visitors who use the church premises. → Example: It will be the responsibility of the church custodian to care for the driveways and walking paths around the property to ensure that they are clean and free of hazards.
Training	It is appropriate that those who have responsibility for various aspects of health and safety also be given the necessary training to discharge their role. Training might include courses in first aid and CPR, fire prevention, Workplace Hazardous Materials Information System (WHMIS) and using protective equipment. → Example: All church employees must receive basic certification in first aid and CPR.
Procedures and Practices	This is a set of rules and procedures that will serve to implement effectively the policy and form the basis for the achievement of its objectives. → Example: No scents or perfumes may be worn on the premises out of respect for those who suffer from environmental or chemical sensitivities.

Health and Safety Committee	Depending on the number of employees working for the church, the establishment of a committee to oversee health and safety concerns may be required by provincial legislation. Even where it is not required, it may nonetheless be desirable to have such a body in place to take charge of health and safety matters. This aspect of the policy would set out all aspects of the health and safety committee, including its composition, rules, procedures and mandate.
Record Keeping	It is important that the church keep records of all matters pertaining to health and safety, including information about any hazardous materials on the premises. All steps taken to ensure health and safety should be well documented. This type of record could prove essential if there was an allegation that the church was negligent or failed to address health and safety concerns.

Harassment policy

Harassment is an issue of concern in Canadian society, especially in the employment context. It takes many forms, including verbal, physical, emotional and sexual. Those who fall victim to acts of sexual harassment have recourse to either provincial, territorial or federal human rights legislation,[8] the terms of which apply to all employers and service providers. Human rights commissions oversee the application of such legislation and also work to increase public awareness of human rights concerns. These bodies are active in emphasizing to employers and other organizations the importance of developing internal policies pertaining to issues of harassment[9] (see Chapter 16 for a discussion of human rights). The formulation of a policy in relation to harassment is a positive step toward preventing its occurrence and provides a framework to deal effectively with complaints when they arise.

Policy components

The following chart contains some suggested elements that might serve as a basis for the development of a harassment policy by a church.[10]

| Statement of Purpose | An organization should state its position on harassment at the beginning of the policy. Included in this statement would be the overall purposes and objectives that the organization wishes to achieve through the implementation of the policy.

→ Example: The church is committed to creating and maintaining an environment that is free from all forms of harassment, including (but not limited to) verbal, physical, emotional and sexual. |

Scope	This section identifies those who are subject to the policy; this might include members of the church staff, members of the congregation, and those who make use of the premises for group activities. The context(s) in which the policy applies should also be made clear, as well as the particular types of harassment that are being targeted. → Example: This policy applies to all current employees of the church while acting in the course of their employment, both on and off church property.
Procedures and Practices	It is important to establish procedures so that those who allege harassment will know what steps to take. Internal complaint procedures might be identified, in addition to the complaint processes of provincial and territorial human rights commissions. Procedures will typically relate to the reporting, investigation and settlement of harassment complaints. Resources may also be identified to assist those who are affected. → Example: Anyone wishing to make a complaint under this policy will provide a statement in writing to the church officer responsible for these matters, who will then follow the procedures set out in the policy.

Record Keeping	It is essential that a mechanism be in place to keep records of reported incidents of harassment. It should be emphasized that all such records will be kept confidential and private, unless disclosure is required by law.

Sexual abuse policy

The issue of sexual abuse, especially involving members of the clergy, has in recent years come to the forefront as a significant challenge facing churches in North America. Churches need to develop effective screening, testing and monitoring in order to prevent these harms from occurring. They also need to develop better approaches to dealing with incidents of abuse when they do occur. Developing a sexual abuse policy clarifies what a church intends to do to prevent sexual abuse from happening, and how a church would respond if it were to occur.

Policy components

The following chart contains some suggested elements that might serve as a basis for the development of a sexual abuse policy by a church.

Statement of Purpose	As with all other kinds of policies, it is useful at the outset to provide a broad statement of the principles and purposes that animate the policy. This establishes a framework for the body of the policy.
History and Context	As a further means of framing the issue, it is helpful to look at the history of sexual abuse within the particular church preparing the policy. Identifying what has happened in the past and what steps were previously taken to deal with the matter will serve as a foundation for looking to the future.
Risk Assessment	In order to prepare effectively for the future, it is necessary to evaluate the main areas of risk. What situations might lead to allegations or actual incidents of abuse? What groups or individuals are most at risk? Answering these types of questions will provide a direction for the policy and will identify the risks that need to be addressed.

| Procedures and Practices | This section deals with the particular procedures that will be employed to implement the policy. One aspect might be screening procedures, which are an effective means of ensuring that people who are struggling with certain issues or tendencies are not placed in positions in which they could engage in abusive behavior. Another critically important matter is to set out how the church will respond to incidents of abuse should they occur. Procedures might also be included for dealing with people who are experiencing difficulties in the course of their ministry.

→ Example: Those being considered for ministerial roles within the church will be required to undergo psychological testing, the purpose of which will be to identify any issues that might be or become impediments to ministry. |
|---|---|
| Record Keeping | It is essential that records be kept of incidents that occur and what the church did to deal effectively with them. The emphasis must always be on confidentiality and privacy, but the involvement of law enforcement and the justice system in instances of criminal conduct should be acknowledged. |

Transferring risk: insurance, waiver of liability agreements and indemnity agreements

Avoiding or reducing risk by developing and following policies and procedures is an essential aspect of risk management, but even with the best policies and procedures in place, harm can still occur. Given this reality, churches are wise to consider ways to transfer the risk of loss. Three common methods to transfer risk are insurance, waiver of liability agreements, and indemnity agreements.

Insurance

In today's society – in which everyone must be insured to drive a car and where most people have at one time or another taken out life, disability or property insurance – it hardly seems necessary to stress the importance of organizations such as churches having insurance. The potential for a fire to destroy church property, for church valuables to be stolen or for a successful lawsuit against a church all speak to the need for churches to maintain insurance policies that will cover these and other kinds of risks.

Indemnity insurance is the most common type of insurance. To indemnify means to compensate for a loss suffered. Indemnity insurance is a contract between insurer and insured in which the insurer agrees to compensate the insured for specified losses. By entering into an insurance contract, a church transfers the risk of loss to the insurance company.

> Most insurance other than life insurance is indemnity insurance. Indemnity insurance provides for financial loss flowing from misfortune such as damage to property, the incurring of liability to pay damages [in a lawsuit], or personal injury. The arrangement is that the financial loss will be made good [by the insurer]. But the principle of indemnity requires that no more than that be paid. A claimant is not permitted to profit from the situation by receiving more from the insurer than was lost.[11]

Property insurance is an example of indemnity insurance. Churches should be insured against loss or damage to their property, whether that is a church building or other forms of property, such as sacred vessels, musical equipment or vestments.

Liability insurance is another example of indemnity insurance. Liability insurance indemnifies an insured for civil liabilities incurred, such as liability for injuries caused to a third party by a church employee's careless driving, or a slip and fall on faulty church steps. Churches owe a duty of care toward their members, volunteers and any other people who enter upon their premises. When a person is injured on church property because of the failure of the church to take reasonable care, a church could be sued and found liable for the loss suffered and ordered to pay damages to the injured party. A church may be liable for significant claims, depending on the severity of injury and the person injured. For example, someone injured by the careless act or omission of a church and who is unable to work as a result may have a claim of several million dollars for his or her future loss of income claim. (For a discussion of occupiers' liability, see Chapter 20. Other areas of civil liability are covered in Part II.)

Liability insurance is sometimes obtained for directors and officers of the church's governing body. These policies indemnify directors and officers for claims made against them in their capacity as a director or officer of the organization. Whether directors' and officers' liability insurance is necessary or advisable will depend on the facts of the particular situation. A church should obtain advice from its lawyer and insurance representative. Advice is especially important on this issue because there is some question about the legality of directors' and officers' liability insurance for certain organizations.[12] (See below for a discussion of indemnity agreements that are sometimes used in tandem with directors' and officers' liability insurance.)

In addition to indemnification, a liability policy usually states that the insurer will provide a defence and pay the costs of the defence should the insured church, cleric or director be sued by a third party for losses covered under the policy. This latter aspect of liability insurance is often overlooked or undervalued when considering whether liability insurance is needed.

Insurance: excluded risks

It is important to appreciate that any insurance policy only covers the risks accepted and agreed to by the insurer that occur in a specified period of time. An insured must be aware of both what is covered and what is excluded from coverage. Certain sorts of risks are rarely covered by liability insurance:

Generally, liability insurance is available to cover only civil liability to pay damages. For public policy reasons, a person cannot transfer the risk of criminal liability to an insurer, since this would defeat the punitive purpose of criminal sanctions. ...

Liability arising from unintentional torts, i.e. negligent acts or omissions, is the most common form of liability covered by liability insurance. Generally acts committed with intent to cause injury or damage are expressly excluded in most policies ....[13]

Insurance is a complex subject. The best advice is to talk with your insurance representative and your lawyer. It is important to underscore the necessity of full and accurate disclosure of all relevant information to the insurer when entering into an insurance contract and anytime the facts relevant to the insurance contract change. For example, if the church vehicles are insured for a particular use and that use changes, this new information should be immediately brought to the attention of the insurer. Failure to disclose fully all relevant facts to your insurer may result in a denial of coverage after a loss occurs.

Waiver of liability agreements

A church may sometimes organize an event that involves the risk of injury or loss, such as a camping trip for the youth or a skiing expedition. The risk may be quite ordinary, such as the risk of driving to the event, or more unusual, such as the risk of injury on a ski slope. Should one of the participants suffer injury or loss, he or she may allege the church is legally responsible.

The allegation may be that the driver of the vehicle carrying the participants drove negligently, or that the church did not supervise the group properly at the event. In anticipation of a possible lawsuit, it is common to ask participants to sign an agreement beforehand not to sue the church or its employees should one of the participants suffer an injury or loss. These documents are called waiver of liability agreements. Waiver means to relinquish or give up a right. One who signs a waiver of liability agreement is giving up the right to sue. When recognized and enforced by a court, they provide a complete defence to a lawsuit.

These sorts of agreements raise ethical issues. Is it ethical to use them to prevent someone harmed by a church's negligence from seeking redress through the courts? Since reasonable (and ethical) people can disagree over the answer to that question, it is perhaps advisable for a church to consider the issue before using waiver of liability agreements.

Waiver of liability agreements will be valid only when certain conditions are strictly complied with by those relying on them. To be effective, they must be written in clear and comprehensible language. Further, it is essential to include in the waiver document the specific risks that are being waived (e.g., injury to person or property at the skiing expedition). The fact that legal liability for a specific loss or harm suffered is being waived must be stated clearly, and the court must conclude that the person signing the form understood that he or she was waiving the right to sue. In addition, the person signing the form must have the capacity to do so.[14]

It is doubtful whether a waiver signed by a child, the child's parent on behalf of the child or both the child and the parent would be enforced by a court against the child. As one author concludes, "Most contracts made by minors (or "infants") are only valid if they are for the minor's benefit. Since a release or exclusion of rights is to the minor's disadvantage, such contracts are not enforceable, even when co-signed by the parent or guardian."[15] In other words, if a child was injured because of a church's negligence, the fact that the child and his or her parents had signed a waiver of liability form would not prevent the child from starting a lawsuit. The court would not recognize the validity of the agreement.

Indemnity agreements

Risks can also be transferred or avoided through indemnity agreements. An indemnity agreement is a contract in which one person agrees to repay or compensate (i.e. indemnify) the other for a loss he or she may suffer.

For example, the parents of a child participating in a church event could be asked to sign an indemnity agreement, whereby they agree to repay the church for any damages (i.e. money) the church is required to pay as a result of a lawsuit brought by the child against the church for personal injuries arising from participation in the event. Or, suppose a situation in which a person taking part in a church event injures someone else, who in turn sues the church. If the participant who caused the injury has signed an indemnity agreement with the church, he or she would be obligated to repay the church any amount it pays to the injured person.

Indemnity agreements are also sometimes entered into between the directors and officers of a church and the church. Pursuant to the agreement, the church agrees to indemnify the officers and directors for losses a director or officer sustains as a result of a lawsuit brought against them. Any church entering into such an indemnity agreement would want to consider obtaining directors' and officers' liability insurance to cover any losses the church incurs as a result of the agreement.

As noted previously, there is a caveat with respect to liability insurance for directors and officers. The same caveat applies to indemnity agreements for directors and officers: the law is somewhat unclear in this area.[16] It is therefore important that a church obtain advice from its lawyer before entering into an indemnity agreement with the directors of the church's governing body. Indeed, a lawyer should be retained to draft any agreement, whether for indemnification, waiver or something else.

Obtaining legal advice

A leitmotif that runs through this book is the wisdom of seeking legal advice before legal issues become legal problems. One of the best ways to eliminate or reduce risk is to get legal advice in a timely manner. Suppose, for example, an employee alleges that she was harassed by a co-worker. If you do not already know the steps the law requires you to take to deal with this situation, then you should speak to a lawyer.

It is important that the lawyer you retain be knowledgeable and experienced in the subject area about which you are seeking advice. Although all lawyers receive the same legal education, most specialize in certain areas of practice. You would be wrong to assume that all lawyers have the same level of skill and experience. For example, many – perhaps most – lawyers are not experienced in real estate law, family or criminal law, to name but three. The same is true for employment law. The very best personal injury lawyer in your province may never have drafted a will, or may have been involved in only a few real estate transactions some 30 years ago. To make the point as clear as possible, he or she would be a fine choice if you had been injured in a car accident and wanted to sue the other driver, but not if you wanted a will drafted or wanted legal help arranging the sale of the church camp.

How, then, do you find a lawyer with relevant practice experience? Lawyers often list themselves in the yellow pages by area of expertise or preferred practice. You can do further research by reviewing the information found on law firm websites. Other church members, business colleagues and friends may be a source of information. A lawyer you already know may also be an excellent resource to suggest names of legal counsel experienced in particular areas of law.

Many people make the mistake of thinking that the best lawyers are always in the bigger law firms. This is not true. Or that the higher a lawyer's hourly rate, the greater his or her expertise. Again, not true. What a lawyer charges reflects, in part, operating costs and years of seniority, not necessarily expertise. Highly competent legal counsel practise at firms of all sizes, and charge various rates depending on numerous factors, only one of which is expertise.

Initial meeting with prospective lawyer

Once you have the names of a few prospective lawyers, you should speak with them before making any decisions about whom to retain. Many lawyers do not charge for an initial short consultation. Do not hesitate at this meeting to ask the lawyer about his or her expertise in the subject area. When you are looking for a lawyer to advise you on employment matters, for instance, you will want to know how much of his or her time is spent practising in this area, the type and complexity of the matters he or she has handled, the number of years he or she has been practising in that field and what, if any, education he or she has received on the subject since law school.

You will also want to know what hourly rate he or she charges or whether you will be billed a fixed cost for a specific task, such as drafting an employment contract. If you eventually retain a lawyer on a hourly fee basis, you should set a spending limit and instruct the lawyer to call you before billing above that amount. Depending on the sort of matter that has led you to seek legal advice, you may want to know whether the lawyer can be retained on a contingency arrangement, whereby the fee is a percentage of any money recovered from the opposing side or elsewhere (sometimes expressed as "no fee if no recovery"). Questions about time are often as important as questions about money, and therefore you should also ask how long the work in question will take to complete.

Conclusion

Risk management is not difficult or complex. No person or church should feel daunted, discouraged or intimidated by the task. Risk management calls mainly for "healthy doses of common sense, deliberate foresight, and good planning."[17] Of equal importance, it requires a solid and ongoing commitment by all members of the church community, from the top down and the ground up.

What needs to be done is usually obvious. When questions or problems arise, there is an abundance of resources and expertise available to meet and overcome any obstacle. It is also helpful to consider what other organizations have done to address issues of risk management, especially when approaching the task of drafting a policy.[18]

Preventing Harm and Reducing Risk: Questions and Answers

Q. What is risk?

A. Risk is the possibility of loss or injury.

Q. What is risk management?

A. Risk management involves identifying, evaluating and controlling risks.

Q. How can risks be controlled?

A. Risks can be controlled by avoiding risky activity, taking appropriate steps to reduce risks, or transferring the liability for risks through insurance or other means.

Q. What is the purpose of policies and procedures?

A. They serve as a focus for addressing risk management issues.

Q. What is indemnity insurance?

A. Indemnity insurance is a contract between insurer and insured, in which the insurer agrees to compensate the insured for specified losses. Property and liability insurance are both examples of indemnity insurance.

Q. What is a waiver of liability agreement?

A. It is an agreement not to sue someone.

Q. What is an indemnity agreement?

A. It is an agreement in which one person agrees to repay or compensate (i.e. indemnify) the other for a loss he or she may suffer.

Notes

1   Linda L. Graff, *Better Safe… Risk Management in Volunteer Programs & Community Service* (Dundas, Ont.: Linda Graff & Associates Inc., 2003), p. 19 [*Graff*]. Emphasis omitted. There are many other resources available on issues of risk management, some of which are cited at Chapter 2, note 8.

2   *Ibid.* Emphasis in original.

3   *Ibid.*, p. 11.

4   *Ibid.*, pp. 55 and 65.

5   *Ibid.*, p. 140.

6   See, for example, Nova Scotia's *Occupational Health and Safety Act,* S.N.S. 1996, c. 7, s. 27.

7   Of particular usefulness in identifying key components of health and safety policies: Human Resources in the Voluntary Sector, *Occupational Health and Safety* (www.hrvs-rhsbc.ca); Government of Newfoundland and Labrador, *Developing Occupational Health and Safety Policies and Programs* (www.gs.gov.nl.ca).

8   See, for example, *Human Rights Code,* R.S.O. 1990, c. H.19; *Human Rights Act,* R.S.N.S. 1989, c. 214; *Canadian Human Rights Act,* R.S.C. 1985, c. H-6.

9   See Ontario Human Rights Commission, *Policy on Sexual Harassment and Inappropriate Gender-Related Comments and Conduct* (www.ohrc.on.ca).

10   Of great assistance in identifying the key components of a sexual harassment policy: Human Resources in the Voluntary Sector, *Harassment* (www.hrvs-rhsbc.ca).

11   Craig Brown et al., *Insurance Law in Canada* (Scarborough, Ont.: Thomson Carswell, 2002), vol. 1, p. 1–4 [*Brown*].

12   See generally, Donald J. Bourgeois, *The Law of Charitable and Not-for-Profit Organizations,* 3rd ed. (Markham, Ont.: Butterworths, 2002), pp. 270 and following [*Bourgeois*].

13   *Brown*, note 11, vol. 2, p. 18-2.

14   G. H. L. Fridman, *The Law of Torts in Canada,* 2nd ed. (Toronto: Carswell, 2002), pp. 455–456.

15   John Barnes, *Sports and the Law in Canada*, 3ʳᵈ ed. (Markham, Ont.: Butterworths Canada Ltd., 1996), p. 278.

16   See generally, *Bourgeois*, note 12, pp. 270 and following.

17   *Graff*, note 1, p. 19.

18   See the resources cited at Chapter 2, note 8. Many churches have developed policies on these and other issues. For example,

- **Health and Safety:**
  – Anglican Church of Canada Diocese of Toronto, *Health and Safety Information* (www. toronto.anglican.ca);
  – Anglican Church of Canada Diocese of Huron, *Sample Health and Safety Policy* (www.diohuron.org);

- **Harassment:**
  – Anglican Church of Canada Diocese of Toronto, *Sexual Misconduct Policy: sexual harassment, exploitation and assault* (www.toronto.anglican.ca);
  – Evangelical Lutheran Church in Canada Eastern Synod, *Sexual Abuse or Harassment Policy* (www.easternsynod.org);
  – Presbyterian Church in Canada, *Policy of the Presbyterian Church in Canada for Dealing with Sexual Abuse and/or Harassment, 1998 & Statements of Clarifications, 2001* (www.presbyterian.ca);
  – United Church of Canada, *Sexual Abuse (Sexual Harassment, Pastoral Sexual Misconduct, Sexual Assault) and Child Abuse* (www.bc.united-church.ca);

- **Sexual abuse:**
  – Anglican Church of Canada Diocese of Ottawa, *Sexual Exploitation Policy* (www.ottawa.anglican.ca);
  – Baptist Church of Canada, *Church Ministry Guidelines and Procedures Regarding Child Safety* (www.baptist.ca);
  – Mennonite Church Canada, *Safe Church Policy* (www.mennonitechurch.ca);
  – Presbyterian Church in Canada, *Leading with Care: A policy for ensuring a climate of safety for children, youth and vulnerable adults in the Presbyterian Church in Canada* (www.presbyterian.ca).

Part II:

Civil Liability

There is no special legal immunity from a civil lawsuit or protection of any kind for churches or clergy in Canada. Given this fact and our increasingly litigious society, churches and clergy are well-advised to consider ways to reduce or avoid the risks of litigation. Being knowledgeable about civil liability generally, and the various grounds for civil liability more specifically, is an important step toward addressing the risk of liability. Part II deals with issues related to civil liability.

Chapter 6 sets the stage by discussing the three grounds of civil liability: contract, tort and statute.

Chapter 7 focuses on the secular courts. It notes that the secular courts have authority or jurisdiction over all Canadian churches and provides a short description of the main courts. Chapter 8 outlines the civil trial process, beginning when the plaintiff files the requisite documents and ending with the possibility of an appeal to the Supreme Court of Canada.

The concepts of direct and vicarious liability are discussed in Chapter 9. Direct liability arises when the wrongful actions of a person or corporation cause harm. A person or corporation, although innocent of any wrongdoing, may be liable for the wrongdoing of another person because of their relationship to that person; this is referred to as vicarious liability. Churches can be vicariously liable for the wrongdoing of both employees and volunteers, a fact that significantly broadens the ambit of potential liability.

Civil liability in tort is of particular importance, and chapters 10 to 12 discuss several torts: battery, intentional infliction of mental suffering, negligence and defamation. Liability for intentional torts, such as battery, arises in situations in which someone means to cause harm. Negligence, a far more common ground of liability, is careless action that causes harm. The tort of defamation involves false statements that disparage a person's reputation. Two other areas of tort liability, nuisance and occupiers' liability, of particular relevance to property issues, are discussed in Chapters 20 and 21. The tort of trespass is discussed at Chapter 19.

Chapter 13 describes the characteristics of fiduciary relationships, an area of law that exists to protect the integrity of relationships in which a vulnerable party relies on a more powerful party. Several courts have found a church or cleric liable for breach of fiduciary duty.

Issues of privilege will be of significance to clerics or churches involved in lawsuits, and are discussed in Chapter 14. The general rule is that all relevant information, even confidential communications between a cleric and church member, must be disclosed to the court.

Anyone interested in learning more about the background of Canadian law may wish to read Part V, which sets out the three sources of law: the Constitution, legislation and the common law.

6

Civil Liability Overview

I am by no means sure that if a man kept a tiger,
and lightning broke his chain, and he got loose and did mischief,
that the man who kept him would not be liable.
—Lord William Bramwell, Exchequer Court,
Nichols v. Marsland (1875)

The central claim of the plaintiff in a lawsuit is usually that the defendant is the person liable for the loss or harm the plaintiff has suffered. The court's task is to determine whether, in fact and in law, the defendant is indeed liable and, if so, what consequences flow from that conclusion. Whether it is a case about a man who kept a tiger or a person who drove a car carelessly, refused to honour a contract in which he or she promised to build a cottage, or dumped garbage into a river contrary to a statute, the issue of liability must be decided.

This chapter begins with a definition of the concept of liability and describes the distinction between civil and criminal liability. It then sets out the three grounds or bases of civil liability: contract, tort and statute. Liability in tort is of particular importance; Chapters 10 to 12 look more closely at various torts. The concepts of direct and vicarious liability are dealt with in Chapter 9.

To be liable means to be responsible for or obligated by law. A person can be found liable for committing a tort, breaching a contract or disobeying a statute.

It is important to distinguish between civil and criminal liability. Criminal liability generally involves a breach of the *Criminal Code of Canada*. Civil liability involves the breach of a contract, the commission of a tort or the breach of a stat-ute. Criminal proceedings are prosecuted by the state against a citizen, the Queen v. X (the accused). Civil proceedings are generally disputes between private citizens, Plaintiff v. Defendant. Criminal proceedings usually end with either an acquittal or a finding of guilt. Civil proceedings usually end with either a plaintiff being awarded a sum of money in lieu of the loss caused by the defendant, or the plaintiff's claim being dismissed. The same behaviour by an individual may attract both civil and criminal liability, such as stealing or drunk driv-ing that results in an injury. A person who drives drunk and causes an accident may be tried in criminal court under the relevant *Criminal Code* provision, found guilty and sentenced to prison or fined. That person could also be sued in civil court by the injured person, found liable and ordered to pay a sum of money to the plaintiff equal to the amount of the loss.

Civil liability in contract

A contract is a legally enforceable promise. The three basic elements of a contract are agreement, consideration and contractual intention.

Agreement

An agreement involves an offer and an acceptance. An agreement is made when one party accepts the other party's offer. For example, one party offers to sell his or her car for $30,000, and the other party accepts the offer by agreeing to pay $30,000 for the car.

Consideration

Consideration has a specific legal definition. It can be defined as something of value given in return for the performance of an act or the promise of performance.[1] "[E]ach party [to a contract] must give or promise something in return for the other party's act or promise to act. A bare, voluntary, gratuitous act or promise, unsupported by any reciprocal undertaking, will not be enough. There must be mutuality: a contract must show that both parties are bound ...."[2]

One person promises to pay another $30,000 for a car. The seller promises to deliver it to the buyer. The buyer's promise to pay is consideration for the seller's promise to deliver; the seller's promise to deliver the car is consideration for the buyer's promise to pay $30,000. Each party to the contract has given something of value (i.e. consideration) in exchange for the other party's promise. The idea of consideration distinguishes a contract from a gift, such as a promise to donate to a charity. A promise to donate a car to a charity does not create a contract, because it lacks consideration: the intended recipient, the charity, has not promised anything of value in return for the car. If the car was not donated as promised, and the charity sued, a court would say that no contract was made because there was no consideration given by the charity.

Contractual intention

The third essential element of a contract is the presence of an intention by the parties to be legally bound – that is, an intention to enter into an agreement enforceable by the courts. It is presumed that parties to a social or domestic agreement do not intend to be legally bound by any agreement they make. Thus, an agreement to meet someone for lunch or to drive a friend to work does not create any legal obligations (although it may give rise to moral obligations). By contrast, the courts presume that parties to an agreement made in a commercial or business context intended to create a legally enforceable agreement (i.e. a contract).

Generally, a contract can be written or oral. (Certain types of contracts, such as contracts for the sale of land, must be written). Oral contracts, made with a handshake and a smile, should be avoided. Although enforceable by a court, it is often difficult to prove the terms of the contract after relations between the parties have broken down and disagreements have arisen.

When a contract is broken and the promises made are not kept, the party who broke the contract can be sued for damages (i.e. money). In some situations, the defaulting party can be sued for an injunction (a remedy that prohibits a party from doing a particular act) or for specific performance (a remedy that requires the party in breach to fulfill his or her obligations under the contract).

General advice on contracts

- Contracts should be written in clear and comprehensible language. The parties to a contract should be able to read and understand what they are signing.

- Never sign a contract without first reading and understanding it. The law is clear that a competent adult who signs a contract is bound by the contract, whether he or she read and understood it or not.[3]

- Always consider including a mediation and/or arbitration clause, by which the parties agree on a method to resolve any dispute that arises over the contract (see Chapter 4).

The importance of legal advice

Churches enter into contracts of various sorts. Building, employment, property and insurance contracts are some of the most common. Each type of contract has its own complexities, issues and risks that need to be addressed. It is a fair rule of thumb that no one should enter into a contract of any consequence without first receiving advice from a lawyer knowledgeable in the particular field.

Civil liability in tort

It is difficult to give a precise definition of the word *tort*. The root meaning of the word is the Latin word *tortus*, which means twisted. One of the simplest and perhaps most useful definitions is that a tort is a civil wrong for which a court will award damages (i.e. money). Put very generally, one can be civilly liable for certain sorts of actions or behaviour considered wrongful that cause certain sorts of harmful consequences. A person who injures another, or his or her property, either intentionally or negligently, may be liable to compensate the injured party for the harm. Negligent behaviour is unintentional in the sense that the person who carelessly caused a loss did not intend to cause the harm: for example, negligent driving that causes harm. Negligent behaviour can be contrasted with a situation in which a person acts intending to cause harm to another: for example, one person punches another in the face.

Broad and expansive potential tort liability

Liability in tort can arise in almost any area of life. The first paragraph of the first page of the torts book read by most first-year Canadian law students says:

> The law of torts hovers over virtually every activity of modern society. The driver of every automobile on our highways, the pilot of every aeroplane in the sky, and the captain of every ship plying our waters must abide by the standards of tort law. The producers, distributors and repairers of every product, from bread to computers, must conform to tort law's counsel

of caution. No profession is beyond its reach: a doctor cannot raise a scalpel, a lawyer cannot advise a client, nor can an architect design a building without being subject to potential tort liability. In the same way, teachers, government officials, police and even jailers may be required to pay damages if someone is hurt as a result of their conduct. Those who engage in sports, such as golfers, hockey-players, and snowmobilers, may end up as parties to a tort action. The territory of tort law encompasses losses resulting from fires, floods, explosions, electricity, gas and many other catastrophes that may occur in this increasingly complex world. A person who punches another person in the nose may have to answer for it in a tort case as well as in the criminal courts. A person who says nasty things about another may be sued for defamation. Hence, any one of us may become a plaintiff or a defendant in a tort action at any moment. Tort law, therefore, is a subject of abiding concern not only to the judges and lawyers who must administer it but also the public at large, whose every move is regulated by it.[4]

The main area of potential tort liability is in negligence, which is liability for careless actions that cause harm (see Chapter 11). A person or organization that exercises reasonable care in the ordering of their affairs will not be found liable for negligence, which, by definition, is liability for harm caused by a lack of reasonable care. The fact that most tort liability can thus be avoided is important to keep in mind, and puts the unsettling spectre of liability raised by the above quotation in perspective.

Liability and fault

A basic premise of tort law is that (with a few important exceptions)[5] there is no liability unless the defendant is judged to be at fault in one of two ways. A person is said to be at fault when he or she intentionally causes a loss: for example, by punching someone else in the face. That is the tort of battery. A person is also said to be at fault when he or she causes a loss through carelessness: for example, by a driver taking his or her eyes off the road for a second to tune the car radio, crossing the centre line and striking an oncoming car. That is the tort of negligence. A defendant who is able to prove that he or she neither intentionally nor carelessly caused the loss in question will not often be found liable in tort.

The difference between contract and tort

Contract law is different from tort law. A contract is sometimes described as a private law that is created by the parties to the contract and governs their relationship. Tort law, by contrast, is defined by the courts and legislatures. Duties in tort are owed "towards persons generally; in contract, it is toward a specific person or persons"[6] (i.e. the other party or parties to the contract).

There are numerous individual torts, some of which are well known while others are quite obscure. Battery, defamation, negligence and nuisance are four of the most common torts. Subsequent chapters are devoted to a discussion of these and other torts.

Civil liability for breach of statute

Another potential basis of liability, in addition to breach of contract and tort, is breach of statute. A statute is an act of a legislature: federal, provincial or territorial. Statutes may, among other things, prescribe conduct and define crimes.[7] A person or corporation that breaches a statute may be liable to pay a fine, lose certain rights or privileges, or be imprisoned.

A few examples may be helpful. The *Criminal Code* contains most of the criminal offenses in Canada. The provisions of the *Criminal Code*, a federal statute, prohibit certain actions, such as driving a car while intoxicated. Every province and territory has civil statutes dealing with occupational health and safety that set out the duties of employers and workers with the goal of creating safe workplaces. A person or corporation failing to comply could be fined or imprisoned. Other statutes, such as the federal *Firearms Act*, mandate who can own and use firearms. Fines and imprisonment are penalties for non-compliance. Every province and territory has statutes that define the requirements for persons to practise certain professions, such as barbers, nurses or lawyers. A person who breaches such a statute may lose the right to practise his or her profession.

Statutes of relevance to a church

There are various statutes of relevance to churches, some specific to churches, most of general application. In the first category are statutes that provide for religious organizations holding property by way of trustees, for example. There is a plethora of general legislation that affects churches, including zoning and building laws, environmental legislation, and health and safety laws. Various statutory obligations are discussed throughout the book. Statutes imposing liability on directors and officers of a church are touched on in Chapter 2. Human rights legislation is discussed in Chapter 16. Legislation relating to church property is covered in Chapter 19.

Conclusion

Knowledge about potential liability is the first step toward avoiding or reducing the risk of liability. Although it may sometimes seem, when canvassing and considering issues of liability discussed throughout the book, that legal liability is difficult or impossible to avoid, this is not so. Liability is rarely imposed unless a defendant is at fault. The law does not often demand perfection and does not impose liability for every error or misstep. The legal theme that we will encounter again and again is that the law requires individuals and organizations to take reasonable care and reasonable steps to avoid causing harm.

Civil Liability Overview: Questions and Answers

Q. What does it mean to be liable?

A. To be liable means to be responsible for or obligated by law.

Q. What are the three grounds or bases of civil liability?

A. There are three possible bases of civil liability: tort, contract and statute.

Q. What are the essential elements of a legally enforceable contract, whether written or oral?

A. The essential elements of a legally enforceable contract are that the parties have reached an agreement on clearly defined terms, intended to be legally bound by the agreement and given or promised something of value to each other (i.e. consideration).

Q. Is an oral contract enforceable?

A. Yes. Although enforceable by a court, the difficulty of proving the terms of the contract after relations between the parties have broken down and disagreements have arisen is one good reason to ensure that contracts of any importance be written.

Q. What are the consequences when one party does not live up to the terms of a contract?

A. When a contract is broken and the promises made not kept, the party in breach can be sued for damages (i.e. money).

Q. What if a signed contract includes a term that the church was unaware of or misunderstood?

A. The law is clear that a competent adult who signs a contract is bound by the terms of the contract, whether he or she read and understood it or not. A church that signs a contract is likewise bound.

Q. What is a tort?

A. A tort is a civil wrong for which a court will award damages (i.e. money).

Q. In what areas could liability in tort arise?

A. Liability in tort is expansive and could arise in almost any activity or occupation or upon any circumstance in the modern world.

Q Can a person who is not at fault be liable in tort?

A. A basic premise of tort law is that (with a few exceptions) there is no liability unless harm was caused either intentionally or carelessly.

Q. What is the main difference between the law of tort and the law of contract?

A. Duties in tort are defined by the courts and legislatures, and are owed to persons generally. By contrast, duties in contract are defined by and owed to the persons who sign the contract.

Q. What is a statute?

A. A statute is an act of a legislature: federal, provincial or territorial.

Q. What is the purpose of statutes?

A. Statutes may, among other things, prescribe conduct and define crimes.

Q. What are the possible consequences of breaching a statute?

A. A person or corporation that breaches a statute may be liable to pay a fine, lose certain rights or privileges, or be imprisoned.

Notes

1   *Canadian Law Dictionary*, 5ᵗʰ ed., *s.v.* "consideration."

2   G. H. L. Fridman, *The Law of Contract in Canada*, 4ᵗʰ ed. (Scarborough, Ont.: Carswell, 1999), pp. 94–95, cited in *ibid.* Emphasis in original.

3   One exception is the doctrine of *non est factum* which, translated, means "it is not his deed." This defence is very narrow, but when recognized by a court the signer will not be bound by the contract. It can be raised only by those who are tricked into signing a document or who, because of illness, innate incapacity, or defective education, did not understand what they were signing: G. H. Treitel, *The Law of Contract*, 7ᵗʰ ed. (London: Sweet & Maxwell Limited, 1987), p. 251. Professor Treitel further explains that "[t]he doctrine may thus apply not only to the blind and illiterate but also to persons who are senile, of very low intelligence or unable to read English. But it will not normally protect literate persons of full capacity."

4   Allen M. Linden, *Canadian Tort Law*, 7ᵗʰ ed. (Markham, Ont.: Butterworths, 2001), p. 1, cited in Allen M. Linden et al., *Canadian Tort Law: Cases, Notes and Materials*, 12ᵗʰ ed. (Toronto: Butterworths, 2004), p. 1.

5   There are several torts for which one can be found liable even when the harm was not caused intentionally or negligently, such as defamation and nuisance (see Chapters 12 and 21). Also, the doctrine of vicarious liability is a form of no-fault liability; an innocent defendant can be found liable simply because of his or her relationship to the person who commits a tort. For example, liability can be imposed on a faultless employer for the wrongdoing of an employee (see Chapter 9).

6   Salmond and Heuston, *The Law of Torts*, 21ˢᵗ ed. (Toronto: Carswell, 1996), p. 10.

7   *Canadian Law Dictionary*, 5ᵗʰ ed., *s.v.* "statute."

7

The Secular Courts

A court may not permit one litigant to sit
and compel the other to stand,
one to speak all his desires and the other to be brief.
—*Talmud*, Shebu'oth 30a

Two basic questions need to be answered by a person who wants a secular court to resolve a dispute involving a church or cleric: Do the secular courts have authority to deal with the matter in dispute; and, if so, which court, because there is more than one?[1] This chapter briefly considers these two questions. The first question was answered by the Supreme Court of Canada in *Brassard v. Langevin*.[2] A description of some of the salient features of the secular court structure answers the second.

Jurisdiction of the secular courts

Brassard v. Langevin, a nineteenth-century decision of the Supreme Court of Canada, sets out the law as it remains in the 21st: Canadian churches and clergy are subject to the authority (i.e. jurisdiction) of the secular courts:

> But while the members of that Church thus have a perfect right to the full and free exercise of their religion in as full and ample a manner as any other Church or denomination in the Dominion, every member of that Church, like every member of every other Church, is subordinate to the law .... "There ... can be no doubt that if the rule in question or any rule of any Church had for its object the exemption of the clergy from secular authority or their immunity from civil jurisdiction or civil punishment, it would be our duty at once to declare that such a rule was utterly illegal. Upon this there ought to be, as there is, no doubt. No church, no community, no public body, no individual in the realm, can be the least above the law, or exempted from the authority of its civil or criminal tribunals. The law of the land is supreme and we recognize no authority as superior or equal to it. Such ever has been and is, and I hope will ever continue to be a principle of our Constitution."[3]

Secular courts, however, defer to ecclesiastical courts or ecclesiastical authority in certain circumstances. Courts do not generally intervene in the purely spiritual or ecclesiastical matters of a church. When an internal church decision or dispute affects the property, tort or contract right of a church member, a secular court may intervene, but generally only after a claimant exhausts his or her ecclesiastical remedies, i.e. pursues the matter to the highest church court. At that point, a claimant could seek judicial review from the secular courts (see Chapter 3).

The Canadian secular court system

Every province and territory in Canada has different levels and types of courts where disputes are adjudicated.[4] The basic division within each province and territory is between superior courts and inferior courts.[5]

Provincial and territorial superior courts

Superior courts have broad jurisdiction that gives them the authority to hear almost any type of case, unless expressly excluded by a statute; by contrast, the inferior courts are limited by statute to certain sorts of disputes.

Each province and territory has a trial court and an appeal court. The trial court generally hears civil disputes involving significant monetary claims and serious criminal matters. An appeal from a decision of a superior trial court may be made to that province's or territory's court of appeal. Appeals from the decision of a court of appeal are made to the Supreme Court of Canada.

Superior courts are sometimes referred to as section 96 courts, a reference to section 96 of the *Constitution Act, 1867*, which mandates that the federal government appoint and pay the judges of the superior courts.

Provincial and territorial inferior courts

Each province and territory has several inferior courts: small claims court, for example. Small claims courts were created to provide a speedy, inexpensive and informal procedure to resolve disputes involving small monetary claims. The adjudicator is often a lawyer, the court usually sits in the evening, the rules of procedure are simplified and decisions are rendered on the day of the hearing or soon after. Claimants usually represent themselves, although representation by a lawyer is allowed. Small claims courts are limited in the amount of the award they can make to the successful party. In Manitoba, the maximum amount that may be awarded is $7,500; in Ontario, the limit is $10,000. These courts are also limited in the sort of matters they may hear. Typically, they are not authorized to hear disputes over land or wills, for example.

Other provincial and territorial inferior courts have jurisdiction over such matters as various criminal offences, young offenders, regulatory offences and traffic violations. Judges of the provincial and territorial courts are appointed and paid by the provincial or territorial governments.

Federal Court of Canada

The Federal Court is a trial court and also an inferior court in the sense that it is limited by statute in the matters it may hear. Its governing statute, the *Federal Courts Act*, gives it exclusive jurisdiction over several matters. In other words, some matters, such as reviewing decisions of certain federal boards, commissions and tribunals, copyright and trademark disputes, and citizenship appeals, can be dealt with only by the Federal Court. Other matters, such as a lawsuit against the federal Crown and cases involving navigation and shipping, may be heard by either the Federal Court or the superior courts (this is referred to as concurrent jurisdiction). Appeals from the Federal Court are made to the Federal Court of Appeal.

There are 32 judges of the Federal Court and a Chief Justice, and thirteen judges of the Court of Appeal, including the Chief Justice, all appointed and paid by the federal government.

Supreme Court of Canada

The highest court in the land and the court of final appeal, the Supreme Court of Canada hears appeals on civil and criminal matters from the provincial and territorial superior courts and the Federal Court of Appeal. The Supreme Court comprises eight judges and the Chief Justice of Canada, and sits in Ottawa for three sessions each year. Judges of the Supreme Court are appointed and paid by the federal government. When a litigant wishes to appeal a civil matter from a superior court to the Supreme Court of Canada, he or she must apply to the Court for leave to appeal (i.e. permission), which is rarely granted. For example, of the 498 leave applications made in 2002, only 53 were granted: a mere 11 per cent.[6] The difficulty of gaining leave means that for most litigants, the court of appeal in their province or territory is, in effect, the final court of appeal. When leave is granted, a hearing is held at the Supreme Court, and a decision is rendered on the appeal.

Conclusion

It is clear that a church is subject to the jurisdiction of the secular courts, whether small claims court or the Supreme Court of Canada. A church, the clergy, church directors and officers, and others involved with the church and its activities could be named as defendants in a lawsuit. In Canada, there is no special legal immunity from a lawsuit or protection of any kind for non-profit or charitable organizations, such as a church. It is equally clear that a church is accorded the same measure of fairness that every litigant receives in our justice system. An Ontario judge gave the following charge to a jury in a recent case:

> The Church Corporation is entitled to the same fair trial at your hands as a private individual. As a Church Corporation you must not extend to it any particular favour, nor must you extend any prejudice against it. All persons, individuals, corporations, partnerships and other lawful organizations stand equal before the law and are to be dealt with as equals in a court of justice. [7]

The Secular Courts: Questions and Answers

Q. Do the secular courts have jurisdiction (i.e. authority) over churches and clergy?

A. Yes. Churches and clergy in Canada are today, and have always been, subject to and subordinate to the law of the land. No person or organization in Canada is above the law or exempt from the authority of the secular courts.

Q. Is there any special legal immunity from a lawsuit or protection of any kind in Canada for non-profit or charitable organizations such as a church?

A. No.

Q. Will the courts intervene in the internal matters of a church?

A. Courts do not generally intervene in the internal matters of a voluntary association, such as a church. When an internal church dispute or decision affects the property, contract or tort right of a church member, a secular court may intervene, but generally only after a claimant exhausts all his or her ecclesiastical remedies, i.e. pursues the matter to the highest church court.

Q. Are churches involved in a lawsuit treated differently than other litigants?

A. No. A church is accorded the same measure of fairness that every litigant receives in the Canadian justice system.

Q. What is the basic difference between superior courts and inferior courts?

A. Superior courts have broad jurisdiction to hear almost any type of case and grant any remedy. By contrast, inferior courts are limited, by statute, to certain sorts of disputes, and are sometimes limited in the remedy they may grant.

Q. What is the role of the Federal Court of Canada?

A. The Federal Court is the only court in Canada that may hear certain matters, such as reviewing decisions of some federal boards, commissions and tribunals, and copyright and trademark disputes. It also deals with lawsuits against the federal Crown, and lawsuits involving navigation and shipping issues.

Q. What sort of disputes are appropriate for a small claims court?

A. Small claims courts provide a speedy and inexpensive forum in which to resolve disputes involving relatively small amounts of money. Small claims courts are always limited in the amount of money they may award to a successful claimant. The limit is usually around $10,000 to $25,000.

Q. What is the role of the Supreme Court of Canada?

A. The Supreme Court of Canada is the highest court in the land and the court of final appeal in Canada. The Supreme Court hears appeals on civil and criminal matters from the superior courts and the Federal Court of Appeal.

Q. How does a civil dispute reach the Supreme Court of Canada?

A. The losing party at the court of appeal would apply to the Supreme Court of Canada for leave to appeal (i.e. permission). If leave was granted by the Supreme Court of Canada, then the case would be heard.

Q. Is leave to appeal in civil matters usually granted by the Supreme Court of Canada?

A. No. Leave to appeal is rarely granted in civil matters. For example, of the 498 leave applications made in 2002, only 53 (11 per cent) were granted. The difficulty of gaining leave means that for most litigants, the court of appeal in their province or territory is, in effect, their final court of appeal.

Notes

1   A secular court could be either a civil or criminal court. A civil court adjudicates disputes between citizens with respect to property, torts and contracts. See Chapter 6 for a discussion of the difference between civil and criminal liability. Throughout the book, when we use the word *court* we are almost always talking about a civil court. If we are referring to a church court we will be explicit.

2   *Brassard v. Langevin* (1877), 1 S.C.R. 145.

3   *Ibid.*, para. 75.

4   See generally, Gerald Gall, *The Canadian Legal System*, 5th ed. (Toronto: Thomson Carswell, 2004); Supreme Court of Canada, *Organization of the Courts* (www.scc-csc.gc.ca). See also the Federal Department of Justice, *Canada's Court System* (www.justice.gc.ca). Most every court has its own website, which can be easily located by entering key search terms, such as "court" and the name of the province or territory.

5   Superior courts have different names in different provinces; for example, the Ontario Superior Court of Justice, the Supreme Court of Nova Scotia, the Nunavut Court of Justice and, in several provinces, the Court of Queen's Bench. Two inferior courts in many provinces are the Provincial Court and Small Claims Court. Other courts include the Tax Court of Canada and the Court Martial Appeal Court of Canada.

6   Supreme Court of Canada, *Bulletin of Proceedings: Special Edition, Summary 1994-2004* (www.scc-csc.gc.ca).

7   *Szczepaniak v. Roman Catholic Episcopal Corp.*, [1992] O.J. No. 2632, para. 74 (Ct. J. (Gen. Div.)) (QL), para. 74.

8

Anatomy of a Lawsuit

A jury trial is a fight and not an afternoon tea.
—Justice W. R. Riddell,
Supreme Court of Ontario (Appellate Division),
Dale v. Toronto R. W. Co. (1915)

Disputes and disagreements are an inevitable part of life. They come in all shapes and sizes, from the trivial to the traumatic. We may be unhappy with a neighbour about the loud music wafting from next door early on a Saturday morning, upset with the local grocer for selling us apples of inferior quality, disappointed by the poor quality of a new computer, or injured in an accident by a careless driver. An American legal scholar has noted, somewhat poetically, that "Disputes are drawn from a vast sea of events, encounters, collisions, rivalries, disappointments, discomforts and injuries."[1]

We respond to the myriad disputes encountered in various ways.[2] Often, when the dispute is minor, we do nothing. When we do decide to do something, we may try to negotiate a settlement, perhaps returning the new computer or asking for a refund or a discount on the apples. If negotiation fails, we might lodge a complaint or ask to speak to someone with greater authority in the company: "I want to talk to the manager." Disputes in which a lot is at stake, such as compensation for injuries sustained in a motor-vehicle accident, are often dealt with in a more formal process, such as mediation or arbitration (see Chapter 4). One way of resolving disputes, and more often than not the method of last resort, is by starting a lawsuit in the civil courts. Few disputes ever turn into lawsuits and, of those that do, few end up in a trial before a judge. According to one study, only nine per cent of lawsuits ever go to trial; most either settle before trial or are abandoned.[3] The reasons are obvious and well known: lawsuits are expensive, time-consuming and stressful; the outcome is unpredictable. A wise judge of years gone by once remarked that a trial "is a fight and not an afternoon tea."[4] It is rarely the best way to resolve a dispute, although there are sometimes sound reasons for taking a matter to trial.

This chapter describes some of the essential features of the civil trial process. A brief outline of the possible parties to a lawsuit and the sort of claims they may make or be obligated to defend is followed by an overview of a lawsuit.

Parties to a lawsuit

Who might be sued in the church environment?

1. When a church is incorporated, the corporation itself could be sued. An incorporated body is a legal person and can be sued in contract and tort and be held criminally liable for its actions. A corporation acts through its directors and officers; they are its directing mind (see Chapters 1 and 2). A church corporation can be directly liable for its own wrongdoing and also vicariously liable for the actions of employees or volunteers (see Chapter 9).

2. When a church is an unincorporated association, members who control the management of the association could be sued in contract and tort and be held criminally liable for its actions, or be held vicariously liable for the wrongdoing of employees and volunteers (see Chapters 1, 2 and 9).[5]

3. The directors and officers of a church, both a church corporation and unincorporated association, can be personally liable under various statutes and also liable for harm caused by breaches of the duties they owe to the church (see Chapter 2).

4. Clergy, employees, members and volunteers can be personally liable, both civilly and criminally, for their own actions.

Who might sue a church?

1.   A cleric or church employee may sue a church for, among other things, wrongful dismissal (see Chapter 15).

2.   Church members, volunteers and visitors could sue a church for injuries sustained in a fall on church property, for example (see Chapter 20).

3.   Children in the care or under the supervision of the church might sue for injuries suffered by the negligence or even intentional wrongdoing of a church, cleric, employee or volunteer (see Chapters 9 and 11).

4.   Church neighbours might sue a church. Lawsuits for nuisance are occasionally brought (see Chapter 21).

Anatomy of a lawsuit

The Canadian justice system is described as an adversarial system, meaning that the parties – plaintiff and defendant – have the responsibility of putting forward the evidence and arguments to prove their respective cases before an impartial judge who, at the end of the trial, renders a decision on the evidence presented.

Although the procedure varies from province to province and between levels of court within a province, the following description highlights the main elements of a proceeding commonly referred to as a lawsuit or civil action.

Facts: the necessary foundation of a lawsuit

In order to commence a lawsuit, a person (the plaintiff) must have a cause of action against another (the defendant). A cause of action is the facts necessary to give a person the legal right to sue.[6] For example, the fact that someone is touched without their consent will give him or her the legal right to sue in battery. Often, a given set of facts or cause of action allows a plaintiff to sue on various theories of legal liability. A person whose property is damaged by the construction of a new church might be able, on the facts, to sue the church in both the torts of negligence and nuisance. The law allows a plaintiff to put forward as many theories of liability as arise from a given set of facts. A defendant found to be liable on the basis of more than one theory of liability (e.g. negligence and nuisance) would still only be awarded damages that compensate for the loss sustained. In other words, double recovery is not allowed.

Time limitations

Every province and territory has a general statute that sets out the time period in which a lawsuit must be commenced.[7] For example, someone injured in a motor vehicle accident in Nova Scotia must begin a claim for injuries within three years of the accident.[8] This means that a person injured in a motor vehicle accident has three years from the date the injuries occurred (or from the date the injuries were discovered, if later) to file documents with the court to launch a lawsuit. Different limitation periods are set out for claims of battery, breach of contract and medical malpractice, etc. There are also other provincial, territorial and federal statutes that may contain limitation periods. A plaintiff who fails to commence a lawsuit within the allotted time may be forever barred from doing so.

Limitation statutes and persons under a disability

A plaintiff who is under a disability is not required to commence a lawsuit while under the disability. A plaintiff younger than the age of majority is considered to be under a disability, as is someone who is of unsound mind. The limitation period for a person under a disability does not begin until the disability ends. For example, the three-year limitation period for a thirteen-year-old child injured in a motor vehicle accident in Nova Scotia does not commence until he or she reaches the age of majority, which is nineteen in Nova Scotia. He or she then has three years from his or her nineteenth birthday to commence a lawsuit.

Can a child sue?

Although the limitation period for a person under a disability, such as a child, does not begin until he or she reaches the age of majority, a child is nevertheless allowed to commence a lawsuit at anytime, but must be represented by a litigation guardian. A litigation guardian is an adult, often a parent, who is responsible for the conduct of the minor's lawsuit.

Starting a lawsuit

A lawsuit is started when the plaintiff files certain documents with the court administration. These documents go by different names but are commonly called the originating notice and statement of claim (other names include writ, complaint or claim). The originating notice contains the name of the parties to the action, styled as John Doe, Plaintiff v. Mary Smith, Defendant. The statement of claim contains the factual details of the claim that the plaintiff is making against the defendant.

Service: giving notice to the defendant

After filing the necessary documents, the plaintiff must then arrange for the defendant to receive notice of the lawsuit, which is accomplished by handing him or her a copy of the documents. This is called service. It is not sufficient to fax or mail the documents. They must be handed to the defendant or someone legally authorized to accept them on the defendant's behalf.

The statement of defence

Once the defendant is served, he or she has a set amount of time, usually about 20 days, to file a defence. The statement of defence contains the factual details denying or disputing the plaintiff's claim or offering some other reason why the defendant is not liable to the plaintiff.

The consequences of failing to file a defence

When no defence is filed within the allotted time, a court, upon application by the plaintiff, may grant judgement in favour of the plaintiff for all or part of the claim.

It is therefore of great importance to contact your lawyer as soon as possible after you receive the originating documents so that a defence may be filed in a timely fashion.

The discovery stage

Once a defence is filed, the proceeding moves into what is called the discovery stage. This is the stage at which each party, plaintiff and defendant, gathers information about the other side. The overall goal of discovery is for each side to learn everything there is to know about the other side's case. Modern courts demand full disclosure of all the facts by each party. The basic rule is that nothing may be hidden or kept secret from the other side, in the hope that such strict disclosure requirements will encourage settlement. The assumption is that if you know the details of the other side's case, you are in a good position to value the claim or weigh the defence and either settle or discontinue the lawsuit.

All relevant documents must be disclosed

During the discovery stage, the parties are obligated by law to exchange copies of all documents (e.g. letters, photos, contracts, videotapes, blueprints, medical reports, etc.) that are relevant to the proceeding, even when the documents contain confidential information. All relevant documents must be disclosed unless the document is privileged (e.g. covered by solicitor–client privilege or some other privilege; see Chapter 14).

Oral discovery

Each party is also obligated to submit to oral discovery examinations, which are examinations under oath during which the opposing party's lawyer may ask any question relevant to the proceeding (called depositions in the United States).

There are also other methods that can be used by the parties to gather information about the claim. These include requiring the adverse party to supply written answers to written questions (called interrogatories); examination by a medical specialist; and the inspection of property.

Restrictions on information learned through discovery

Documents disclosed in the context of a court proceeding may not be used by anyone for any purpose other than the proceeding in which they were disclosed. Likewise, any information learned through oral discovery may not be used for any purpose other than in that proceeding.

Most lawsuits settle before trial

Parties may try to negotiate a settlement of the claim at any time. Most lawsuits do not end up going to a trial. The vast majority of lawsuits settle before trial, thus avoiding the cost, time and publicity of a trial. Parties are often encouraged by the courts to try to settle their claims outside of court. Some courts mandate that parties involved in a lawsuit attempt to resolve the dispute by attending a mediation session. Seeking ways to resolve a dispute, rather than going to trial, is almost always a sensible idea (see Chapter 4 for a discussion of alternative dispute resolution).

Summary judgement

There are various procedural steps a party may be able to take to stop a lawsuit before trial. The most common is called an application for summary judgement. Either party may apply to the court asking it to stop the matter from proceeding to trial because there is no issue that needs to be resolved at a trial. At a summary judgment hearing, the defendant would argue either that the plaintiff's claim is groundless or that there is a complete defence to the claim and would request that the plaintiff's claim be dismissed. The plaintiff would argue that the defendant has no defence to the claim that merits a hearing at trial, and ask that all or part of the plaintiff's claim be granted immediately.

The trial

When a proceeding is not discontinued, does not settle or is not dealt with by way of summary judgment or some other pretrial manoeuvre, it will eventually proceed to a trial. Trials are forums in which a judge, or a judge and jury, decide contested issues by weighing the evidence in light of the governing law. Evidence is given by witnesses in open court; open in the sense that the public may attend and the media may report on what occurs.

Weighing the evidence

In a civil trial, the plaintiff must prove his or her case on the balance of probabilities, which is referred to as the standard of proof. Put more generally, the plaintiff must convince the judge that it is more likely than not that his or her allegations are true (this could be expressed as a greater than 50 per cent likelihood). Contrast the civil standard of proof with the criminal standard, which is proof beyond a reasonable doubt. If, after hearing all the evidence in a criminal trial, the judge has any real doubt about the accused's guilt, the judge must acquit him or her. These two standards of proof sometimes lead to the situation in which a person is acquitted in a criminal trial but found liable in a civil trial, based on the same set of facts.

What is a remedy?

A remedy is the means employed by the courts to enforce a right or redress an injury. The most common remedy of the courts is an award of damages (i.e. money) to the winning party. In tort, the principle is that an award of damages should put the injured party in the same position he or she would have been in had the loss not occurred. In contract, the principle is that an award of damages should put the party not in breach in the same position he or she would have been in had the contract been performed. Another common remedy is an injunction, which is a court order prohibiting a person from doing a particular act.

Monetary penalties against the losing party

Sometime after the trial ends, the judge renders a decision, either finding in favour of the plaintiff or dismissing the plaintiff's claim. The losing party is obligated to pay a portion (about one half) of the legal fees charged by the winning party's lawyer to his or her client. This is referred to as an award of costs.

In addition to paying these legal costs, the losing party must pay all the winning party's reasonable disbursements. Disbursements are out-of-pocket expenses incurred during the lawsuit, such as the cost of travel, photocopying, long-distance phone calls, and expert reports. A party's disbursements can be a large amount of money: $5,000 for one expert's report and testimony, for example.

This is a significant consideration when contemplating whether to commence, defend or settle a lawsuit. When you are the defendant and you lose, you must pay your own lawyer plus pay a portion of the plaintiff's legal fees and all of his or her reasonable disbursements. When you are the plaintiff and you are unsuccessful, you must pay your own lawyer and will be ordered to pay a portion of the defendant's legal fees and all of his or her reasonable disbursements.

Appeal by the losing party

The losing party may appeal the decision, usually within 30 days. To succeed on appeal, the appeal court must be convinced that the trial judge made an error of law or a serious error on the facts. Very few appeals succeed. A party who loses on appeal may seek leave (i.e. permission) to appeal to the Supreme Court of Canada. If leave is granted (only about 11 per cent per year are granted),[9] the case will be heard by the Supreme Court of Canada, Canada's highest court and court of final appeal.

Conclusion

Given that disputes and disagreements are an inevitable part of life and that courts have civil authority over churches and clergy, it is almost inevitable that some churches and clergy will be involved in civil lawsuits in the secular courts. Litigation is costly – in time, money and often one's peace of mind. Settlement is almost always the wisest choice. But settlement is not always possible and is sometimes ill-advised. An understanding and appreciation of a lawsuit's anatomy may be a spur to settlement and will most certainly be of value when a dispute ends up in a court.

Anatomy of a Lawsuit: Questions and Answers

Q. Who might be sued in a church environment?

A. Possible defendants include a church corporation, members of an unincorporated church association, directors and officers of a church, church employees and volunteers.

Q. Who might sue a church?

A. Possible plaintiffs include clergy and church employees, church members, volunteers and church neighbours.

Q. Must a lawsuit be commenced within a certain time period?

A. Yes. Every province and territory has a general statute that sets out the time period in which a lawsuit must be commenced. Different limitation periods are set out for claims of battery, breach of contract, medical malpractice, etc.

Q. Do limitation periods apply to children?

A. The limitation period for a child does not begin until he or she reaches the age of majority.

Q. May a person under the age of majority commence a lawsuit?

A. Yes, but he or she must be represented by a litigation guardian. A litigation guardian is an adult, often a parent, who is responsible for the conduct of the minor's lawsuit.

Q. How is a lawsuit started?

A. A lawsuit is started by filing the appropriate documents with the court administration.

Q. What is a statement of claim?

A. A statement of claim is one of the documents filed to commence a lawsuit. It contains the factual details of the claim that the plaintiff is making against the defendant.

Q. Is the defendant obligated to file a statement of defence?

A. Once a defendant is served with the originating documents by the plaintiff, he or she has a set amount of days, usually about 20, to file a defence. Failure by the defendant to do so may result in the court granting judgment on the claim in the plaintiff's favour.

Q. What is the discovery stage of a lawsuit?

A. The discovery stage of a lawsuit is when each party gathers information about the other side. During the discovery stage, the parties are obligated by law to exchange copies of all relevant, non-privileged documents and to answer, under oath, all questions posed by the other side.

Q. Do most lawsuits settle before going to a trial?

A. Yes. The vast majority settle. According to one study, only nine percent of all lawsuits started ever end up going to trial.

Q. **Is the losing party to a lawsuit obligated to pay a portion of the winning party's legal fees?**

A. Yes. The losing party is obligated to pay a portion (about one half) of the winning party's legal fees plus all reasonable disbursements, which are out-of-pocket expenses incurred in the lawsuit. This is an important fact to consider when deciding whether to commence, defend or settle a lawsuit.

Notes

1   Marc Galanter, "Reading the Landscape of Disputes: What We Know and Don't Know (and Think We Know) About Our Allegedly Contentious and Litigious Society" (1983–1984) 31 *University of California, Los Angeles Law Review* 4, p. 12 [*Galanter*].

2   See generally, *ibid.*

3   D. Trubek et al., *Civil Litigation Research Project: Final Report, Volume II: Civil Litigation as the Investment of Lawyer Time* (Madison, Wis.: University of Wisconsin Law School, 1983) II-53-56, cited in *Galanter*, note 1, p. 28.

4   Riddell J. in *Dale v. Toronto R.W. Co.* (1915), 34 O.L.R. 104 (S.C. (A. D.)), para. 15.

5   See generally, Robert Flannigan, "The Liability Structure of Nonprofit Associations: Tort and Fiduciary Liability Assignments" (1998) 77 *Canadian Bar Review* 73.

6   *Canadian Law Dictionary*, 5th ed., *s.v.* "cause of action."

7   For example, the Alberta *Limitations Act*, R.S.A. 2000, c. L-12; British Columbia *Limitation Act*, R.S.B.C. 1996, c. 266.

8   *Limitation of Actions Act*, R.S.N.S. 1989, c. 258, s. 2(1) (f).

9   Supreme Court of Canada, *Bulletin of Proceedings: Special Edition, Summary 1994-2004* (www.scc-csc.gc.ca).

9

Direct and Vicarious Liability

The safety of the people shall be the highest law.
—Marcus Tullius Cicero, statesman, orator, lawyer,
106–43 BC, *On the Laws*

A person or church that harms someone by its own wrongful acts or omissions is sometimes described as being directly liable to the person harmed. A person or church, although innocent of any wrongdoing, can be held liable for the wrongdoing of someone else, a form of liability referred to as indirect or vicarious liability. It is important to understand the meaning of, and the difference between, each of these concepts. The idea of direct liability is quite straightforward and usually grasped rather intuitively. By contrast, the concept of vicarious liability is often misunderstood. This chapter discusses each in turn. It concludes with a discussion on liability issues and volunteers.

Direct liability

It is not hard to think of situations in which a person's own actions cause harm. A careless driver crosses the centre line and hits an oncoming car. The driver of that oncoming car could claim against the careless driver because he or she caused the accident. In other words, the careless driver is directly liable to the person he or she injured. A waitress carelessly spills soup in your lap, ruining your best suit. Her own careless actions caused your loss, and she therefore is directly liable to you.

Direct liability of a church corporation

A corporation is a legal person and can also be directly liable for harm caused by its own acts. (See Chapter 1 for a discussion of the differences between a church that is incorporated and a church that exists as an unincorporated association.) Corporations are said to act through their directors and officers; they are considered the directing mind of the corporation. Suppose a church corporation fails to clean snow and ice off the front steps of the church and someone falls, breaking an arm. The injured person could sue the church directly, naming the corporation as the defendant.

Direct liability and unincorporated church associations

By contrast, an unincorporated association has no legal status and cannot sue or be sued. However, members of a church that exists as an unincorporated association can be directly liable in both contract and tort. Members who commit torts will be directly liable for their own actions. Members that control the affairs of the association will be directly liable for contractual obligations.[1]

Illustrative cases

A brief synopsis of two cases further illustrates the concept of direct liability.

Some of the relevant facts of *John Doe v. Bennett* were set out as follows by the Supreme Court of Canada:

> Over a period of almost two decades, Father Kevin Bennett, a Roman Catholic priest in Newfoundland in the Diocese of St. George's, sexually assaulted boys in his parishes. Two successive bishops failed to take steps to stop the abuse. Ultimately, in 1979, a victim revealed the abuse to the Archbishop of the neighbouring diocese, St. John's …. He referred the complaint to Bennett's Bishop but again nothing was done. The unnamed plaintiffs, 36 in number, suffered greatly as a consequence of the abuse. Now adults, they remain deeply wounded.[2]

The plaintiffs sued Father Bennett, the Roman Catholic Episcopal Corporation of St. George's and others. One of the main issues in the appeal to the Supreme Court of Canada was whether the Roman Catholic Episcopal Corporation of St. George's was directly liable to the plaintiffs.

First, the court concluded that the episcopal corporation is the secular arm of the bishop or archbishop. In other words, they are the directing mind of the corporation. "All temporal or secular actions of the bishop are those of the corporation. This includes the direction, control and discipline of priests, which are the responsibility of the bishop. If the bishop is negligent in the discharge of these duties, the corporation is directly liable."[3]

The court then concluded that the Roman Catholic Episcopal Corporation of St. George's was, on the facts of the case, directly liable to the plaintiffs because "[t]he bishops of St. George's in charge of Bennett … knew or ought to have known that Bennett was abusing [children] and negligently did nothing to stop the assaults from continuing."[4] The church corporation, acting through the bishops, caused harm to the plaintiffs by its careless omission to stop the abuse. Father Bennett was also held directly liable for the harm he caused to the plaintiffs.

Another case involving a finding of direct liability against a church is *Chartrand v. Grace Lutheran Church Society*.[5] In this case, a septic tank built on church land in 1948 fell into disuse after the church was attached to the municipal sewer system. Mrs. Chartrand, the plaintiff, was injured in 1998 when the concrete pad over the tank gave way and she fell into the tank, suffering a moderate whiplash-type injury. She sued the church. The court concluded that:

> The church, through its trustees, took no steps to fill in the septic tank once it was no longer in use. It appears that over time the knowledge of that situation was not actually passed from trustee to trustee with the result that by the time the sidewalk was constructed the then

trustees were unaware that there had ever been a septic tank on the property.[6] ...

Here the question is whether the knowledge that the church had, through its trustees, at the time the septic tank was abandoned is deemed to be the knowledge of the church at the time of the incident giving rise to this action.[7]

The court found that the church was directly liable because it created the dangerous situation and had a continuing reason to know of its existence. Having created the danger, the church could not avoid its responsibilities to take reasonable care for the safety of people such as Mrs. Chartrand by "'forgetting' that it was there."[8]

Vicarious liability

Vicarious liability occurs "when the law holds one person responsible for the misconduct of another, although he is himself free from personal blameworthiness or fault. It is therefore an instance of strict (no fault) liability."[9] It is sometimes also described as indirect liability, in contrast to direct liability. Vicarious liability is not a tort; rather, it is a legal doctrine that imposes liability on a party because of his or her relationship to the person who has committed a tort.[10]

Relationship of employer and employee

The most common situation in which vicarious liability arises is in the employer–employee relationship.[11] The general rule is that employers are vicariously liable for the torts committed by employees in the course of their employment.

Often, therefore, courts have to determine whether the person who committed the tort was an employee and whether the church was the employer. A British Columbia judge explained the relevant factors courts consider when determining whether an entity such as a church is classified as an employer for purposes of vicarious liability.[12] They include whether the church:

(1) exercises direction and control over the person;

(2) bears the burden of remuneration;

(3) imposes discipline;

(4) hired the person;

(5) has authority to dismiss the person;

(6) is perceived to be the employer by the person.[13]

The key question, according to the courts, "is whether the alleged employer had the power of selecting, controlling and dismissing the alleged employee .... Control, sometimes referred to as 'overriding control' is an important factor in determining the existence of the employer-employee relationship ...."[14]

Whether clerics are employees for purposes of vicarious liability

When assessing whether a cleric is an employee for the purposes of vicarious liability, courts look beyond internal ecclesiastical agreements that define the relationship, and focus on the factors of the employer–employee relationship set out above. In a civil action for sexual assault against a priest, a British Columbia court responded as follows to the argument made on behalf of the church that "the relationship between a priest and the bishop or church is merely a voluntary one and not, therefore, a relationship of employer/employee."[15]

> I was referred to a number of cases which decided that the relationship between the church and its priests is an ecclesiastical one, governed by the Code of Canon Law .... Two of these cases were concerned with the rights and obligations as between the priest and the church. They did not hold that there can be no employer/employee relationship for the purposes of protecting third party rights.[16]
>
> ...
>
> In the present case, all the common law indicia of the employer/employee relationship are present as between the Bishop of Nelson and Paul Pornbacher [the defendant priest]. Those include power to select, control and dismiss, payment of wages, right to exclusive services, determination of place of work and control of hours of work. Although as between the church and its priests the relationship may be governed by ecclesiastical law, the church operates within the secular community. The church cannot insulate itself from the laws and sanctions of the secular community through the implementation of its own internal law. The church must be, and is, subject to the laws of the secular community in its dealings with the members of that community. I have no hesitation in find-

ing that the relationship of employer/employee
does exist in so far as that relationship affects
the rights of third parties.[17]

(The issue of whether a cleric will be classified by the courts
as an employee arises also in the area of employment law and
wrongful dismissal claims. In that context, the issue is much
less clear. See Chapter 15.)

Policy justification for vicarious liability

Vicarious liability is justified by the courts largely on the
basis of two policy considerations.[18] First, it provides the victim with a likely source of compensation for the harm done,
a so-called deep pocket. The employer is usually in a better
financial position than the employee to pay damages. The
theory is that "the employer puts in the community an enterprise which carries with it certain risks. When those risks
materialize and cause injury to a member of the public despite
the employer's reasonable efforts, it is fair that the person or
organization that creates the enterprise and hence the risk
should bear the loss."[19]

Second, the imposition of vicarious liability may deter
future harm. An employer will be motivated to do everything
possible to prevent the harm from occurring, knowing that it
will be liable for its employees' wrongdoing. An employer is
often in the best position to reduce the risks of harm occurring.
When harm occurs, however, the fact that the employer took
every imaginable precaution will not help it escape liability.

Examples of vicarious liability

A typical situation in which vicarious liability will be imposed is when a person employed to drive a delivery truck drives negligently and causes an accident. The person injured by the driver's carelessness could, of course, sue the driver for negligence. His or her employer could also be sued by the injured person, based on the principle of vicarious liability. Even though the accident occurred solely as a result of the driver's careless operation of the truck, the employer will be liable if the accident occurred during the course of employment. An employer held vicariously liable would be obligated to compensate the injured party for his or her entire loss. It is important to realize that the employer's liability does not arise because the employer has done something wrong; liability arises from the employer–employee relationship. A second example is a waitress at a restaurant who carelessly spills soup, ruining a customer's suit. The customer could sue the waitress for negligence; the customer could also sue the restaurant that employed her, on the basis of vicarious liability.

The same reasoning applies to a church. For example, it can be vicariously liable for an employee or volunteer who drives the church van carelessly and causes an accident. (A volunteer is often treated the same as an employee for purposes of vicarious liability. The key question is the extent of control the organization exercised over the volunteer. See the discussion below.) Anyone injured could sue the careless driver for negligence and also sue the church on the basis of vicarious liability. To take another example, the parents of a child injured through the carelessness of a church employee or volunteer could sue (on behalf of the child) the careless caregiver and also could sue the church on the principle of vicarious liability.

In these examples, it is assumed that the church did nothing wrong. It did not fail, for example, to take steps to ensure that the driver or caregiver was competent to do the job. Vicarious liability is no-fault liability; it arises when a church does nothing wrong but is held legally liable for the wrongdoing of an employee or volunteer.

A defendant can be both directly and vicariously liable

It is important to note, so as to avoid confusion, that there are many cases in which one defendant is found to be directly liable because of its own wrongdoing and also vicariously liable because of its relationship to another defendant. In these situations, the finding of vicarious liability does not turn on the finding of direct liability. For instance, the employer of the careless waitress who spills soup on a customer would be vicariously liable for her carelessness. Even if the employer has done nothing wrong, that will not change the finding of vicarious liability; it arises even in the absence of fault. However, if the employer was negligent, say in training or supervising the waitress, and that carelessness was a factor in her spilling the soup, then the employer might also be found directly liable, in addition to being vicariously liable.

Vicarious liability and intentional wrongdoing by an employee

Employers are not often found vicariously liable for the intentional wrongdoing of their employees, but there are exceptional circumstances in which liability is imposed. (Vicarious liability most commonly arises when an employee carelessly causes harm in the course of employment.) In one case, an employer of a bouncer at a nightclub who used excessive force in removing a patron was held vicariously liable for the bouncer's tort of intentional battery.[20] Vicarious liability has sometimes been imposed on employers in situations in which an employee is found liable for sexual assault. The relevant considerations for determining when a court will impose liability on an employer for intentional wrongdoing by the employee were set out by the Supreme Court of Canada in *Bazley v. Curry*.[21] The essential conclusion of the court is that there must be something about the employment relationship that materially increased the risk of the harm occurring before an employer will be found vicariously liable for intentional wrongdoing by an employee.

The case of *Bazley v. Curry* involved a young child living in a residential care facility who was sexually abused by an employee, Mr. Curry. Mr. Curry's employer, the Children's Foundation, was found vicariously liable for his wrongdoing. The Foundation was a non-profit organization that operated two residential care facilities for the treatment of emotionally troubled children. The Foundation provided care for the children in all aspects of their lives, in effect acting as substitute parents. The Supreme Court stated:

> The Foundation hired Mr. Curry, a paedophile, to work in its Vancouver home. The Foundation did not know he was a paedophile. It checked and was told he was a suitable employee. Into this environment, too, came the

child Patrick Bazley, young and emotionally vulnerable. Curry began a seduction. Over the months, step by subtle step, bathing became sexual exploitation; tucking in in a darkened room became sexual abuse.[22]

After someone complained about Curry, the Foundation made further enquires; upon finding that he had previously abused a child, it immediately fired him. Curry was convicted of nineteen counts of sexual abuse, two of which related to Bazley. "[Bazley] sued the Foundation for compensation for the injury he suffered while in its care. The Foundation took the position that since it had committed no fault in hiring or supervising Curry, it was not legally responsible for what he had done."[23] Curry had died by the time the civil suit was launched.

The legal issue before the Supreme Court of Canada was whether the Foundation (the employer) could be held vicariously liable for the intentional tort (sexual assault) committed by Curry (the employee). To reiterate, it was not a question of whether the Foundation was at fault in any way; the court assumed that it was not at fault.

The Supreme Court summarized its legal conclusions as follows:

> The fundamental question is whether the wrongful act is sufficiently related to conduct authorized by the employer to justify the imposition of vicarious liability. Vicarious liability is generally appropriate where there is sufficient connection between the creation or enhancement of a risk and the wrong that

accrues therefrom, even if unrelated to the employer's desires. ...

In determining the sufficiency of the connection between the employer's creation or enhancement of the risk and the wrong complained of, subsidiary factors may be considered and may vary with the nature of the case. When related to intentional torts, the relevant factors may include, but are not limited to, the following:

(a) the opportunity that the enterprise afforded the employee to abuse his or her power;

(b) the extent to which the wrongful act may have furthered the employer's aims (and hence be more likely to have been committed by the employee);

(c) the extent to which the wrongful act was related to friction, confrontation or intimacy inherent in the employer's enterprise;

(d) the extent of power conferred on the employee in relation to the victim; and

(e) the vulnerability of potential victims to wrongful exercise of the employee's power.[24]

The court in *Bazley v. Curry* then discussed these general considerations about vicarious liability for intentional wrongdoing by an employee in the context of sexual abuse by employees. The court underscored that there must be "a strong connection between what the employer was asking the employee to do (the risk created by the employer's enterprise) and the wrongful act."[25] The greater the opportunity to commit the wrongdoing the employment afforded, the more likely the employer will be held vicariously liable. The court will consider how much time the employee was permitted to spend with the child, whether the two were allowed to be alone and the intimacy of the tasks assigned to the employee. The risk is also increased by the nature of the relationship between the employee and the child. Employment that puts the employee in a position of power over the child may "enhance the risk of the employee feeling that he or she is able to take advantage of the child and the child submitting without effective complaint."[26]

On the facts in *Bazley v. Curry*, the Foundation was held vicariously liable for the sexual abuse by Curry:

> The opportunity for intimate private control and the parental relationship and power required by the terms of employment created the special environment that nurtured and brought to fruition Curry's sexual abuse. The employer's enterprise created and fostered the risk that led to the ultimate harm. The abuse was not a mere accident of time and place, but the product of the special relationship of intimacy and respect the employer fostered, as well as the special opportunities for exploitation of that relationship it furnished. Indeed it is difficult to imagine a job with a greater risk for child sexual abuse.[27]

The employer, Foundation, was vicariously liable for the intentional wrongdoing by its employee, Curry, because its enterprise, caring for young children, materially increased the risk of the harm occurring. A defendant employer, such as Foundation, found to be vicariously liable for the actions of an employee, is legally obligated to compensate the plaintiff for the harm he or she has suffered.

Illustrative case: churches and vicarious liability

There have been several cases in which churches were found vicariously liable for the intentional wrongdoing of an employee.[28]

In the case of *John Doe v. Bennett*,[29] discussed above, the Roman Catholic Episcopal Corporation of St. George's was found directly liable and also vicariously liable for the wrongdoing of the defendant, Father Bennett. The Supreme Court of Canada applied the law of the *Bazley* case and reasoned as follows on the issue of whether vicarious liability should be imposed:

> The relationship between the bishop and a priest in a diocese is not only spiritual, but temporal. The priest takes a vow of obedience to the bishop. The bishop exercises extensive control over the priest, including the power of assignment, the power to remove the priest from his post and the power to discipline him. It is akin to an employment relationship. … Applying the relevant test to the facts, it is also clear that the necessary connection between the employer-created or enhanced risk and the wrong complained of is established.

> First, the bishop provided Bennett with the opportunity to abuse his power. As noted by

the trial judge, 'the vast majority' of all the activities which [Bennett] organized and in which he was always accompanied by boys, were activities which he organized and controlled in his capacity as parish priest.

...

Second, Bennett's wrongful acts were strongly related to the psychological intimacy inherent in his role as priest. As explained by [the Court of Appeal Judge] ...: "the Church encourages psychological intimacy between a priest and members of the parish. A priest may not have to bath children [as in *Bazley*] but he, like parents, teaches them right from wrong, he represents God and they are to accept his instructions in spiritual matters." This psychological intimacy encourages victims' submission to abuse and increases the opportunity to abuse ....

Third, the bishop conferred an enormous degree of power on Bennett relative to his victims ....[30]

In summary, the evidence overwhelmingly satisfies the tests affirmed in *Bazley* [and other cases]. The relationship between the diocesan enterprise and Bennett was sufficiently close. The enterprise substantially enhanced the risk which led to the wrongs the [plaintiffs] suffered. It provided Bennett with great power in relation to vulnerable victims and with the opportunity to abuse that power.[31]

The court found the defendant Episcopal Corporation of St. George's vicariously liable for the wrongdoing of Bennett and, as discussed above, directly liable because of its negligent failure to stop the abuse. Father Bennett was held directly liable for his wrongful acts.

Is there an exemption for non-profit organizations?

The idea that non-profit organizations such as a church should be granted an exemption from vicarious liability for the intentional wrongdoing of their employees or volunteers was considered by the Supreme Court of Canada in *Bazley v. Curry*.[32] The following three arguments were put forward in support of an exemption for non-profit organizations, each rejected by the Supreme Court.

1. It is unfair to impose liability without fault on organizations engaged in necessary and important community work. Although sympathetic to this argument, the Supreme Court stressed that the issue must be considered from the perspective of the injured plaintiff, who is an innocent victim. If the church or other non-profit is exempted from liability, then the innocent victim will likely receive no compensation for his or her injuries. Forced to make this choice, the court concluded that it is fair to impose liability on the organization that enhanced the risk of harm. Doing so may reduce the incidence of wrongdoing by motivating organizations

to take all possible precautions. (An organization that takes all possible precautions can nevertheless still be found vicariously liable.) "When all perspectives are considered," the court noted, "it is difficult to conclude that the fact that the [non-profit organization] does good work in the community without expectation of profit makes it unjust that it should be held vicariously liable for the abuse of the [innocent child]."[33]

2. It is unfair to impose liability without fault on non-profit organizations because they are less able to control and supervise those who carry out their work, many of whom are volunteers. The court rejected the premise of this argument that "an organization's responsibility and control over its operations diminish when it employs volunteers."[34] Non-profit organizations, the court concluded, have the same legal duty to screen and supervise their employees and volunteers as any other organization.

3. Holding a non-profit vicariously liable will put many non-profits out of business and have a negative effect on society, since it will be deprived of their important work. The argument is that non-profits, unlike commercial enterprises, cannot pass on to consumers the cost of liability, nor can they usually obtain insurance for intentional wrongdoing by their employees or volunteers. The court saw this as a variation on the first argument and concluded that "if, in the final analysis, the choice is between which of two faultless parties should bear the loss ... I do not hesitate in my answer. Neither alternative is attractive. But given that a

choice must be made, it is fairer to place the loss on the party that introduced the risk and had the better opportunity to control it."[35]

The court then stated:

> I conclude that the case for exempting non-profit institutions from vicarious liability otherwise properly imposed at law has not been established. I can see no basis for carving out an exception from the common law of vicarious liability for a particular class of defendants, non-profit organizations. ... [I]t is for the legislature to consider whether relief should be granted to limit the legal exposure of non-profit organizations to prosecution for sexual abuse.[36]

Volunteers

A volunteer is a person who does a job or provides a service without being paid. Volunteers play an integral part in every church organization. Indeed, volunteers are the lifeblood of most church activity, from teaching Sunday school to helping out with building repair, serving on the board of trustees or decorating the Christmas tree.

While this section is really just a restatement of issues already canvassed in this chapter, looking at things from the perspective of the volunteer, we thought it important to underscore two points. Churches may be directly liable to volunteers who suffer loss caused by the church or someone associated with the church, and churches may be vicariously liable for the harms volunteers cause to others. This second point is surprising to many people. It most certainly extends the ambit of potential church liability. The section concludes with advice on developing church policy around volunteers.

Churches may be directly liable to volunteers

A person who is harmed while volunteering for a church may have a claim against the church if the church was at fault. A case may help to illustrate typical fact situations.

Mr. Bibby, a roofer by trade, was a member of Ebenezer Baptist Church Inc. He volunteered to help build a new church, and would sometimes also visit the construction site to view the progress of construction. On the day of the incident, he was viewing the site with another member of the congregation. After touring the main floor, the two proceeded up a set of stairs to the second floor. While viewing the second floor, Mr. Bibby noticed a room that he had not seen on the blueprints. Taking a few steps backward to view the room from a different angle, he fell through the stairwell opening down onto the concrete floor. There were no guardrails or other barriers around the stairwell.

Mr. Bibby sued the church and the project manager for the injuries he sustained. The legal issue for the court to decide was whether the church had taken reasonable care in the circumstances. The court noted that the church had not complied with provisions of the *Occupational Health and Safety Act* and found in favour of the plaintiff. The court concluded:

> The defendants knew that members of the congregation visited the work site. There was nothing to prevent them entering the building.

There was no indication that they were not welcome on the site. There were no signs to warn them of any danger. In the circumstances, I find that the defendants by not providing a guard-rail and a toeboard failed to take reasonable care.[37]

The law of occupiers' liability requires that a church take reasonable care for the safety of people who enter upon church premises (see Chapter 20). By failing to take reasonable care for the safety of a volunteer, Ebenezer Baptist Church Inc. was directly liable to him for the harm he suffered.

Churches may be vicariously liable for volunteer wrongdoing

For purposes of vicarious liability, the law often treats a volunteer the same as an employee. This is an exceptionally important area of liability for several reasons. Churches usually exercise care in choosing employees, but sometimes are less careful regarding volunteers. Employees usually have training and expertise, something not always true of volunteers. Combining these sometimes lax standards by churches with the law of vicarious liability broadens the ambit and increases the risk of liability for churches.

When will a volunteer be treated like an employee for purposes of vicarious liability? The key question is the extent of control that the church exercised over the volunteer.

A person can be [an employee] on and for a single occasion, even though acting gratuitously. As long as the person doing the work is under the direction and control of the one for whom he is working while carrying out his duties for which he volunteered his assistance the necessary [employer-employee] relationship will arise.[38]

Given that most volunteers are under the direction and control of the church, volunteers will almost always be treated like employees for the purposes of vicarious liability. A church can be vicariously liable for a volunteer who negligently causes harm to someone in the course of doing his or her appointed duties. Although uncommon, a church could be held vicariously liable even for intentional wrongdoing by a volunteer.

The facts of a case in which a non-profit organization was held vicariously liable for the wrongdoing of a volunteer help to illustrate further these principles.

Ms. Chung was in charge of a Boy Scout camp where a young camper was sexually abused. The court found that Ms. Chung had seen the abuse take place but took no action until three days later; she had the power as camp leader to "expel anyone from camp, but she chose not to."[39] Her failure to act in this situation was negligent. Concluding that the Boy Scouts of Canada were vicariously liable for her negligence, the court stated:

> Volunteers like Ms. Chung are still considered [employees] for the purposes of vicarious liability .... Further, there is no exemption from vicarious liability for non-profit organizations ....

The basic precondition to the imposition of vicarious liability is that the employees must have been acting in the course of their employment. Here, Ms. Chung's employment duties were directly related to her negligence. She was to supervise and ensure the safety of the children in the camp. She did not do so in respect of the incidences which ground this action. Her negligence goes to the core of what the law regards as the employment duties for the Boy Scouts.[40]

The Boy Scouts of Canada, a non-profit organization, was held vicariously liable for the negligence of a volunteer, Ms. Chung. For the purposes of vicarious liability, she was treated by the court as an employee, and because her negligent failure to assist the young camper occurred in the course of employment, her employer was held vicariously liable for the harm he suffered.

Church policy and volunteers

Given the importance of volunteers in the life of most churches and the issues of potential liability around volunteers, developing appropriate policies and procedures should be a high priority. The Panel on Accountability and Governance in the Voluntary Sector recommends that organizations that work with volunteers consider doing the following (and notes that "the degree of formality with which these duties are carried out will vary with the size of the organization").[41]

Organizations that rely on volunteers should

- have in place a clear set of policies addressing the recruitment, preparation, oversight and recognition of volunteer resources. (Volunteer programs should be designed and assessed with the same stringency as other programs.);

- give volunteers a clear statement of the tasks and activities that they are to carry out, perhaps including job descriptions or volunteer agreements;

- adopt and adhere to codes of ethical conduct for managers and volunteers themselves;

- provide adequate orientation, training and evaluation;

- publicly recognize the contributions of volunteers;

- screen volunteers, particularly if the organization works with vulnerable populations; and

- establish explicit expectations about the claiming of expenses.[42]

Conclusion

A person or church will not be found directly liable unless its acts or omissions have caused harm. With few exceptions, direct liability is avoided by ensuring that harm is not caused either negligently or intentionally (two of these exceptions, the torts of defamation and nuisance, are discussed at Chapters 12 and 21). By contrast, churches can be found vicariously liable for harm caused by employees and volunteers, even though the church took all measures and did everything humanly possible to ensure that the harm would not occur. There is no doubt that the doctrine of vicarious liability provides a great incentive to take preventative measures, but the hard fact remains that a claim of vicarious liability cannot be defeated by showing that the organization was careful and is itself innocent of any wrongdoing.

Direct and Vicarious Liability: Questions and Answers

Q. Can a church corporation be found directly liable for decisions made by its directors and officers?

A. Yes. Corporations are said to act through their directors and officers, who are considered the directing mind of the organization.

Q. What is vicarious liability?

A. Vicarious liability is a legal doctrine that imposes liability on a person or church because of its relationship to the wrongdoer. It is a form of no-fault liability – a defendant can be found vicariously liable even though he or she did nothing wrong. Vicarious liability most commonly arises in the employer–employee relationship.

Q. Are non-profit organizations such as churches exempt from vicarious liability?

A. No. The Supreme Court of Canada has ruled that there are no persuasive reasons to exempt a non-profit organization from vicarious liability. If such immunity were to be established, the Supreme Court concluded that it would have to be done through an act of a legislature.

Q. What is a volunteer?

A. A volunteer is a person who does a job or provides a service without being paid.

Q. Can a church be sued by a volunteer?

A. Yes. A volunteer who suffers a loss caused by the church or someone associated with a church could sue.

Q. Can a church be found vicariously liable for the intentional wrongdoings of its employees or volunteers?

A. Yes. Organizations are not often found vicariously liable for the intentional wrongdoing of their employees or volunteers, but there are circumstances in which liability is imposed. The key question is whether the employment relationship materially increased the risk of the harm occurring. Courts will consider such factors as the opportunity given the employee or volunteer to abuse power; the relationship of the wrongful act to contact or intimacy inherent in the employer's enterprise; the power conferred on the employee or volunteer in relation to the victim; and the vulnerability of potential victims to the employee's or volunteer's power.

Notes

1   Robert Flannigan, "The Liability Structure of Nonprofit Associations: Tort and Fiduciary Liability Assignments" (1998) 77 *Canadian Bar Review* 73, p. 75 [*Flannigan*].

2   *John Doe v. Bennett*, [2004] S.C.R. 436, para. 1 [*Bennett*]. *John Doe* is a pseudonym. Pseudonyms are sometimes allowed by courts to protect the identity of a party.

3   *Ibid.*, para. 15.

4   *Ibid.*, para. 8.

5   *Chartrand v. Grace Lutheran Church Society*, 2003 BCSC 1377.

6   *Ibid.*, para. 50.

7   *Ibid.*, para. 52.

8   *Ibid.*, para. 53.

9   John G. Fleming, *The Law of Torts*, 9th ed. (Sydney: Law Book Company, 1998), p. 409.

10 The doctrine of vicarious liability applies to unincorporated associations as well as corporations. "Members [or employees of an unincorporated association] who commit [torts] will be directly and primarily liable for their conduct. Where those acts are within the scope of the undertaking of the association, the possibility of vicarious liability will also arise. The appropriate analysis will then be to determine which members participated in generally controlling the management of association affairs. Those members will be vicariously liable." *Flannigan*, note 1, p. 77.

11 Vicarious liability can also arise between two separate but related church entities, a type of liability referred to as cross-over liability. In the January 2003 *Charity Law Bulletin*, authors Esther Oh and Terrance S. Carter explain, in part, as follows:

> The review of the relevant case law suggests that the courts will attribute cross-over liability between two separately incorporated associated church entities if one entity can be characterized as an employer of employees of the second entity. At the same time, courts have been quick to dismiss the attribution of liability

to an incorporated national Church entity for the acts of a separately incorporated associated entity where the national Church entity had no involvement whatsoever in the operation or control of the separately incorporated entity, such as a residential school ....

Based on the reasoning in the *Plint* case [*W.R.B. v. Plint* (1998), 161 D.L.R. (4th) 538], it appears that a national organization that has significant control over the operations of an associated entity will likely be found vicariously liable, whether or not the latter associated entity is separately incorporated.

The authors also provide practical advice on avoiding cross-over liability. Esther S. J. Oh and Terrance S. Carter, *Cross-over Liability: Principles from the Residential Schools Cases* (2003) (www.carters.ca).

[12] The issue of determining whether a person is considered an employee for the purposes of vicarious liability is sometimes analyzed as a choice between whether the person should in law be classified as an employee or as an independent contractor. An employer is not vicariously liable for persons classified as independent contractors. To determine whether someone is an employee or independent contractor, courts look to such factors as the level and amount of control exercised over the individual, who owned the tools and who bore the risk of profit or loss from the relationship. A person is likely to be considered an employee for the purpose of vicarious liability when, within the relationship, he or she was told what to do and how to do it. By contrast, an independent contractor is hired to do a certain job and does it in the way he or she considers appropriate. The use of independent contractors rather than employees for certain tasks is a common strategy for risk reduction or risk shifting.

[13] *B.M. v. Mumford*, 2000 BCSC 1787, para. 23.

[14] *Ibid.*, paras. 24–25.

[15] *W.K. v. Pornbacher*, [1998] 3 W.W.R. 149 (B.C.S.C), para. 51 [*Pornbacher*].

[16] *Ibid.*, para. 52.

[17] *Ibid.*, para. 54.

[18] *Bazley v. Curry*, [1999] 2 S.C.R. 534, paras. 26–36 [*Bazley*].

[19]   *Ibid.*, para. 31.

[20]   *Brown v. Doe* (1980), 23 B.C.L.R. 34 (S.C.).

[21]   *Bazley*, note 18.

[22]   *Ibid.*, para. 3.

[23]   *Ibid.*, para. 5.

[24]   *Ibid.*, para. 41. Emphasis omitted.

[25]   *Ibid.*, para. 42.

[26]   *Ibid.*, para. 44.

[27]   *Ibid.*, para. 58.

[28]   For example, see *J.R.S. v. Glendinning* (2004), 237 D.L.R. (4th) 304 (Ont. Sup. Ct. J.); *Bennett*, note 2; *Doe v. O'Dell* (2003), 230 D.L.R. (4th) 383 (Ont. Sup. Ct. J.); *P.D. v. Allen*, [2004] O.T.C. 645 (Sup. Ct. J.); *Blackwater v. Plint*, [2005] 3 S.C.R. 3; *Pornbacher*, note 15.

[29]   *Bennett*, note 2.

[30]   *Ibid.*, paras. 27–29.

[31]   *Ibid.*, para. 32.

[32]   *Bazley*, note 18, paras. 47–56.

[33]   *Ibid.*, para. 51.

[34]   *Ibid.*, para. 52.

[35]   *Ibid.*, para. 54.

[36]   *Ibid.*, para. 56.

[37]   *Bibby v. Ebenezer Baptist Church Inc.* (1994), 127 Sask. R. 199 (Q.B.).

[38]   G. H. L. Fridman, *The Law of Torts in Canada* (Toronto: Carswell, 2002), p. 601.

[39]   *C.S. (Next friend of) v. Miller* (2002), 1 Alta. L.R. (4th) 120 (Q.B.), para. 8. This case is also discussed in Chapter 11.

[40]   *Ibid.*, paras. 34–35.

[41] Panel on Accountability and Governance in the Voluntary Sector, *Building on Strength: Improving Governance and Accountability in Canada's Voluntary Sector* (www.vsr-trsb.net/pagvs/book.pdf), p. 28.

[42] *Ibid.*

10

Intentional Torts

Justice is a kind of compact not to harm or be harmed.
—Epicurus, Greek philosopher,
341–270 BC, *Principal Doctrines*

It may be stating the obvious to say that the essence of intentional torts is intention, or desiring the consequences of one's actions: deliberately causing harm. Contrast this with negligence, in which someone does not desire to cause harm, but rather did so because of a careless but not intentional act. The difference is simple: I hit you on purpose versus I hit you as a result of my careless actions.

There are several intentional torts, including trespass to land, battery and the intentional infliction of mental suffering. Trespass to land is covered in Chapter 19. This chapter discusses the intentional torts of battery and the infliction of mental suffering.

Battery

Battery involves intentionally making physical contact with a person without their consent or some other lawful justification. An English court stated the law on battery eloquently when it said that "the fundamental principle, plain and incontestable, is that every person's body is inviolate. It has long been established that any touching of another person, however slight, may amount to a battery."[1] Battery is sometimes referred to as assault. For example, in the sexual abuse context, civil courts use the terms *sexual battery* and *sexual assault* synonymously. In criminal law, the term *assault* is always used instead of *battery*.

Battery protects a person's right to be free from physical interference and reflects society's belief in the inherent dignity and sanctity of the person. Many of the sexual abuse claims against clergy and churches are framed in battery and negligence. The issue of sexual abuse is discussed in Chapter 11.

Intentional infliction of mental suffering

Another intentional tort is called the intentional infliction of mental suffering. The first case in which this tort was recognized, in the late nineteenth century, had a colourful set of facts.[2] The plaintiff, Mrs. Wilkinson, was told by the defendant, Mr. Downton, that her husband had broken both his legs in an accident and that she should "go at once in a cab with two pillows to fetch him home."[3] It was a lie: Mr. Wilkinson had not been in an accident. Apparently, Mr. Downton thought it was a funny practical joke. Poor Mrs. Wilkinson, shocked by what she was told, suffered a mental breakdown and serious physical illness. She sued Mr. Downton for the harm he caused. The court recognized the justice of her claim, concluding that anyone who says something intending to cause harm should be liable when a person suffers serious psychological or physical harm as a result. More recent courts have made it clear that the statements must be judged "flagrant and extreme"[4] by community standards.

The tort is an interesting one, not least of all because it shows the courts' willingness to provide compensation for the harm often caused by words, at least words classified as flagrant and extreme.

A plaintiff who sues for intentional infliction of mental suffering must prove that the defendant intentionally did or said something flagrant and extreme, intending to cause harm to the plaintiff. The plaintiff also has to prove that, as a consequence, he or she suffered a physical illness or a recognized psychological illness, such as depression or a nervous breakdown. Mere emotional upset or psychological turmoil is not sufficient.

Illustrative case

A few claims of intentional infliction of mental suffering have been made against clergy, although none successfully.[5] One such case is *Zecevic v. Russian Orthodox Christ the Saviour Cathedral*, in which a 51-year-old widower claimed more than $350,000 in damages "because he was humiliated in front of dozens of his closest friends and relatives" at his wife's funeral.[6] It was "also alleged that he suffered excruciating mental anguish as a result of his inability to honour his beloved wife's wishes in a simple, calm and dignified manner."[7] The plaintiff,

Vlatko Zecevic, and his wife were born in Yugoslavia and had connections over the years to the Serbian Orthodox Church. The defendants included two priests: Father Boldireff of the Russian Orthodox Church and Father Doder of the Serbian Orthodox Church.

The plaintiff's wife stated in her will that she wanted a modest funeral with family and friends, and to be cremated. After her death, while the plaintiff was making funeral arrangements, he learned that a priest of the Serbian Orthodox Church would not officiate at a funeral if the deceased was to be cremated, and so he made funeral arrangements with Father Boldireff of the Russian Orthodox Church. Father Doder of the Serbian Church believed that it was improper for Father Boldireff to officiate because the deceased was connected to the Serbian Church, and accused Father Boldireff of interfering in the affairs of the Serbian Church. This dispute became known to the plaintiff, and led to a commotion and turmoil during a prayer service and the cancellation of the funeral service in the Russian Orthodox Church. Instead, the funeral was held in a funeral home. Cremation was postponed a day. Six months later, a memorial service was held in an Anglican church.

The plaintiff said he felt humiliated because he did not fulfill his wife's last wishes. His claim for intentional infliction of mental suffering was against Father Doder, who he alleged "intended to stop the funeral and did not take into consideration the impact on the plaintiff."[8] Further, the plaintiff alleged that the priest "intended to make an example of these people ...."[9] The judge rejected this claim, concluding that the priest did not intend to cause mental suffering but, rather, honestly believed in what he did. The court also doubted that the emotional upset the plaintiff experienced (nervousness, insomnia and tension) was sufficiently severe to meet the requirements of this tort.

Conclusion

No one would dispute the ancient wisdom that not to harm or be harmed goes to the essence of justice. Ensuring that everyone associated with the church understands and complies with the limits of acceptable behaviour, in both their actions and words, is of fundamental importance in avoiding harm and either eliminating or reducing the risk of liability.

Intentional Torts: Questions and Answers

Q. What is an intentional tort?

A. When a person acts desiring or wanting to cause harm, they are said to be acting intentionally. Intentional torts can be distinguished from the tort of negligence. Negligence involves situations where harm is caused unintentionally by a careless act.

Q. What is battery?

A. The tort of battery involves intentionally making physical contact with a person without their consent or some legal justification. Battery is sometimes called assault.

Q. Can a person be liable for words that cause harm?

A. Yes. A person who says something flagrant or extreme, intending to cause harm, may be liable if someone suffers a physical or psychological illness. This tort is called the intentional infliction of mental suffering.

Notes

1   *Collins v. Wilcock*, [1984] 3 All E.R. 374 (Q.B.), p. 378.

2   *Wilkinson v. Downton*, [1897] 2 Q.B. 57.

3   *Ibid.*, p. 57.

4   *Rahemtulla v. Vanfed Credit Union* (1984), 29 C.C.L.T. 78 (B.C.S.C.).

5   *Deiwick v. Frid*, [1991] O.J. No. 1803 (Ct. J. (Gen. Div.)) (QL); *Greco v. Holy See (State of the Vatican City)*, [2000] O.J. No. 5293 (Sup. Ct. J.) (QL).

6   *Zecevic v. Russian Orthodox Christ the Saviour Cathedral*, [1988] C.L.D. 1613 (H.C.J.).

7   *Ibid.*, para. 1.

8   *Ibid.*, para. 73.

9   *Ibid.*

11

Negligence

The rule that you are to love your neighbour becomes in law
you must not injure your neighbour; and the lawyer's question,
Who is my neighbour? receives a restricted reply.
You must take reasonable care to avoid acts or omissions
which you can reasonably foresee would be likely to injure
your neighbour. Who, then, in law, is my neighbour?
The answer seems to be – persons who are so closely
and directly affected by my act that I ought reasonably
to have them in contemplation as being so affected
when I am directing my mind to the acts
or omissions which are called in question.
—Lord Atkin, House of Lords,
Donoghue v. Stevenson (1932)

Liability in negligence is perhaps the most common basis of legal liability. In other words, if you find yourself the defendant in a lawsuit, chances are you are being sued for negligence. For that reason, it is important to have a good working sense of the tort of negligence. Understanding its essential features will enable you to detect situations that present a risk of negligence liability and take the appropriate steps to remove or reduce the risk.

After setting out the primary purposes of the law of negligence, this chapter focuses on the elements of a negligence action and a few areas of potential liability in negligence relevant in the church context, including motor vehicle accidents, negligent counselling, sexual abuse and relationships of supervision or control.

Purposes

A primary purpose of the law of negligence is to prevent careless behaviour that causes harm. Negligence law establishes reasonable standards of conduct, and failure to meet these standards will likely result in liability when harm is caused. A second purpose is to provide compensation for those injured by careless behaviour.

The elements of a negligence action

The tort of negligence is comprised of four basic elements: duty, standard of care, causation and damage.

Duty is a legal obligation to conform to a standard of behaviour or action. For example, the law imposes a duty on drivers to operate their vehicles safely; a duty rests on doctors to treat their patients with skill and care; carpenters are under a duty to meet the standards of their trade. Likewise clergy, church staff, directors and others involved in the various operations and activities of the church are under a duty imposed by law to perform their activities to a certain standard of care.

A legal duty is said to arise in those situations in which a reasonable defendant would have foreseen that his or her careless actions would cause a loss to the plaintiff. As Lord Atkin explained in the case of *Donoghue v. Stevenson*,[1] a duty is owed to your neighbour: persons who are likely to be harmed by your careless acts or omissions. Courts will impose a duty in these situations unless there is some policy reason that weighs in favour of not doing so. One of the most common is the policy concern that imposing a duty in a particular situation would result in too many claims being brought to the courts, the so-called floodgates argument. For many years, courts denied recovery for this reason to individuals who had suffered psychiatric harm. Policy concerns are also manifested in the belief that certain sorts of activities should be immune from liability. Judges, for example, cannot be sued in negligence for any errors they make in their professional capacity.

Perhaps the first question a person who is told they are under a legal duty would be expected to ask is "What am I required to do?" Or "How can I fulfill this duty?" The answer to these questions raises the issue of standard of care, and the general answer is "You are expected to do what a reasonable person in similar circumstances would do." What is reasonable depends, as Justice Major of the Supreme Court of Canada explained, "on the facts of each case, including the likelihood of known or foreseeable harm, the gravity of that harm and the burden or cost which would be incurred to prevent the injury."[2]

To determine what is reasonable, courts also look to external standards such as custom or industry practice. Compliance with the customary practice of an industry or profession is usually considered to be reasonable conduct. Conversely, failure to comply with customary practice is usually considered unreasonable, i.e. a breach of the standard of care. For example, if there was an allegation against a church that it was negligent in training or supervising an employee who harmed a third party, the court would look closely at whether the church followed current and accepted practices and procedures for training and supervising employees.

Standard of care is usually the main issue in lawsuits alleging negligence. A judge or a jury is asked to decide whether the defendant breached the standard of care. To put it another way, the inquiry is whether he or she did something that a reasonable person would not have done, or failed to do something that a reasonable person would have done.

The standard of care is the same for churches as it is for individuals and corporations, both non-profit and for-profit. The standard of care for those who work for churches, including volunteers, is the same as the standard for any other individuals.[3]

The general rule is that no person will be liable in negligence (or for any other tort, for that matter) unless it can be proven that his or her actions caused the loss or harm suffered by the plaintiff. (Vicarious liability is an important exception. Under the doctrine of vicarious liability, a person can be found liable for a loss caused by someone else. See Chapter 9.) To decide the issue of causation, the courts employ the "but for test." The question asked is whether the plaintiff would not have suffered loss but for the defendant's actions. If the loss suffered by the plaintiff would have occurred regardless of what the defendant did, then the defendant was not the cause. Put more simply, the plaintiff must prove to the court that his or her loss occurred because of the careless actions of the defendant.

Damage, another of the essential elements in a negligence claim, is simply the legal term for the loss, harm or injury suffered by the plaintiff. Damage can be a broken bone, a dented car fender or lost income. The goal of tort law is to compensate the successful plaintiff fully for the losses suffered, often expressed as an attempt by the court to put the plaintiff in the same position he or she would have been in had the tort not happened.

An example may help clarify the way these concepts are used by the courts. Suppose a motor vehicle accident in which a car hits a pedestrian. The court would first ask whether a reasonable driver in the position of the defendant would have realized that careless driving on his or her part might injure someone such as the plaintiff. The court will easily conclude that the driver was under a legal duty to take care, because the loss was foreseeable and there are no policy reasons not to impose a duty. The key question will be whether the driver did something a reasonable driver would not have done, and whether, but for that unreasonable conduct, the accident would not have occurred. Was the driver speeding, inattentive or intoxicated? If the plaintiff is able to prove that he or she suffered a loss (damage) and it was caused by (causation) the unreasonable actions of the driver in the operation of his or her car (breach of standard of care), then the plaintiff will be successful and the court will award a sum of money in lieu of the loss sustained.

Two other elements of the tort of negligence are also sometimes relevant: remoteness and contributory negligence. A person who carelessly causes a loss will not be held legally responsible when the harm caused is a completely unexpected and unforeseeable consequence of the careless act. Loss that is unforeseeable is said to be remote, and the plaintiff is denied recovery for such loss. The principle of remoteness, however, is rarely invoked.

Contributory negligence is a partial defence to negligence. When a plaintiff's own negligence plays a role in the loss suffered, a court will reduce the damages he or she receives. For example, suppose a defendant drives his or her car carelessly and runs into the plaintiff's car, causing property damage and personal injury. If the plaintiff was not wearing a seatbelt and his or her injuries are worse because of this, a court would say that the plaintiff was contributorily negligent and reduce the amount of money he or she is awarded (i.e. the damages) by a certain percentage. If in this example the plaintiff was entitled to $100,000 for personal injury, a court might reduce the award by ten per cent to take account of the plaintiff's careless failure to wear a seatbelt, i.e. his or her contributory negligence.

Motor vehicle accidents

If a church employee driving a church vehicle, or his or her own vehicle, in the course of employment negligently causes an accident, the church will be vicariously liable for the loss to the third party (see Chapter 9). In several provinces, the owner of a motor vehicle is, by statute, vicariously liable for the actions of anyone (not just employees) who drives the vehicle with the owner's consent.[4]

The church may also be vicariously liable for volunteers using their own or church vehicles for church purposes, depending on the degree of control exercised by the church over the volunteer. Volunteers are often treated the same as employees for the purpose of vicarious liability (see Chapter 9).

Note should be taken that vicarious liability can flow to a church even when vehicles not owned by the church are being used. To recap the law on vicarious liability, the doctrine imposes liability on the basis of a relationship, usually the employer–employee relationship. When an employee commits a tort in the course of employment (for example, negligent driving), the employer can be held liable for that loss, whether or not the car being driven was owned by the employer.

The main concerns and considerations to avoid this risk are to ensure that competent drivers are driving reliable vehicles suitable for the occasion and are covered by adequate motor vehicle liability insurance. Insurers should always be fully apprised of all relevant information concerning the use and operation of motor vehicles. Failure to do so may result in a denial of coverage should a loss occur.

Negligent counselling

The general rule in negligence law is that everyone is expected to meet the standard of a reasonable person. Professionals, however, are held to a higher standard in light of their superior knowledge, skill and training. A doctor is held to the standard of a reasonably competent doctor; a lawyer to the standard of a reasonably competent lawyer. When a doctor is sued for negligence, the central focus of the case is likely to be whether he or she did something that a reasonably competent doctor would not have done. If he or she failed to meet that standard of care and that failure caused the plaintiff's loss, then he or she would be liable. The lawsuit is framed in negligence and is often referred to as a claim of professional malpractice.

A psychiatrist, psychologist or professional counsellor is also held to a higher standard of care than the average person. Malpractice lawsuits against such professionals are common. When a psychologist, for example, fails to provide treatment that a reasonably competent psychologist would have provided, he or she may be liable to the plaintiff who suffers a loss because of the substandard treatment. What about clergy? Are clergy liable for professional malpractice?

Clergy malpractice has been defined in an American case as "the failure to exercise the degree of care and skill normally exercised by members of the clergy in carrying out their professional duties."[5] Clergy malpractice claims in the United States usually involve a claim of negligent counselling. Do clergy, as with other professionals, owe a duty of care to people they counsel? If so, to what standard of care should they be held? The standard of the reasonable person or something higher? Should the court impose liability when, in the course of counselling, they breach the standard of care and cause harm?

Courts in the United States have refused to impose tort liability on clergy for professional malpractice,[6] concluding that to do so would be a violation of the First Amendment to the United States Constitution, which states, in part, "Congress shall make no law respecting an establishment of religion, or prohibit the free exercise thereof …."[7] American courts have held that "civil tort claims against clerics that require the courts to review and interpret church law, policies or practices in the determination of claims are barred by the First Amendment …."[8] Deciding clergy malpractice claims "would embroil the courts in establishing the training, skill and standards applicable for the members of the clergy in this state in a diversity of religions professing widely varying beliefs. This is as impossible as it is unconstitutional."[9]

By contrast, the recent Canadian court decision B. (V.) v. Cairns imposed liability for negligent clergy counselling.[10] The decision is important "as it establishes a precedent for liability being imposed against churches, clergy and pastoral counselors in situations where they provide negligent counseling or advice."[11]

The plaintiff in Cairns was raised as a Jehovah's Witness. At the age of nineteen, she told an elder of the church that she had been abused by her father. The elder, after consulting with more senior advisors at the head office of the Jehovah's Witnesses church, advised her that she must confront her father about the abuse and give him a chance to repent. The elders were adhering to a practice grounded in a particular interpretation of a New Testament passage.[12] The plaintiff felt compelled to follow what she was told was the teaching of her church. The elder knew the plaintiff was beginning to have emotional problems caused by her father's abuse and that she was terrified about confronting him. A meeting was held where the plaintiff, accompanied by two other elders, confronted her father. She found the meeting traumatic.

The plaintiff sued several elders of the church and the Watch Tower Bible and Tract Society of Canada (the governing body of the Jehovah's Witnesses in Canada). She alleged that two of the elders were liable for negligence "in directing her to confront her father and knew or ought to have known she would be psychologically harmed by that process."[13] She alleged that a senior elder at the Watch Tower head office and the Watch Tower instructed and supported the other elders in their handling of the matter and were equally responsible for the damages she sustained.[14]

On the question of whether a duty of care was owed by the defendants, the court in *Cairns* drew the following conclusion:

> There is obviously a close and direct relationship between a member of the clergy and a parishioner who goes to him for advice. In that situation the clergyman would know that the person seeking his advice would be directly affected by the advice he provides. ... Given the direct relationship, it is easily foreseeable that harm may befall the parishioner if the member of the clergy is negligent in dealing with the matter before him. In my view, this situation is precisely the kind of close and direct relationship to which courts have recognized it would be just to impose a duty of care on the person providing the advice.[15]

Having ruled that the elders in *Cairns* had a duty of care toward the plaintiff, the court then turned to the issue of standard of care. The court concluded that the elders should not be held to the standard of care expected of psychiatrists, psychologists or social workers. No evidence was provided by the parties to help the judge determine what the standard of care should be in the circumstances. The court stated that "in the absence of specific evidence as to the standard, it is appropriate to apply the general standard of care for negligence, that of a reasonable person in like circumstances."[16] In other words, the standard of care issue in this case turned on determining whether the elders did what a reasonable person would have done in the circumstances. The court concluded that a reasonable person in the position of the elders would have known that "being a victim of sexual abuse is traumatic and that for any such victim to confront her abuser about such conduct in front of others would also likely be emotionally difficult."[17] The particular elders involved in counselling the plaintiff had knowledge about the plaintiff's emotional problems caused by her father's abuse, and they knew she was terrified about confronting her father.

> Fixed with that knowledge, and aware of their own lack of expertise, it was incumbent upon the elders to make enquiries of a professional as to how the potential harm to the plaintiff could be minimized, if not avoided entirely. In my opinion, failure to take this very basic precaution was a breach of the standard of care.[18]

The court further reasoned that the breach of the standard of care caused psychological harm to the plaintiff, and found the defendant Watch Tower liable because it was the Watch Tower, acting through its elders, that advised the plaintiff to confront her father.[19] The court found two of the three elders sued not liable because they were completely unaware of the subject matter of the meeting where the plaintiff confronted her father.[20] A third elder was found not personally liable because he did not advise anyone that it was theologically mandated for the plaintiff to confront her father.[21]

Avoiding liability for clergy counselling

It is a principle of negligence law that professionals in general, or indeed anyone who undertakes work requiring special skills, are expected to possess at least a certain minimum level of relevant knowledge and ability.[22] Professionals cannot escape liability by performing to the standard of the ordinary person. As Justice Linden has noted, this higher standard is to be expected given that professionals "hold themselves out as being possessed of extra skill and experience. This is why people consult them."[23] Clergy who hold themselves out as counsellors will also no doubt be expected to possess a minimum level of knowledge, skill and experience. The court in *Cairns* did not think it appropriate to expect clergy counsellors to meet the standard expected of psychiatrists, psychologists or social workers. Future courts will have to determine the standard of care appropriate for clergy counsellors. In other words, what level of skill and expertise will a court require of them? Against what standard will their actions or omissions be judged? A related question is whether courts will develop one standard of care for all clergy counsellors, regardless of church affiliation, or a standard for each specific denomination, based on the training and practices within that group.

This area of potential liability calls for appropriate policies and training by churches. One American commentator recommends that all clergy counsellors acquire at least basic skills in diagnostic screening in order to be able to identify the problems faced by the person seeking counselling.[24] Second, he suggests that clergy counsellors know when to refer to another professional someone they are counselling or considering counselling. Without question, knowing when to refer is essential to avoiding harm and legal liability. An expert in the field of clergy counselling recommends referral to an appropriately qualified health professional in the following situations:

> The first category of individual who should be referred consists of those who are psychotic, who are out of touch with reality to a major degree. These are people who show delusional thinking or very inappropriate or bizarre behavior. ...

> The second group includes those people who are overtly suicidal or who have a history of making suicide attempts in the past. ...

> Third is the group of people with significant problems of drug addiction or alcohol abuse. ...

> In the fourth category of people who should be referred are those who show signs of severe depression which interferes with their physical functioning and their day-to-day activities. ...

> The last category includes those people who show signs of brain disease – signs which include confusion, disorientation, and memory loss. ...

The majority of people who consult a clergy-person, however, usually do not fall into any of the five categories listed above. The majority are people with problems in living, with anxieties and fears, with mild depression, and with personality traits which get them into difficult situations. With this large group of people there are no hard-and-fast rules as to whom the clergyperson should refer. The decision depends on a number of factors, including the clergyperson's training and competence, available time, and degree of interest in counseling. It also depends upon whether or not the clergyperson's own personality makes a workable match with the personality of the one who is seeking help. ... One of the most important skills of counseling is the ability to recognize as early as possible those persons whom one is not able to help, and to refer these people as smoothly and rapidly as possible in the appropriate direction.[25]

Cairns marks the first time in Canada a church was found liable for negligent counselling. It is but one trial decision, and it is difficult to predict how the law will develop. However, it is at the very least a caution to churches and clergy counsellors that, if other claims follow, the courts will expect a certain level of skill and expertise.

Sexual abuse

Sexual abuse claims against churches, clergy, church employees or volunteers have been framed in various theories
of legal liability. There is inevitably a claim that someone
employed by or associated with the church has committed the
intentional tort of sexual battery (also called sexual assault). As
noted in Chapter 10, proving battery involves showing that the
defendant made harmful or offensive physical contact to the
plaintiff's person without consent or any other legal justification. Often an accompanying claim is that the church is vicariously liable for the actions of the defendant who committed the
battery. As previously discussed, vicarious liability is liability
without fault that arises because of the relationship between
the church and the defendant who battered the plaintiff. The
employer–employee relationship is the most common situation
in which vicarious liability is imposed (see Chapter 9).

In some suits, a plaintiff will allege negligence against the
church directly, i.e. that the church itself, acting through its
directors and officers, failed to meet the standard of reasonable
care. The allegation may be, for example, that the church was
negligent in hiring, training or supervising the person who
sexually abused the plaintiff.[26]

Another sort of claim made by plaintiffs in sexual abuse
cases is that a church or cleric breached a fiduciary duty owed
to the plaintiff (see Chapter 13).

Each of these claims – sexual assault, vicarious liability,
negligence and breach of fiduciary duty – was advanced by the
plaintiffs in *J.R.S. v. Glendinning*.

Father Glendinning was a priest and a faculty member at a local seminary. Over a period of several years, he developed a close relationship with a family, including the parents and their four children, a girl and three boys. He took the children to movies and camping.[27]

> The children stayed overnight with Glendinning on several occasions. The boys claimed they were sexually assaulted by Glendinning .... The female child, MS, claimed that she had witnessed several of Glendinning's assaults on her brothers. ... All the children had suffered from alcohol and drug abuse, left school and had been involved in prostitution as they became adults.[28]

The court found Father Glendinning liable for sexually assaulting the children. He was also liable for breach of his fiduciary duty toward the children. The diocese was vicariously liable for his wrongdoing on the basis of the principles enunciated by the Supreme Court of Canada in *Bazley v. Curry* (see Chapter 9).

With respect to the claim of negligence against the diocese, it acknowledged that it had a legal duty "to prevent the abuse of a parishioner by a member of the clergy,"[29] but took the position that it was not in breach of the standard of care. The diocese submitted that it complied with the standard of care because its "screening procedure for would-be priests in place in 1963 were appropriate for the times, and that it was not negligent in supervising its professors at the seminary."[30] The diocese was arguing that the measures it took to prevent the harm that occurred were reasonable, i.e. that they met the standard of care and should not be held liable. The court rejected this argument.

In concluding that the diocese was liable for negligence, the court considered the following facts as relevant breaches of the standard of care expected of the diocese. The extensive list is a verbatim excerpt from the decision of the trial judge. It underscores the scrutiny a court brings to bear on a defendant's actions and omissions. It also illustrates that general policies, such as the requirement to screen and supervise employees, must be fulfilled in particular and concrete ways.

a) It failed to appreciate that Glendinning had children in his apartment overnight when it ought to have known such was the case.

b) It ignored the high frequency of children's visits and Glendinning's unusual conduct in bringing children to his rooms.

c) It took no notice of the fact that Glendinning alone of all other residents of the seminary entertained children alone in his rooms.

d) It was willfully blind to the fact that on occasion the children stayed with Glendinning overnight at the seminary.

e) No official at the seminary made any enquiry concerning those activities when one ought to have been made under the circumstances.

f)   It disregarded the fact that he took young boys on overnight camping trips where he was the only adult.

g)   It failed to keep proper records of Glendinning's past conduct.

h)   It failed to provide education or counselling on sexual matters.

i)   It treated the issue of sex as taboo, result-ing in inappropriate and unusual behavior going unchecked.

j)   Rector Carrigan failed to interview any of the visiting children personally, or make any enquiries as to their activities, and as a result failed to learn about their activities with Glendinning.

k)   It failed to render assistance to the Plaintiffs after Glendinning was exposed, and failed to take steps to reduce the impact of his assaultive behaviour.[31]

Churches are now taking appropriate action in response to the scourge of sexual abuse. This is evidenced in many ways, not least by a clear institutional commitment embod-ied in thoughtful and thorough policies and procedures (see Chapter 5). One commentator, a practising lawyer, suggests that a church should take the following steps, at a minimum, to address concerns about potential sexual abuse: examine confidentiality guidelines to ensure, among other things, that members are aware of mandatory reporting requirements (see

Chapter 18); review internal church rules of ethical conduct; examine hiring practices; establish procedures for situations in which a church or employee is subject to criminal charges or a civil suit; ensure that internal disciplinary procedures meet the duty of fairness (see Chapter 3); review insurance coverage; and consider corporate restructuring to limit liability.[32] Within the context of a solid and ongoing commitment by each church community, the proper focus is always twofold: safety and prevention, coupled with training and support of leaders and members.[33]

Duty to help others

The duty that arises in negligence is simply to avoid doing careless things that cause harm. Historically, the common law never imposed on a person the duty to help someone in need. The classic illustration is that "one can, with immunity, smoke a cigarette on the beach while one's neighbour drowns and, without a word of warning, watch a child or blind person walk into certain danger ...."[34] A noted legal scholar wrote:

> ... however revolting the conduct of the man who declined to interfere, he was in no way responsible for the perilous situation, he did not increase the peril, he took away nothing from the person in jeopardy, he simply failed to confer a benefit upon a stranger. As the law stands today, there would be no legal liability, either civilly or criminally, in any of these cases. The law does not compel active benevolence between man and man. It is left to one's con-

science whether he shall be the good Samaritan or not.[35]

While it is still true today that the common law imposes no general duty to assist or help others, there are a few relationships on which such a duty is imposed by law: sellers of alcohol have duties to their customers, and those who supervise children have a legal duty to protect them from harm. In addition, while there is no common-law duty imposed to go to the assistance of a stranger in an emergency, duties arise when you decide to intervene and help. (Note, however, that there is a duty imposed under child welfare statutes in every province and territory to report to the appropriate government authority information about child abuse. A duty is also imposed under various adult welfare statutes to report information about adults who are at risk. See Chapter 18.)

Sellers of alcohol and their customers

Jordan House v. Menow[36] was a groundbreaking decision of the Supreme Court of Canada. In that case, a patron of a local hotel bar, Mr. Menow, drank to the point of intoxication. Knowing he was intoxicated, the hotel employees nevertheless turned him out into the night. Menow was injured when he wandered onto a highway and was struck by a car. The court held the hotel partially responsible, concluding that in situations in which a commercial business profits from the sale of alcohol, it owes a duty to its customers to take positive steps to protect them from harm. The court suggested that such things as calling a taxi, the police or his employer, or asking another patron to drive Menow home would have been reasonable to do in the circumstances. Failure to take any of these reasonable steps resulted in liability.

The principle of *Jordan House* has been applied in many subsequent cases, and not only to bars and restaurants, but also to organizations holding special events at which alcohol is sold.[37] Plaintiffs have been people, such as Mr. Menow, who consumed alcohol and were later injured, and also people injured by someone who consumed alcohol, such as a pedestrian run down by a drunk driver.

No liability has yet been imposed on a social host, someone who serves alcohol at a private house party or some other function, for example. Nevertheless, even in the social host context, it is prudent to take reasonable steps to ensure that anyone leaving a party or event intoxicated will not be operating a motor vehicle, and that anyone walking will be able to get home safely.

Supervisors of children

Anyone who assumes responsibility to control or supervise another is under a legal duty to help that person when the need arises and also to prevent him or her from hurting someone else. This duty can arise between adults, for example in an employer–employee relationship. It most often arises between an adult and a child. Common relationships where the duty is imposed are parent and child or teacher and child.

Consider the case of *C.S.* (*Next friend of*) *v. Miller and The Boy Scouts of Canada*,[38] in which a court found that a camp director was under a duty to help a child visiting the camp because she assumed a supervisory role over him. (Next friend is another name for a litigation guardian, someone who is appointed by the court to conduct a lawsuit on behalf of a person under a disability, such as a minor.)

C.S. was a five-year-old boy who was introduced to Mr. Miller by his mother. Mr. Miller was a family friend and C.S.'s mother felt that her son would be safe with him. Mr. Miller offered to take C.S. to visit a Boy Scout camp. While visiting the camp, Mr. Miller "fondled C.S.'s genitals for approximately five minutes while the Camp Chief in charge, Ms. Khris Chung, watched in disbelief and discomfort."[39]

C.S.'s mother sued Mr. Miller on her son's behalf and also sued the Boy Scouts of Canada. Mr. Miller conceded that he was liable for battery and breach of fiduciary duty (see Chapter 13). The main issue at trial was whether Ms. Chung had a duty to intervene and help C.S. If she breached a legal duty to intervene, she would be liable for the tort of negligence and the Boy Scouts would be vicariously liable for her wrongdoing (see Chapter 9). The court noted that "volunteers like Ms. Chung are still considered [employees] for the purposes of vicarious liability .... Further, there is no exemption from vicarious liability for non-profit organizations."[40]

> The Boy Scouts argue that they did not assume a right of control over C.S. since C.S. was never a registered camper. They argue that C.S. was a stranger to them, and that they were never delegated parental responsibilities by C.S.'s mother. In the absence of that delegation, the Boy Scouts argue, they not only had no duty to assist C.S., it would have been illegal for them

to interfere with Miller, who had been given parental authority by C.S.'s mother.

I do not accept this argument. The Boy Scouts, through Ms. Chung, accepted control over C.S. when she permitted him to stay at the Camp. As Camp Chief, she undertook to supervise everyone at the Camp, and thereby to supervise C.S.'s participation in the same activities the registered children were engaged in. Ms. Chung had ultimate control over whether C.S. and Miller could be a guest of, or remain at, the Camp. She willingly and knowingly undertook to care for children in a situation where the children's parents would not be present. Mr. Miller's presence did not derogate from that duty. ...[41]

This relationship of supervision, care and control raises a duty of care to all those children using the facilities at the camp, not just in relation to those who were registered or who were Boy Scouts. This special relationship is an exception to the usual rule that there is no duty to ... rescue. Ms. Chung owed the same duty of care to every child there, including C.S., a duty which was breached when she did not stop the assault ....[42]

The Boy Scouts took the position that Ms. Chung was under no duty to rescue. The court rejected that argument. Ms. Chung was not in the position where she could choose to intervene and thereby take on the role of a Good Samaritan, or choose not to intervene and nevertheless be legally blameless. Because she had assumed a supervisory role, she was under a legal duty to assist the young camper and her failure to do so was negligence.

Helping a stranger in an emergency

When a person goes to the assistance of another, even though there is no duty to do so, the common law imposes a duty to act reasonably in the circumstances. If, for example, you encounter a stranger in need of assistance, the law imposes no duty on you to help. In other words, you cannot be sued for passing by. Should you choose to intervene (and in effect take on the role of Good Samaritan), then you also assume a legal duty to act reasonably in providing assistance. Mr. Justice Cardozo, a famous American judge of the early 20th century, stated that "it is ancient learning that one who assumes to act, even though gratuitously, may thereby become subject to the duty of acting carefully, if he acts at all …."[43]

This, then, is the common-law standard: when you go to someone's assistance, you are under a duty to take reasonable care.

However, several provinces and territories in Canada have statutes, sometimes referred to as Good Samaritan statutes, that state that a person who renders assistance in an emergency will be liable only when he or she is grossly negligent.[44] As noted in Chapter 22, statutes take precedence over the common law, and so a person who goes to the assistance of someone in an emergency *will not be liable* in these provinces or territories when he or she fails to act reasonably: only when, according to the statute, he or she does something considered grossly negligent.[45]

Conclusion

The biblical injunction to love your neighbour is transmuted in law to the rule that you must not injure your neighbour. The essence of the tort of negligence is the requirement to take reasonable care, and churches, clergy, employees and volunteers are held to the same standard of reasonable care as any other person or organization in Canada. To determine whether a defendant's actions were reasonable, courts look at what precautions were taken in light of the chance of harm occurring, the gravity of the harm and the cost of prevention. Compliance with the customary practice of an industry or profession is usually considered to be reasonable conduct.

As this chapter illustrates, liability in negligence can arise in numerous activities and encompasses broad areas of life. It is important to know the various risks and determine if reasonable measures are in place to prevent harm from occurring. Are church vehicles in good repair? Do clergy counsellors know when to refer? Have those who work with youth been adequately screened and trained? Asking and answering these sorts of questions is part of the process of risk management. Putting in place and following reasonable policies and procedures will ensure that the standard of care in negligence is met.

Negligence: Questions and Answers

Q. What is the purpose of negligence law?

A. The primary purpose of negligence law is to prevent careless or unreasonable behaviour that causes harm.

Q. **What is required for a finding of negligence?**

A. The tort of negligence is comprised of four main elements: duty, standard of care, causation and damage.

- Duty is a legal obligation to conform to a particular standard of behaviour or action.

- Standard of care is what a reasonable person would do in similar circumstances.

- Causation is found if the plaintiff would not have suffered a loss but for the defendant's actions.

- Damage is the legal term for the loss, harm or injury suffered by the plaintiff.

Q. **Is a different standard of care expected of churches, church employees or volunteers?**

A. No. The standard of care in negligence is the same for churches as it is for any other organization or corporation, whether non-profit or for-profit. The standard of care for those who work for churches, including volunteers, is the same as the standard for anyone else.

Q. **Can a church be liable for the careless driving of an employee or volunteer?**

A. Yes. A church can be vicariously liable for the carelessness of employees or volunteers driving their own or church vehicles for church purposes.

Q. Can clergy or church be held liable for negligent counselling?

A. Yes. Clergy counsellors owe a duty of care to those they counsel. A church could be held vicariously liable for a cleric's negligent counselling that causes harm.

Q. Can a church be liable if someone consumes alcohol at a church event and hurts themselves or someone else?

A. Yes. If a church is profiting from the sale of alcohol, then the church may be liable if a person becomes intoxicated and hurts himself or someone else. The Supreme Court of Canada has held that, in situations in which an organization profits from the sale of alcohol, it owes a duty to take positive steps to prevent harm from occurring.

Q. Is there a legal duty to assist someone in need?

A. No, except in limited situations. Historically, the common law has never imposed a duty to help someone in need. While it is still true today that the common law imposes no general duty to assist or help others, there are a few relationships where such a duty is imposed: sellers of alcohol and their customers, and relationships of control or supervision, to name two.

Notes

1   *Donoghue v. Stevenson*, [1932] A.C. 562 (H.L.).

2   *Ryan v. Victoria City*, [1999] 1 S.C.R. 201, para. 28.

3   *Oppedisano v. Agustino* (1997), 26 O.T.C. 60, para. 19 (Ct. J. (Gen. Div.)), para. 19, cited in *Gallant v. Roman Catholic Episcopal Corp. for Labrador* (2001), 200 Nfld. & P.E.I.R. 105 (Nfld. C.A.), para. 35.

4   See generally, G. H. L. Fridman, *The Law of Torts in Canada* (Toronto: Carswell, 2002), pp. 286 and following.

5   *Byrd v. Faber*, 565 N.E. 2d 584, p. 586 (Ohio 1991), p. 586, cited in Constance Frisby Fain, "Clergy Malpractice: Liability for Negligent Counseling and Sexual Misconduct" (1991) 12 *Mississippi College of Law Review* 97, p. 98.

6   See *Franco v. The Church of Jesus Christ of the Latter Day Saints*, 21 P. 3d 198 (Utah 2001) [*Franco*] and other American cases cited within *B. (V.) v. Cairns* (2003), 65 O.R. (3d) 343 (Sup. Ct. J.), paras. 122 and following [*Cairns*]. *Cairns* is also discussed in Chapter 4.

7   U.S. Const. amend. I.

8   *Franco*, cited in *Cairns*, note 6, para. 122.

9   *Ibid.*, para. 123.

10   *Cairns*, note 6. This case is also discussed in Chapter 4.

11   Mervyn F. White, assisted by Suzanne E. White, *Recent Decision Casts Doubt on Use of Matthew 18:15-18 to Address Church Disputes* (www.carters.ca).

12   The elders were following the teaching of their church on Matthew 18:15-18, which "sets out a formal procedure for settling disputes within the church" Wayne A. Meeks et al., eds., *HarperCollins Study Bible: New Revised Standard Version* (New York: Harper Collins Publishers, 1993), p. 1891.

13   *Cairns*, note 6, para. 120.

14   *Ibid.*, para. 21.

15   *Ibid.*, para. 146.

16   *Ibid.*, para. 176.

17   *Ibid.*

18   *Ibid.*, para. 177.

19   *Ibid.*, para. 181.

20   *Ibid.*, para. 179.

21   *Ibid.*, para. 180.

22   W. Keeton, *Prosser and Keeton on the Law of Torts*, 5th ed. (St. Paul, Minn.: West Publishing Co., 1984), p. 185.

23   Allen M. Linden, *Canadian Tort Law*, 7th ed. (Markham, Ont.: Butterworths, 2001), p. 149.

24   Lawrence M. Burek, "Clergy Malpractice: Making Clergy Accountable to a Lower Power" (1986–1987) 14 *Pepperdine Law Review* 137, pp. 156 and following.

25   Dana Charry, *Mental Health Skills for Clergy* (Valley Forge, PA: Judson Press, 1981), pp. 18–19. See also Richard W. Roukema, *Counseling for the Soul in Distress*, 2nd ed. (New York: The Haworth Pastoral Press, 1997).

26   Another case where the court made a finding of negligence against a church is *John Doe v. Bennett*; see Chapter 9, note 2.

27   *J.R.S. v. Glendinning*, [2004] O.J. No. 285 (Sup. Ct. J.) (QL), headnote.

28   *Ibid.*

29   *Swales v. Glendinning* (2004), 237 D.L.R. (4th) 304 (Ont. Sup. Ct. J.), para. 208.

30   *Ibid.*

31   *Ibid.*, para. 220.

32   A. L. Kirby, "Sexual Abuse by a Member of a Religious Organization: Obligations and Preventative Measures" (1995) 12:3 *Philanthropist* 13, p. 26.

33   Presbyterian Church in Canada, *Leading with Care: A Policy for Ensuring a Climate of Safety for Children, Youth and Vulnerable Adults in the Presbyterian Church in Canada*, p. 7.

34   *Horsley. v. MacLaren*, [1970] 2 O.R. 487 (C.A.), para. 34.

35   James Barr Ames, "Law and Morals" (1908–1909) 22 *Harvard Law Review* 97, p. 112.

36   *Jordan House Ltd. v. Menow*, [1974] S.C.R. 239.

37   *Crocker v. Sundance Northwest Resorts Ltd.*, [1988] 1 S.C.R. 1186; *Stewart v. Pettie*, [1995] 1 S.C.R. 131.

38   *C.S. (Next friend of) v. Miller* (2002), 1 Alta. L.R. (4ᵗʰ) 120 (Q.B.). This case is also discussed in Chapter 9.

39   *Ibid.*, para. 2.

40   *Ibid.*, para. 34.

41   *Ibid.*, paras. 25–26.

42   *Ibid.*, para. 28.

43   *M.R. Moch Co. v. Rensselear Water Co.*, 159 N.E. 896 (N.Y.C.A. 1928), cited in A. M. Linden and L. N. Klar, *Canadian Tort Law: Cases, Notes and Materials*, 12ᵗʰ ed. (Toronto: Butterworths, 2004), pp. 331–332.

44   For example, British Columbia *Good Samaritan Act*, R.S.B.C. 1996, c. 172; Ontario *Good Samaritan Act, 2001*, S.O. 2001, c. 2.

45   Gross negligence is difficult to define. It refers to acts that could be characterized as extremely careless, involving a reckless disregard for another's safety. For example, suppose in an emergency one went to the assistance of an unconscious person and, trying to help, forced water down his or her throat. The rescuer would be liable for harm caused if this action was characterized as something more than ordinary negligence, an action rising to the level of gross negligence.

12

Defamation

Good name in man and woman, dear my lord,
is the immediate jewel of their souls:
Who steals my purse steals trash; ...
But he that filches from me my good name
Robs me of that which not enriches him,
and makes me poor indeed.
—William Shakespeare, English poet and playwright,
1564–1616, *Othello*

T he tort of defamation protects a person's reputation against false statements. In the leading Canadian case, *Hill v. Church of Scientology of Toronto*, Justice Cory of the Supreme Court of Canada stated:

Democracy has always recognized and cherished
the fundamental importance of an individual.
That importance must, in turn, be based upon

the good repute of a person. It is that good repute which enhances an individual's sense of worth and value. False allegations can so very quickly and completely destroy a good reputation. A reputation tarnished by libel can seldom regain its former lustre. A democratic society, therefore, has an interest in ensuring that its members can enjoy and protect their good reputation so long as it is merited.[1]

To succeed in a defamation claim, a plaintiff must prove that a defamatory statement was made about him by the defendant to a third person. The defendant then must raise a defence or be found liable.

This chapter begins by noting the difference between libel and slander. What is meant by a defamatory statement is then discussed. Next, we look at two other elements of the tort: the requirement that the defamatory statement be communicated to a third person, and the need for the plaintiff to prove that the statement made was about him or her. The defences to a defamation action play an important role; we conclude with an overview of some of the defences available.

Defamatory statements

Defamatory statements may be either written or oral. Libel is written words (or pictures, drawings, films, etc.) that are defamatory; slander is spoken words that are defamatory.[2]

A court must first decide whether the statements made are defamatory. A defamatory statement is a false statement that "has the tendency to harm, injure, disparage or adversely affect the reputation of the plaintiff ...."[3] Words tending "to lower a person in the estimation of his fellows by making them think less of him" are considered defamatory.[4]

The test for determining whether words are defamatory is, as a leading torts scholar has concluded, "extremely minimal." "The cases indicate that virtually all critical comment, whether it be in the form of fact or opinion, which portrays a person in an uncomplimentary light will be considered to be defamatory."[5] For example, courts have concluded that it is defamatory to call someone a liar, to call a lawyer "a shyster" or a doctor "a quack." Statements that someone is "hideously ugly," a drunk or heavily in debt have also been held by courts to be defamatory.[6] Courts have held that it is defamatory "to state of a clergyman that he is guilty of immorality or drunkenness, or that he preaches sedition, lies, or that he knows less about his religion than an adolescent, or that he has used his pulpit to throw out personal invectives against a member of the congregation ... or that he has desecrated a part of his church by turning it into a cooking department."[7]

It is not relevant whether the person making the defamatory statement intended to defame or knew that the statement was defamatory. The test is objective: Would a reasonable person conclude that the statement was defamatory?

Publication

The statement must be communicated to a third person. A person will not be liable for statements made only to the plaintiff. When the words are communicated to a third person, they are said to be published. When a defamatory statement is overheard or read by another, the defendant can escape liability if he or she can show that he or she did not intend another to hear or read the statement and is able to prove that it was reasonable to believe that a third person would not read or hear the statement.

Each communication or publication of a defamatory statement is a separate tort. For example, a person who says something defamatory about X to a third person could be sued for defamation. A newspaper that publishes the statement could be sued. Someone reading the newspaper who repeats the statement could also be liable.

Of and concerning the plaintiff

The plaintiff must prove that the defamatory statement was made about him or her, the legal phrase is that the statement was "of and concerning the plaintiff." The question the court asks is whether a reasonable person hearing the statement would believe it was about the plaintiff. Intention to defame a particular person, or indeed any person, is not relevant. A person can be liable for defamation even if he or she did not know that the person he or she defamed existed. There are several cases, for example, in which a writer who created a fictitious character was sued by someone who resembled the character.[8] There was no intent by the writer to defame anyone, certainly not the plaintiff. The court concluded nevertheless that it is no defence to defamation to say "'I never heard of A and did not mean to injure him.' If he publishes words reasonably capable of being read as relating directly or indirectly to A and, to those who know the facts about A, capable of a defamatory meaning, he must take the consequences of the defamatory inferences reasonably drawn from the words."[9]

Individual persons can be defamed, as can non-natural persons, such as a church or charitable corporation.[10] For a non-natural entity such as a corporation to be a successful plaintiff in a defamation claim, it must show that the defamatory statement negatively affected its business reputation.[11] Corporations can be sued for defamatory statements made by agents or employees of the corporation.[12]

A person claiming that he was defamed by statements made about a group of which he or she is a member would need to prove that a reasonable person would conclude that the statement referred to him or her as a member of that group. A statement such as "Everyone who volunteered at last week's fundraiser is incompetent" might be actionable by a member of that group.

The Hunger Project v. Council on Mind Abuse[13] is an example of a successful defamation action by a corporation. The Hunger Project was a company incorporated as a charity under the British Columbia *Societies Act*. It was the Canadian arm of a group of related companies around the world whose aim was the elimination of hunger by the year 2000. The defendant company, the Council on Mind Abuse, and another person published in Toronto a pamphlet that alleged that the Hunger Project was engaged in a scam, raising money but not using the money to alleviate hunger in the Third World. The Hunger Project sued for defamation, claiming that its fundraising efforts had been harmed by the libel. In their defence, the defendants pleaded qualified privilege (see the discussion below), claiming that it had a social and moral duty to communicate the information in issue. In finding for the plaintiff, Justice MacDonald wrote:

If companies have business reputations, then charitable companies have reputations for the charitable work which they undertake. To the extent that they have been damaged, they are entitled to damages like any other person or corporation, to the extent the law provides such redress. It is however relevant to the measure of damages in this case that a charitable corporation has been attacked as being a front for a cult, has been accused of being a scam and a rip-off and on the basis that donations to it bypass the Third World poor.[14]

The statements in the defendants' pamphlet were found to be false. The allegations by the defendants were considered defamatory, and the plaintiff Hunger Project was awarded $25,000 in damages.

Defences

Given the low threshold for what constitutes a defamatory statement, the various defences available play an important role. The tension in this area is between a plaintiff's concern for his or her reputation and the defendant's right of free speech. The law tries to strike an appropriate balance between the two. Once the plaintiff proves that the defendant made a defamatory statement about him or her to a third person, the defendant must offer a defence to escape a finding of liability. Defences include truth, fair comment, absolute privilege and qualified privilege. A privilege, in this context, means an exemption from liability for speaking or publishing defamatory words.

Truth (or justification)

Truth is a complete defence. When a statement is proven to be true, no matter how harmful it is to the plaintiff, the plaintiff's claim of defamation will fail. It is not enough for a defendant to show that he or she believed the statement to be true or relied on a competent authority that said it was true. However, a defendant does not need to prove that every detail of the statement is true, as long as he or she can show that the statement is substantially true.[15]

Fair comment

Comments and opinions on matters of public interest are protected, even when they are defamatory. A fair comment is one based on true facts, made honestly and not motivated by malice.[16] The English Court of Appeal gave the following lively explanation. Fair comment is "the right of the public, which means you and me, and the newspaper editor, and the man who, but for the present bus strike, would be on the Clapham omnibus [judicial shorthand in English law for the ordinary or reasonable person], to express their views honestly and fearlessly on matters of public interest, even though that involves strong criticism of the conduct of public people."[17]

Absolute privilege

There is an absolute privilege for statements made in certain forums, including judicial proceedings, parliament and statutory tribunals. Privilege attaches even if the defamatory statements made are known to be false and uttered with an intention to harm. This defence reflects society's belief that in certain situations an individual should be free to speak his or her mind without any fear of legal action. Take, for example, the absolute privilege that attaches to statements made by witnesses in court. A witness would hesitate to provide full and candid testimony if he or she worried about being sued for defamation.

Qualified privilege

Defamatory statements made on certain occasions are protected by a qualified privilege. The privilege is qualified by the requirement that the defamatory statement be made without malice. In other words, on those occasions recognized by law, a person will not be held liable for making false and defamatory statements about someone, unless these statements were made maliciously.

Malice is defined broadly. In *Crandall v. Atlantic School of Theology* the court stated that it includes "spite or ill will; an unjustifiable intent to inflict injury; stating what the defendant knows to be untrue; recklessly for the gratification of his anger or other wrong motive; using language stronger than the circumstances of the case warrant."[18]

The defence of qualified privileged "is justified on the basis of public policy. It is in the general interest and to the general advantage of society that a person on limited occasions should be free to speak out honestly without fear of retribution even though others may be defamed."[19]

It is not easy to define the occasions on which a qualified privilege arises. The classic description is that "a privileged occasion is, in reference to a qualified privilege, an occasion where the person who makes the communication has an interest or duty, legal, social or moral, to make it to the person to whom it is made, and the person to whom it is so made has a corresponding interest or duty to receive it. This reciprocity is essential."[20]

These occasions can be divided into four categories: communications in the public interest; communications to protect one's own interest; communications between persons with a common interest; and communications to protect another's interest. It may be helpful to set out these four categories and provide examples to try to describe the ambit of the qualified privilege defence.

Communications in the public interest. The law recognizes a qualified privilege to "make charges and complaints against all public officials, but such communications ought to be addressed only to those who have power to punish the offenders or otherwise to redress the grievance."[21] Examples include reporting an alleged crime to the police or complaining about the conduct of a schoolteacher to the principal or school board.

Communications to protect one's own interest. A qualified privilege arises when a person makes statements "in his own interest, in defence either of his property or his character."[22] An employer making enquiries and conducting an investigation into a suspected theft by an employee would be protected by a qualified privilege.[23] He or she would not be liable for any defamatory statements made in the course of, and related to, the investigation. A person whose property was stolen would be protected by qualified privilege when asking neighbours about its whereabouts and naming possible suspects.[24] A person whose character or reputation is attacked by another has a right to defend himself or herself and "he or she is privileged to meet the attack with an appropriate rejoinder. A person is entitled to deny or explain the defamatory matter ... and in an appropriate case, even defame the assailant in the process."[25]

In an old English case, *Whitely v. Adams*, a clergyman was asked by a colleague to help resolve a dispute between two church members. He decided not to get involved, and, in the course of explaining to his colleague his reasons for declining, made defamatory statements about one of the disputants. He was sued for defamation. The defence of qualified privilege was recognized because the court concluded that the clergyman had a right to disclose his reasons and explain his conduct to the person who asked him to get involved.[26]

The plaintiff in *Pleau v. Simpson-Sears Ltd.* had his wallet stolen.[27] Later, someone (probably the thief) began cashing forged cheques in Mr. Pleau's name. The defendant department store posted 55 notices near its cash registers that contained the name and address of Mr. Pleau and the words "IF ANY CHEQUE IS PRESENTED, DETAIN PERSON AND CALL SECURITY." The notices were easily visible by customers. Mr. Pleau sued the store for defamation, but his claim was defeated by the defence of qualified privilege because the court concluded that the store was acting to protect its own property interests.[28]

Communications between persons with a common interest. Another occasion of qualified privilege involves "communications between parties who are alike concerned in the condition of some property or the management of some undertaking ...."[29] Internal communications within a business, professional or religious organization are communications between persons with a common interest in an undertaking and are therefore covered by privilege. The communications must be made without malice. The person who communicates the information must have a duty or interest to do so and the person receiving the information must have a corresponding duty or interest.

Members of a church are protected by qualified privilege when discussing or dealing with church affairs. An oft-cited case that illustrates this is *Slocinski v. Radwan*.[30] In *Radwan*, three church members who circulated to other members of the church information that a priest had in the past been found guilty of criminal conduct were sued by the priest for defamation. In finding that the defence of qualified privilege was available to the defendants, the court concluded that:

> It is hard to imagine a more obvious example of common interest than that which is shared by the members of a church in the character and conduct of the minister, since these factors determine his capacity for spiritual leadership. No minister can expect, nor should he desire, that the question whether he measures up to the standards of behavior or ability demanded by his parishioners will not be debated in private conversations by members of his congregation.[31]

Following is an excerpt from the leading Canadian text, *The Law of Defamation in Canada*, by Professor Raymond E. Brown, that sets out the ambit of the law on the defence of qualified privilege arising from communications between persons with a common interest as related to churches and clergy.

> (A) *General Affairs*. It is to the advantage and in the interest of all members of a church, or other

religious bodies, that information concerning its affairs be circulated to its members. If statements are published in good faith and in the honest performance of official or moral duties on behalf of the members of the church, and for the benefit of the church, they are protected by a qualified privilege. Thus, individuals within a congregation may discuss among themselves matters of interest to the church, and resolutions agreed upon in church conventions may be distributed to the membership. Statements made from the pulpit to a church congregation commenting on religious practices within the church are protected if they are made in good faith. ...

(B) *Competency and Qualifications of Church Leaders.* Within religious bodies, members have a common interest in the affairs of the organization and the competency and qualifications of its leaders. Any member of the church may forward information to an appropriate official of the church regarding the behaviour of a clergyman. Members of a congregation may discuss the character [and] the conduct of a minister in their private conversations. ...

Not every communication will be protected. If a defendant persists in repeating his remarks after the occasion which gives rise to the privilege in the first instance has ended, the court may treat the subsequent communications as motivated by malice, and no longer protected.

(C) *Conduct and Standing of Members.* There is a privilege on the part of leaders and members of a religious body to circulate information about the conduct and standing of individual members. Thus complaints preferred against members of a congregation for infractions against church discipline are protected by a qualified privilege. ...

Any communication of information about members of a congregation must be done with a view to discipline, or as a step in a proper procedure, and not with a purpose to injure or spread malicious gossip. The pulpit, particularly, must not be used as a pretext to intentionally defame a member of the congregation or any-one else. Thus, unsolicited information about the sexual proclivities of a parishioner, given to some members and one adherent of the church by the minister, were held not to be protected by a qualified privilege.[32]

This category of qualified privilege is of particular relevance to a church organization because it is perhaps the most likely de-fence to a defamation claim. The above excerpt makes clear that it is a broad category that covers a range of communications.

Communications to protect another's interest. A qualified privilege arises when the defamatory statements were made by a person who has a legal, moral or social duty to protect another person's interests. This privilege would protect a brother who warns his sister about the unsuitability of her boyfriend[33] or a father who complains to a school board about one of his child's teachers.[34] A bishop is protected by qualified privilege when he or she conveys information and advice to his or her clergy.[35] The rationale is that the bishop has a moral and legal duty to protect the clergy's interests. A church asked to comment on the *bona fides* of someone soliciting funds would be protected by a qualified privilege.

A former employer asked by a prospective employer to comment on a job applicant would be protected by qualified privilege; the former employer is said to be acting from a social and moral duty to protect the interests of the prospective employer.

Likewise, this area of privilege protects statements made by someone who has a duty to appraise or assess a candidate's fitness for a profession.[36] *Crandall v. Atlantic School of Theology*[37] involved a defamation lawsuit brought by Crandall, formerly a divinity student and a postulant for ordination as an Anglican priest. The Anglican bishop obtained assessments and recommendations about Crandall's fitness for the priesthood from the faculty of the Atlantic School of Theology, statements that Crandall claimed were defamatory. In concluding that the statements were covered by a qualified privilege, the court made the following comments:

> The framework of assessing, appraising and reporting on a candidate's progress towards professional status is an extremely important process, leading to society's eventual recognition of the profession's special status, its attendant duties

and privileges. Many subjective factors must be considered. They must be considered frankly and honestly and without fear of legal reprisal. Mistakes may be made but if made honestly and without malice, there should be no legal liability arising from them, and indeed that is the law.[38]

...

If frank and honest appraisals of students of all professions are being constrained by [the fear of lawsuits] then indeed the professions are permitting the entry to their ranks of unworthy candidates. That must not be allowed to happen. That is, the empty threat of imagined lawsuits or futile lawsuits should be exposed and eliminated. I encourage and applaud the process complained of by the plaintiff. It must be fostered and protected so that unworthy candidates for the professions will not achieve the privileges of their professions. I am not saying here that the plaintiff in this case is unworthy. That is not for me to decide. That is for the process of assessments to determine.[39]

The words of the court in *Crandall v. Atlantic School of Theology* should be underscored. The law recognizes the value of frank and honest communication without fear of legal reprisal, and therefore on certain occasions there is no liability even for defamatory communications, absent malice. That is the public policy justification for the defence of qualified privilege.

Conclusion

The test for what is defamatory is so low, some people may be surprised to learn that they have unwittingly defamed another. In addition, defamation is a tort of strict or no-fault liability: a person can be liable even if they were not negligent and did not intend to defame. These two facts alone suggest the importance of being knowledgeable about this area of potential liability.

A sound and simple piece of advice is to be very careful about what you say or write about other people. Whether speaking from the pulpit, talking to a colleague or chatting at a social gathering, avoid words that defame – that is, words that have "the tendency to harm, injure, disparage or adversely affect the reputation of" a person.[40]

It is essential to appreciate the ambit of the defences available, in particular the defence of qualified privilege. The general question to ask to determine whether an occasion is protected by a qualified privilege is whether you have an interest or duty to communicate the information and whether the person to whom it is made has a corresponding interest or duty to receive it. Thus, a person involved in a formal process of assessing a candidate's fitness for the ministry is protected from liability by a qualified privilege. Church members discussing church affairs at a church meeting need not fear liability in defamation.

But the qualified aspect of the privilege must be kept in mind at all times. It fails when the communications are made with malice or outside the privileged occasion. In the absence of malice, the court allowed the defence of qualified privilege because the clergyman in *Whitely v. Adams* had the right to justify or explain his conduct in refusing to intervene in the dispute. The person to whom he spoke the defamatory words had a corresponding interest in hearing his explanation. But if the clergyman had made the statement to someone other than the person who asked him to intervene in the dispute, he may have had no defence. Likewise, if a faculty member in *Crandall v. Atlantic School of Theology* had made defamatory comments about the plaintiff outside the postulant assessment process, the defence would not be available. The defence will also fail if a church member discussing church affairs at a church meeting makes defamatory statements he or she knows to be false – that is, with malice.

Defamation: Questions and Answers

Q. What is a defamatory statement?

A. Words tending "to lower a person in the estimation of his fellows by making them think less of him" are considered defamatory.

Q. Is it necessary that the person making the statement intended it to be defamatory?

A. No. It is not relevant whether the person making the defamatory statement intended to defame or knew that the statement was defamatory. The test is objective: would a reasonable person conclude that the statement was defamatory?

Q. Can a claim of defamation arise from a conversation between the defendant and plaintiff only?

A. No. The statement must be communicated to a third person. A person will not be liable for statements made only to the plaintiff. If a defamatory statement is overheard or read by another, the defendant can escape liability when he or she can show that he or she did not intend another to hear or read the statement and is able to prove that it was reasonable to believe that a third person would not read or hear the statement.

Q Can someone be held liable for a defamatory statement merely by repeating information given to him or her?

A. Yes. Each communication or publication of a defamation is a separate tort. For example, a person who says something defamatory about X to a third person could be sued for defamation. A newspaper that publishes the statement could be sued. Someone reading the newspaper who repeats the statement could also be liable.

Q. What are the defences to a claim of defamation?

A. Truth is a complete defence. No matter how harmful to the plaintiff, when a statement is proven to be true, the plaintiff's claim in defamation will fail. There is an absolute privilege for statements made in certain forums, including judicial proceedings, parliament and statutory tribunals. There is a qualified privilege for statements made on certain occasions, and there is a defence of fair comment.

Notes

1   *Hill v. Church of Scientology of Toronto*, [1995] 2 S.C.R. 1130, para. 111.

2   Legislation in several provinces has eradicated the distinction between libel and slander. In those provinces where the distinction still exists, it is relevant to the issue of damages. In a libel suit, a plaintiff need not prove that the defamatory statement caused loss or harm. By contrast, with some exceptions, loss or harm must be proved in an action for slander. See G. H. L. Fridman, *The Law of Torts in Canada* (Toronto: Carswell, 2002), pp. 652 and following. For the most part, the statutes codify and clarify the common law.

3   Raymond E. Brown, *Defamation Law: A Primer* (Toronto: Carswell, 2003), p. 23 [*Defamation Law Primer*].

4   John G. Fleming, *The Law of Torts*, 9th ed. (Sydney: Law Book Company, 1998), p. 581.

5   Lewis Klar, *Tort Law*, 3rd ed. (Toronto: Thomson Carswell, 2003), p. 673.

6   Allen M. Linden, *Canadian Tort Law*, 7th ed. (Markham, Ont.: Butterworths, 2001), pp. 686–687 [*Linden*].

7   Patrick Milmo and W. V. H. Rogers, eds., *Gatley on Libel and Slander*, 10th ed. (London: Sweet & Maxwell, 2004), p. 64.

8   *Cassidy v. Daily Mirror Newspapers Ltd.*, [1929] All E.R. Rep. 117 (C.A.).

9   *Ibid.*, para. 5.

10   An incorporated church body can be defamed. Churches that exist as unincorporated associations cannot sue or be sued for defamation, although their members may be able to do so. "[A] voluntary unincorporated association cannot maintain an action for libel on itself …. If one says of the Longbeach Angler's Association that at the competition last Saturday they cheated, there is a defamatory statement; but the Longbeach Angler's Association cannot maintain an action in respect of it. It may be that the individuals of the association who were partaking in the competition could successfully sue by saying that, although they were not named, the defamatory statement pointed at them …; but the association could not do so … on the principle that it has no personality of its own which is capable of being defamed ….

So you have got to give personality which is capable of being defamed
before a plaintiff can bring an action for libel." *Electrical, Electronic,
Telecommunication and Plumbing Union v. Times Newspapers Ltd.*, [1980]
3 W.L.R. 98 (Q.B.D.), p. 101, cited in Raymond E. Brown, *The Law
of Defamation in Canada*, 2nd ed. (Scarborough, Ont.: Carswell, 1994)
vol. 2, p. 1201 [*The Law of Defamation in Canada*]. See also p. 1203
and footnotes regarding the legal status of churches to sue or be sued
for defamation.

11   *Linden*, note 6, p. 695.

12   *Defamation Law Primer*, note 3, p. 86.

13   *The Hunger Project v. Council on Mind Abuse* (1995), 22 O.R. (3d) 29
(Ct. J. (Gen. Div.)).

14   *Ibid.*, para. 34.

15   See generally, *Defamation Law Primer*, note 3, pp. 95 and following.

16   The facts upon which the comment or opinion is made must be true.
The defence covers the comment or opinion that defames; it does not
extend to a statement of fact. False statements of fact are not protected.
Professor Brown gives the following helpful example to illustrate this
tricky point: "If it is reported that a city councilman was seen taking
money in exchange for political favours, that is a statement of fact. If it
is suggested that this conduct is disgraceful or dishonourable that is an
expression of opinion. The statement of fact is defamatory on its face,
and an action by the plaintiff may be defeated only by showing it is
true, or by demonstrating it was published on an occasion of privilege.
Assuming the fact to be true, the opinion expressed, which may also
be defamatory, may be protected by the defence of fair comment on a
matter of public interest." *The Law of Defamation in Canada*, note 10,
vol. 1, p. 954.

17   *Silkin v. Beaverbrook Newspapers Ltd.*, [1958] 1 W.L.R. 743 (C.A.),
p. 746, cited in J.F. Clerk, *Clerk & Lindsell on Torts*, 16th ed. (London:
Sweet & Maxwell, 1989), p. 1167 [*Clerk & Lindsell on Torts*].

18   *Crandall v. Atlantic School of Theology* (1993), 120 N.S.R. (2d) 219
(S.C. (T.D.), para. 34 [*School of Theology*]. Professor Brown notes: "Any
motive other than the sense of duty or furtherance of the appropriate
interest which gave rise to the privileged occasion in the first instance
is what the law calls malice." *Defamation Law Primer*, note 3, p. 188.

19   *Defamation Law Primer*, note 3, p. 129.

20   *Adam v. Ward*, [1917] A.C. 309 (H.L.), p. 334.

21   *Clerk & Lindsell on Torts*, note 17, p. 1164.

22   *Ibid.*, p. 1162.

23   *The Law of Defamation in Canada*, note 10, vol. 1, p. 728.

24   *Ibid.*, p. 730.

25   *Ibid.*, p. 742.

26   *Whitely v. Adams* (1863), 15 C.B. (N.S.), p. 392, cited in *Clerk & Lindsell on Torts*, note 17, p. 1163.

27   *Pleau v. Simpson-Sears Ltd.* (1976), 15 O.R. (2d) 436 (C.A.).

28   *Ibid.*, para. 2-3.

29   *Clerk & Lindsell on Torts*, note 17, p. 1160.

30   *Slocinski v. Radwan*, 144 A. 787 (N.H. 1929).

31   *Ibid.*, p. 789.

32   *The Law of Defamation in Canada*, note 10, vol. 1, pp. 789 and following.

33   *Ibid.*, p. 756.

34   *Ibid.*, p. 757.

35   *Ibid.*, p. 1156.

36   The rationale for the existence of a qualified privilege on this occasion could also be explained as a communication between persons with a common interest.

37   *School of Theology*, note 18.

38   *Ibid.*, para. 27.

39   *Ibid.*, para. 40.

40   *Defamation Law Primer*, note 3, p. 23.

13

Breach of Fiduciary Duty

Vulnerable: Capable of being physically wounded.
Open to attack or damage.
—Webster's New Collegiate Dictionary

A fiduciary is a person who has a duty to act solely and faithfully for the benefit and in the interests of another, the beneficiary. A fiduciary has an obligation of loyalty to the beneficiary, must avoid conflicts of interest and is prohibited from profiting at the expense of the beneficiary. Numerous relationships have been recognized by the courts as fiduciary in nature, including parent and child, doctor and patient, director and company. Fiduciary duties have been imposed in two different types of relationships within a church environment. First, courts have found a fiduciary relationship when a church or cleric assumes the role of guardian of children or of other vulnerable members of society. Second, courts view the relationship between a spiritual advisor or clergy counsellor and a church member as fiduciary in nature.[1] This chapter describes the key characteristics of a fiduciary relationship. It concludes with descriptions of two cases in a church context in which a fiduciary relationship was found to exist and a fiduciary duty was breached.

Characteristics of a fiduciary relationship

Fiduciary law is concerned with preventing persons in positions of trust and confidence from abusing their power. By doing so, it protects the "integrity of socially valuable or necessary relationships ...."[2] Perhaps the clearest example of a fiduciary relationship is that of parent and child. The parent holds a position of power over the child, and the child places his or her trust and confidence in the parent. The child is particularly vulnerable to the parent's power and authority. Vulnerability has been identified by the Supreme Court of Canada as the one feature that is indispensable to the existence of a fiduciary relationship. "There is ... the notion underlying all the cases of fiduciary obligation that inherent in the nature of the relationship itself is a position of disadvantage or vulnerability on the part of one of the parties which causes him to place reliance upon the other."[3] In *Frame v. Smith*, the Supreme Court stated that the relationships in which fiduciary obligations have been imposed share three general characteristics:

1) The fiduciary has scope for the exercise of some discretion or power.

2) The fiduciary can unilaterally exercise that power or discretion so as to affect the beneficiary's legal or practical interests.

3) The beneficiary is peculiarly vulnerable to or at the mercy of the fiduciary holding the discretion or power.[4]

The relationship between a professional advisor, such as a tax accountant and his or her clients, is usually seen by the courts as fiduciary in nature. To illustrate the characteristics of a fiduciary relationship, suppose a situation where a tax accountant gives investment advice to a client. The client is in a vulnerable position because he or she lacks knowledge about tax matters and trusts the accountant to give honest advice. The accountant is in a position to affect the interests of the client. These sorts of relationships, where a person in a vulnerable position trusts a more powerful person to act in his or her best interests, are often categorized in law as fiduciary. Fiduciary duties are imposed on the more powerful person, who must act solely in the best interests of the vulnerable person, the beneficiary. If the accountant were to betray that trust, for example by advising the client to make an investment in which the accountant had an undisclosed interest, the accountant would be in breach of fiduciary duty. The accountant has put his or her own interests ahead of the interests of the beneficiary.

The duties of a fiduciary are significant. A fiduciary is held to an exceptionally high standard of conduct, the highest standard of care imposed by a court. Fiduciary law is sometimes described as "the law of faithfulness or fidelity. It has often been called the law of loyalty."[5] As noted, a fiduciary is expected to be loyal to the beneficiary and to always put the interests of the beneficiary above his or her own personal interest. A fiduciary must not "allow his professional duty to come into conflict with his personal interests."[6]

Illustrative cases

A brief overview of two cases in a church context, focusing on the breach of fiduciary duty claim, may help clarify this difficult and often confusing area of law.

F.S.M. v. Clarke was a lawsuit by F.S.M. against the Anglican Church of Canada, the federal government and Clarke for negligence, breach of fiduciary duty and vicarious liability.[7] Clarke was a dormitory supervisor at an Indian residential school run by the Anglican Church, and F.S.M. was a young resident who was repeatedly sexually assaulted by Clarke. Clarke eventually pled guilty to sexual assault and was imprisoned.

As employers of Clarke, both the government and the Anglican Church were found vicariously liable for his actions (see Chapter 9). Both were also found liable for negligence because they failed "to take reasonable steps to ascertain that the parental and pastoral power given to their joint employee was exercised properly. This necessarily required adequate and reasonable supervision"[8] (see Chapter 11).

The court considered the characteristics of a fiduciary relationship set out in *Frame v. Smith* (above) and determined that the Anglican Church of Canada was in a fiduciary relationship with the plaintiff, F.S.M., noting that he "was vulnerable as a child isolated in an Anglican institution under the control of an Anglican dormitory supervisor and principal."[9]

The relevant facts regarding fiduciary duty were set out as follows:

> The plaintiff absolutely trusted that he would be properly cared for, especially because this was an Anglican institution. The fact of Anglicanism lent a superior moral tone to the residence that created an additional level of assurance. The Bishop of the Diocese knew that dormitory supervisors were in a position to affect the plaintiff's intimate personal and physical interests and encouraged this position of trust through insistence that child care workers be Anglican and follow Anglican practice. When Clarke breached this trust, Harding [the principal of St. George's Indian Residential School] told the plaintiff that he would bring the matter to the appropriate authorities. The Anglicans took control of the matter and took no action. The Anglicans assumed a duty to act on behalf of the plaintiff in this circumstance and did nothing. ... The Anglican Church was in a fiduciary relationship with the plaintiff when it undertook to look after his interests to the exclusion of the federal Crown following the disclosure of Clarke's abuse.[10]

> ...

> It is my conclusion that Clarke's sexual assault of the plaintiff was purposely covered up by Harding and the diocesan personnel who were

in the know so as not to attract attention to St. George's school.[11]

The court in *F.S.M. v. Clarke* concluded that the Anglican Church of Canada, in a role akin to guardian of the plaintiff, breached its fiduciary duty by putting its own interests ahead of the interests of the beneficiary, F.S.M. The breach of fiduciary duty was the church's "failure to report properly and investigate the sexual abuse of F.S.M. and to care for F.S.M. afterwards for reasons related to protection of the interests of the Anglican Church and Harding."[12]

In another case, *Deiwick v. Frid*, the defendant, Rev. Frid, was a minister of the United Church of Canada. Ms. Deiwick was, for many years, a member of Rev. Frid's congregation, and viewed him as an advisor and friend. Ms. Deiwick married in 1971. When problems arose in the marriage, Ms. Deiwick and her husband sought and received marriage counselling from Rev. Frid. In December 1979, Ms. Deiwick and her husband entered into a separation agreement and the counselling ended. Shortly thereafter, Rev. Frid and Ms. Deiwick began a sexual relationship. She eventually sued Rev. Frid for, among others things, breach of fiduciary duty and breach of confidence.[13] (See Chapter 18 for a fuller description of the breach of confidence claim.)

The court in *Deiwick* reviewed the three characteristics of a fiduciary relationship from *Frame v. Smith*, set out above, and found that Rev. Frid "did have the scope for the exercise of some discretion or power and it is a fair inference that the plaintiff was vulnerable to him."[14]

Rev. Frid's lawyer submitted that it could not be a fiduciary relationship because Ms. Deiwick consented. The court rejected this line of argument, concluding that "although it may be a mitigating circumstance, it is no excuse to find, as I do, that the plaintiff was a willing participant. For a person in Frid's position, this was unethical conduct, not in the best interests of the plaintiff."[15]

Another argument put forward by Rev. Frid's counsel and rejected by the court was that "if a fiduciary relationship existed, it ceased to exist upon the separation between husband and wife, i.e. at the conclusion of the counselling."[16] The court found ample authority for the proposition that a fiduciary duty can continue to exist even after the relationship that gave rise to it has ended – in this case, marriage counselling. The court concluded as follows:

> I find that when the plaintiff and her husband sought counselling in relation to their marriage problems, Frid was in a fiduciary relationship with the plaintiff. Also, that when he entered into a sexual relationship with the plaintiff he was in breach of his fiduciary duty.[17]

The court accepted evidence that because of Rev. Frid's breach of his fiduciary duty, the plaintiff suffered mental stress and anxiety and awarded her $20,000 in damages.

Conclusion

A fiduciary relationship and the duties of a fiduciary may arise when a church or cleric stands in the role of guardian or caregiver for the weak and vulnerable: children, the aged and the psychologically troubled. The role of cleric as spiritual advisor or counsellor is always fiduciary in nature. In these fiduciary relationships, cleric and church are subject to exceptionally high standards of faithfulness and loyalty.

Breach of Fiduciary Duty: Questions and Answers

Q. What is a fiduciary?

A. A fiduciary is a person who has a duty to act solely and faithfully for the benefit of another, the beneficiary.

Q. What are the duties of a fiduciary?

A. A fiduciary has an obligation of loyalty to the beneficiary, must avoid conflicts of interest and is prohibited from profiting at the expense of the beneficiary.

Q. What is the key or essential element of all fiduciary relationships?

A. The key element is the vulnerability of one party that causes him or her to rely on another person.

Q. In what sort of relationships have fiduciary duties been imposed by the courts?

A. Fiduciary duties have been imposed in a broad range of professional relationships, including lawyer–client, doctor–patient and cleric–church member. Courts have found a fiduciary relationship when a church or cleric assumes the role of guardian of children or other vulnerable members of society and in the relationship of spiritual advisor and church member.

Notes

1   See generally, Michael Ng, *Fiduciary Duties, Obligations of Loyalty and Faithfulness* (Aurora, Ont.: Canada Law Book, 2005) [*Fiduciary Duties*].

2   Leonard I. Rotman, "Fiduciary Obligations" in Mark Gillen and Faye Woodman, eds., *The Law of Trusts: A Contextual Approach* (Toronto: Emond Montgomery, 2000) 739, p. 742.

3   *Lac Minerals Ltd. v. International Corona Resources Ltd.*, [1989] 2 S.C.R. 574, para. 132.

4   *Frame v. Smith*, [1987] 2 S.C.R. 99, paras. 39–42.

5   *Fiduciary Duties*, note 1, p. 1-1.

6   *Henderson v. Johnston*, [1956] O.R. 789 (S.C.), para. 32.

7   *F.S.M. v. Clarke*, [1999] 11 W.W.R. 301 (B.C.S.C.).

8   *Ibid.*, para. 174.

9   *Ibid.*, para. 193.

10   *Ibid.*, para. 196.

11   *Ibid.*, para. 40.

12   *Ibid.*, para. 191.

13   *Deiwick v. Frid*, [1991] O.J. No. 1803 (Ct. J. (Gen. Div.)) (QL).

14   *Ibid.*, para. 58.

15   *Ibid.*

16   *Ibid.*, para. 59.

17   *Ibid.*, para. 61.

14

Religious Communication Privilege

One of the primary aims of the adversarial
trial process is to find the truth.
—Justice Claire L'Heureux-Dubé,
Supreme Court of Canada,
R. v. Gruenke (1991)

C lergy often receive confidential communications in the course of their ministry: in the confessional, in counselling and in private conversations with church members, for example. There is no doubt that clergy, similar to other professionals such as doctors and lawyers, have an ethical and professional duty not to disclose this confidential information, save in exceptional circumstances (see Chapter 18).

The issue of privilege arises in the context of a legal proceeding. Can a cleric refuse to disclose to a court confidential communications received from a person on the basis that such communications are privileged? Or, in other words, does the common law recognize a privilege for communications made to spiritual or religious advisors, variously referred to as a religious communication privilege, clergy–penitent privilege, spiritual advisor privilege or religious privilege? This chapter sets out the law on the issue, provides an overview of a leading case and then considers some practical issues that may arise about privilege, both in the civil and criminal context.

Class privilege and case-by-case privilege

As Justice L'Heureux-Dubé stated in *R. v. Gruenke*, a primary goal of a trial is to determine the truth. To achieve that goal, the general rule is that any person with relevant information can be compelled to provide that information to the court. Courts have the power to compel all persons with relevant information to testify or to make available for perusal all written communications that are relevant to the proceeding. A person who refuses to comply can be cited for contempt, a finding that could result in a fine or imprisonment.

There are a few exceptions to the general rule. One exception is a claim of privilege. "Courts and legislators have … been prepared to restrict the search for truth by excluding probative, trustworthy and relevant evidence to serve some overriding social concern or judicial policy. The latter are the source of privileges for certain private communications."[1] When a particular communication is designated as privileged, the holder of the privilege may resist disclosing the information to the court.[2]

Courts have recognized two categories of privilege: class privilege and case-by-case privilege. With class privilege, there is a presumption that all communications that occur within the relationship are privileged. Solicitor–client privilege is the most common example of a class privilege. The other category of privilege is referred to as case-by-case privilege in which there is a presumption that all relevant confidential communications are admissible (i.e. not privileged) unless it can be shown why they should not be admitted. [3]

The Supreme Court of Canada has ruled that there is no class privilege for religious communications. All such communications are presumptively admissible. Claims of privilege by clergy are considered by the courts on a case-by-case or ad hoc basis. One commentator has noted several factors that courts have considered relevant when deciding whether a religious communication is privileged:

> a) Is there a practice of confidentiality by the religious organization? b) Was there an expectation of confidentiality by the confider? c) Was the communication required in the course of a discipline or practice of the religious organization? d) Is there evidence that the confider is, or ever was, a member of that religious organization or that he or she has any religious practices or beliefs? e) Does the communication involve some aspect of religious belief, worship or practice? f) Is the religious aspect the dominant feature or purpose of the communication?

g) Would the communication have been called
into being without the religious aspect?[4]

When a claim of privilege on a case-by-case basis fails,
then the communication must be disclosed, or the person who
refuses to comply risks a finding of contempt.

The Supreme Court of Canada has stated that analyzing
claims of religious communication privilege on a case-by-case
basis "will allow courts to determine whether, in the particular circumstances, the individual's freedom of religion will be
imperiled by the admission of the evidence."[5] Further, the
court stressed that the "fact that the communications were
not made to an ordained priest or minister or that they did
not constitute a formal confession will not bar the possibility
of the communications being excluded."[6]

Wigmore criteria

To determine whether to grant a privilege on a case-by-
case basis, courts apply what are called the Wigmore criteria,
developed by Professor John Henry Wigmore, an American
legal scholar who flourished in the first half of the 20th century.
The person claiming a privilege must show the following:

1) The communications originated in a confidence that
   they would not be disclosed;

2) This element of confidentiality must be essential to the
   full and satisfactory maintenance of the relationship
   between the parties [i.e. cleric and confider];

3) The relationship must be of significant importance
   to society; and

4) The injury that would be caused to the relationship by the disclosure of the communications must be greater than the benefit gained by the correct disposal of the litigation.[7]

When these four criteria are proven on a balance of probabilities, then the court grants a claim of privilege and does not require the disclosure of the confidential information. However, it should be noted that few claims of privilege on a case-by-case basis have been successful in Canada. So, although a claim of religious communication privilege can and should be raised when appropriate to do so, the chances of a court recognizing the privilege are slight.

Most claims of case-by-case privilege founder on the fourth branch of the test. The court must balance the interests served by protecting the communications (such as the particular clergy–confider relationship and the privacy interests of the person claiming privilege, as well as the effect disclosure would have on society's interest in encouraging and maintaining religious communications) against the interest in admitting relevant evidence and thereby disposing correctly of the litigation.[8] The commitment of our judicial system to this latter interest, and more broadly our society's commitment, is so strong that the court usually rules in favour of disclosure.

If a religious communication privilege is recognized in a particular case, then either the cleric or the person who confided in the cleric could claim the privilege to resist disclosing documents covered by the privilege and to resist answering any questions the answers to which would reveal the confidence. If the person who confided in the cleric waives the privilege, then the cleric would be compelled to disclose.

Statutory privilege

The legislatures of two provinces – Quebec, and Newfoundland and Labrador – have created a class privilege for religious communications. The Newfoundland and Labrador *Evidence Act* states at section 8 that "[a] member of the clergy or a priest shall not be compellable to give evidence as to a confession made to him or her in his or her professional capacity."[9]

In these two provinces, therefore, confessions to a cleric are privileged, and a cleric cannot be compelled by a court to disclose the confidential information.

Illustrative case

Consideration of the leading case, *R. v. Gruenke*, illustrates the law regarding religious communication privilege.[10]

Ms. Gruenke, 22 years old, was found guilty of murdering 82-year-old Philip Barnett. Mr. Barnett had befriended Ms. Gruenke and helped her in various ways. He had loaned her money to start a business and provided her with a car and an allowance. Although the relationship was at first platonic, Mr. Barnett began to make sexual advances that frightened Ms. Gruenke. At about this time, she moved back home to live with her mother. Thinking that she was sick with leukemia, Ms. Gruenke began attending the Victorious Faith Centre (a fundamentalist Christian church) and started counselling with a Ms. Frovich, a counsellor assigned to her by the church pastor, Ms. Thiessen.

The Crown's theory of the case was that Ms. Gruenke and her boyfriend had killed Mr. Barnett to stop the sexual harassment and to benefit from provisions in his will. Ms. Gruenke said she killed him in self-defence. Two days after the murder, Ms. Frovich and Pastor Thiessen met with Ms. Gruenke, who confessed to them that she and her boyfriend had planned to kill Mr. Barnett.

At trial, Ms. Gruenke applied to have the testimony of the counsellor and pastor ruled inadmissible on the basis of religious communication privilege. She lost at trial and on appeal on that issue, and was convicted of murder. She appealed to the Supreme Court of Canada.

The Supreme Court concluded that these communications did not satisfy the first requirement of the Wigmore test, namely that the communications originate in a confidence that they will not be disclosed. The court noted that "the testimony of Pastor Thiessen and Janine Frovich indicates that they were unclear as to whether they were expected to keep confidential what Ms. Gruenke had told them about her involvement in the murder."[11] The court found that Ms. Gruenke did not approach Ms. Frovich or the pastor with the expectation of confidentiality. Ms. Gruenke spoke to Ms. Frovich and Pastor Thiessen "more to relieve [her] emotional stress than for a religious or spiritual purpose."[12]

Practical issues and considerations

The issue of privilege arises in the context of a court proceeding, either civil or criminal. Following is some practical advice about responding to the different sorts of situations that may confront a church or cleric.

Privilege and the civil process

Church or cleric as party to a lawsuit. Anyone who is a party to a lawsuit is obligated to provide copies of all relevant documents to the other party or parties. This includes information that is confidential. The only ground for refusing to provide relevant information is a claim of privilege. Documents over which privilege is claimed should be withheld, unless the person who is the subject of the document consents to the release. To challenge the claim of privilege, the opposing party must make an application to court where the issue of privilege will be resolved.

Cleric as witness. Every witness (in either a civil or criminal trial) is required to answer all relevant questions, unless the information sought is covered by a privilege. If called as a witness, a cleric should raise a claim of privilege, when appropriate. The judge will then have to decide whether to recognize a privilege in the particular case. If compelled to testify, the cleric witness should ask the court's permission to first seek legal counsel, if he or she has not already done so.

Church or cleric as non-party. A party to a lawsuit may obtain an order compelling the release of confidential information held by a person or organization not a party to the lawsuit, such as a church or cleric. Confidential information should never be released unless compelled by a court order, or unless the person who is the subject of the document consents to its release. If subject to an order to produce confidential information, withhold any documents over which privilege is claimed until a judge rules on the issue of privilege.

Privilege and the criminal process

Church or cleric subject to a search warrant. Law enforcement officials may obtain a search warrant under the *Criminal Code of Canada* and other statutes, both federal and provincial. All documents subject to a search warrant (*but only those documents*) must be released to the authorities with the search warrant. If possible, any documents over which privilege is claimed should be placed in a sealed envelope or container marked "privileged" before being released. Legal counsel should be contacted immediately to arrange for a hearing before a judge to determine the issue of privilege over the sealed documents.

Conclusion

Confidential information must be disclosed to a court unless privileged. Except in two provinces, where a class privilege has been created by statute, religious communications are not protected by a class privilege, as are communications between a lawyer and his or her client. A claim of religious communication privilege will be decided on a case-by-case basis, a determination that will turn on the facts of the case. Few such claims of case-by-case privilege have been successful.

Religious Communication Privilege: Questions and Answers

Q. When does the issue of privilege arise?

A. This issue arises in the context of a legal proceeding and involves the question of when a person has the legal right to refuse to disclose to a court confidential information.

Q. Can a person be forced by the courts to disclose confidential information?

A. Yes. The general rule, to which there are very few exceptions, is that any person with relevant information must comply with a court's request to disclose that information, even when the information is confidential. A person who refuses to comply can be cited for contempt of court, which could result in a fine or even imprisonment.

Q. Are there any exceptions to the general rule that all relevant information must be disclosed at the request of a court?

A. Yes. One of the main exceptions is a claim of privilege. Confidential communications within certain protected relationships, the most well-known being the solicitor–client relationship, are privileged.

Q. **What is the effect of designating a particular communication privileged?**

A. When a communication is privileged, the holder of the privilege can refuse to disclose the information to the court.

Q. **Does the common law recognize a class privilege for communications made to spiritual or religious advisors?**

A. No. All such communications are presumed to be admissible. However, courts will consider claims of religious communication privilege on a case-by-case basis.

Q. **What is a statutory privilege?**

A. Two provinces – Quebec, and Newfoundland and Labrador – have enacted legislation that creates a statutory privilege. Members of the clergy in these provinces are therefore holders of a class privilege, which means that they cannot be compelled to disclose confidential communications that meet the requirements of the statute.

Notes

1   *R. v. Gruenke*, [1991] 3 S.C.R. 263, para. 64 [*Gruenke*].

2   *Canadian Law Dictionary*, 5th ed., *s.v.* "privilege."

3   *Gruenke*, note 1, para. 34.

4   A. L. Kirby, "Sexual Abuse by a Member of a Religious Organization: Obligations and Preventative Measures" (1995) 12:3 *Philanthropist* 13, p. 17.

5   *Gruenke*, note 1, para. 48.

6   *Ibid.*

7   *Ibid.*, paras. 25 and 99.

8   A.M. *v. Ryan*, [1997] 1 S.C.R. 157, para. 29.

9   Newfoundland and Labrador *Evidence Act*, R.S.N.L. 1990, c. E-16, s. 8. See also Quebec *Charter of Human Rights and Freedoms*, R.S.Q. 1977, c. C-12, s. 9.

10   *Gruenke*, note 1.

11   *Ibid.*, para. 52.

12   *Ibid.*

Part III:

Employment

Part III focuses on issues relating to employment. Almost every church has at least one employee, and some churches have many employees. For this reason, churches need to be aware of the legal rights and obligations that apply to the employment relationship. This awareness will help churches to make better decisions and reduce the risks of litigation.

Chapter 15 addresses employment law issues. The chapter starts with the question of when the law considers a cleric an employee. The chapter then discusses issues relating to entering into an employment relationship, managing the employment relationship and terminating the employment relationship.

Human rights are a core aspect of Canadian law. Individuals and institutions are required to treat one another in ways that do not undermine the rights safeguarded in human rights legislation (frequently referred to as human rights codes). For churches, this is particularly relevant in the context of employment decisions. Chapter 16 outlines the ambit of human rights protection and the permitted exceptions, and suggests some practical steps aimed at helping churches review their policies and practices for compliance with human rights law. The chapter concludes with an overview of the human rights complaints process.

Churches frequently have a great deal of information in their hands – information about employees, volunteers and members of the congregation. Sometimes this information is personal and confidential. Chapter 17 looks at recent federal privacy legislation designed to ensure that personal information is collected, used and disclosed in ways that respect individuals' privacy as much as possible. Chapter 18 focuses on the legal duties and obligations concerning confidential information.

15

Employment Law

An ounce of prevention is worth a pound of cure.
—Ancient proverb, first recorded by Henry of Bratton,
clergyman and judge, died 1268,
On the Laws and Customs of England

E mployment law is a specialized and at times complex field, so if an employment-related dispute does occur, it may be necessary to contact a lawyer with expertise in that area of law. On the other hand, an understanding of some fairly basic principles may help church employers meet the requirements of the law. The purpose of this chapter is to highlight employment law issues that could arise within a church setting and to suggest some ways to avoid potential difficulties. A preliminary issue that may come to mind for some churches is the question of whether the law views clergy as employees. We open the chapter with a discussion of that question. We then address entering into the employment relationship (the hiring process and the employment contract); the employment relationship itself (statutory requirements, workplace policies, performance evaluations, and progressive discipline); and termination of the employment relationship (dismissal for cause and dismissal with reasonable notice). Note that this chapter addresses employment issues in a *non-union* setting. When employees are unionized, the employer–employee relationship is governed by a collective agreement negotiated between the employer and the union.

This chapter should be read in tandem with Chapter 3 (on church decision making) and Chapter 16 (on human rights).

When is a cleric an employee?

Many of the topics addressed in this chapter apply to both clergy and laypeople working within the church; however, with regard to clergy, there is the initial question of whether a cleric is, in the eyes of the law, an employee. It seems likely that a cleric hired solely to perform administrative or management tasks within a church organization would be seen as an employee, but what of the cleric who is called by or assigned to a congregation as its spiritual leader?

Traditionally, churches have tended to view their relationship with clergy as something other than one of employment. For many churches, "the status of clergy is conceptualized as one of ecclesiastical office, or as a spiritual office, and remuneration and benefits are conceptualized as a maintenance provision to free clergy from secular employment and concerns for the exercise of their spiritual vocation."[1]

You might ask why this matters. It may make a real difference. If the cleric is an employee, then he or she has a contract of employment, the terms of which cannot be changed by one side alone. If there is no employment relationship, then there is no employment contract. Further, the law gives employees benefits and protections, such as the right not to be dismissed, unless there is just cause or the employee has been given reasonable notice. When a person is simply the holder of a spiritual office, rather than an employee, these benefits and protections may not apply.

A review of the case law shows that there is no definitive answer to the question of whether, in a dispute between a cleric and the church, the cleric will be viewed by the courts as an employee or as a holder of a spiritual office.[2] (Different considerations apply when the dispute involves a third party alleged to have been harmed by the wrongdoing of a cleric, and the courts must determine whether to treat the cleric as an employee for the purpose of vicarious liability. Vicarious liability is discussed in Chapter 9. The discussion here focuses on disputes between the cleric and the church.)

In determining whether to characterize a cleric as an employee of the church, courts take account of the context in which the issue arises. For instance, is the court being asked to interpret a particular statute? Then, the answer will depend on how that statute defines employee and how closely the cleric fits that definition.

Where the issue does not involve the interpretation of a statute, the degree of control exercised over the cleric by an individual within the church (for instance, a bishop) or a church court (for instance, a presbytery) will be a relevant consideration. The courts will try to determine whether the individual or entity alleged to be the employer exerts sufficient control over the cleric to make the relationship akin to that of employer–employee.

Generally, the greater the control, the greater the likelihood the cleric will be found to be an employee. This approach is seen in *McCaw v. United Church of Canada*, where a cleric asked the court to overturn a decision of presbytery to remove his name from the order of ministry or, in the alternative, to award him damages for wrongful dismissal.[3] While the court did not make an explicit finding as to Rev. McCaw's employment status, it did order that his name be restored to the presbytery rolls. In granting this remedy, the court was clearly influenced by the degree of control that the United Church exerts over its clerics:

> What stands out in this case is that the church, through Presbytery and Conference action, has control over a minister's eligibility to earn his living as a minister within the church. If a minister's eligibility to earn his living in the church is unlawfully taken away, it is obvious that the unlawful action will cause pecuniary loss to the minister ....[4]

The question of control is simply one aspect of the broader question that courts consider in determining the status of a cleric: does the relationship between the cleric and the church look like other employment relationships?

This approach, of comparing the relationship between a cleric and a particular church with other employee–employer relationships, is found in the case of *Smith v. Worldwide Church of God*.[5] Two ministers who were dismissed by the Worldwide Church of God brought actions for wrongful dismissal. Interestingly, although one of the ministers was alleging wrongful dismissal (a concept that applies to employees), he argued that "he was a Christian Minister, not an employee of an organization."[6] The court rejected this argument, stating, "The Worldwide Church of God is in the religion business. I do not say this in a derogatory sense but in the sense that it employs Ministers who are paid salaries, are given car allowances, who attend conventions, who are employees of an organization in every sense of the word."[7] Thus, there was an express finding of an employment relationship, based on the similarities between how the Worldwide Church of God dealt with its ministers and how secular employers deal with their employees. The court found that the dismissal of one of the two ministers was justified because of a "flagrant breach of an essential term of employment."[8] With Rev. Smith, however, there did not appear to have been sufficient misconduct to justify the dismissal. The court held that Rev. Smith was entitled to eight months' pay in lieu of notice.

The reasoning in *McCaw* and *Smith* also suggests that if a cleric who has been harshly treated by the church asks for employment law concepts such as wrongful dismissal or reasonable notice to be applied, the courts may be reluctant to deny the existence of an employment relationship, if that would leave the cleric without a remedy.

To summarize, the law is not clear on when a cleric will be seen as an employee. It depends on the context in which the issue arises, how much the relationship between the cleric and the church resembles secular employment relationships and, perhaps, the availability of other remedies if the cleric is found not to be an employee. If the question arises as to whether the law would characterize the cleric in your congregation as an employee, a lawyer with expertise in employment law should be consulted.

The rest of this chapter focuses on entering into, managing and terminating the employment relationship. As noted in the introduction to this chapter, our discussion deals only with a non-unionized setting.

Entering into the employment relationship

Interview questions

Interview questions should be designed to allow the interviewer to determine whether the applicant has the required skills and qualities. If there is more than one applicant for the same position, then the same questions should be asked of each, both in fairness to the applicants, and to provide the interviewer with a basis for comparison. Further, a scheme for evaluating answers should be prepared in advance, so that the hiring committee has something against which to assess each applicant's responses. Employers should be aware of human rights legislation and avoid asking any questions that might create the perception that a hiring decision would be based on discriminatory grounds. Human rights issues are discussed in Chapter 16.

Confidentiality

Whether your congregation has struck a search committee to call a cleric or you are planning to hire office staff,
consideration must be given to the issue of confidentiality. It
is possible that some of the applicants may not have informed
their current congregation or current employer that they are
looking for a new position. Before the search process begins,
the appropriate level of confidentiality must be determined,
and this must be clearly conveyed to applicants.

References

Before someone is hired, references should be checked.
Information received through this process should be evaluated in light of the relationship between the applicant and
the person giving the reference. Your search committee may
also want to go beyond the references given and speak with
others who know the applicant. This is permissible, so long as
it does not breach the applicant's reasonable expectation of
confidentiality, and so long as it is not contrary to any internal
rules developed by your church.

Written contract of employment

Once an offer of employment has been made and accepted,
an employment contract exists; the only question at that point
is whether it is beneficial to have a written contract, signed
by the employer and employee. In most employment settings,
the best advice is to have a written agreement, so as to have
the terms of the relationship clearly agreed to by both parties.
In a church setting, many aspects of the relationship between

the church and clergy may be governed by established rules;[9] however, to the extent that there are specific terms to be agreed upon, it is wise to have those terms reflected in a written contract.

If there is to be a written contract, it should set out the following:

- the employee's responsibilities;

- whether there is to be a probationary period (a period of at least one year is highly recommended);

- the benefits (such as vacation time or education leave) to which the employee is entitled;

- the method by which performance will be reviewed and evaluated;

- the workplace policies that the employee will be expected to adhere to; and

- the period of notice that the employer would be required to give in order to dismiss the employee.

It should be noted that even the written contract is unlikely to be seen as reflecting every aspect of the employment relationship:

> Unless the scope of the employment contract is expressly limited to the written agreement, the contract will be seen to include representations made in the job advertisement, the application form, the interview, or any letter of offer, as

well as any terms that are required by statute
or implied by common law.[10]

Managing the employment relationship

Once an employment relationship is established, the employer should be aware of an employer's statutory obligations; ensure that appropriate workplace policies are developed and that employees are informed of these policies; put in place a system for performance evaluation; and understand the concept of progressive discipline. Each of these issues is discussed below.

Statutory requirements

When an employment relationship exists, the employer is bound by a variety of statutes. An employer's statutory duties include the requirement to deduct income tax, Canada Pension Plan payments and Employment Insurance premiums from the employee's wages and remit these to the government, along with the employer's contributions to the Canada Pension Plan and Employment Insurance.

Employment relationships are also governed by a number of other statutes, including legislation dealing with human rights (see Chapter 16), employment standards, workers' compensation, and occupational health and safety. It should be noted that the protections and benefits afforded employees by these statutes cannot be waived by the employee, unless this is expressly permitted in the statute.[11] It is rare for employment legislation to allow statutory obligations to be "contracted out of." Thus, if an employee signed a contract saying, "I accept that the human rights code and workers' compensation legislation will not apply to this employment," that term of the contract would be invalid.

Employment standards legislation

All jurisdictions within Canada (federal, provincial and territorial) have employment standards statutes. This legislation applies to all employees unless they fall within the categories of employees explicitly excluded by the statute. Some employment standards statutes exclude members of the clergy and others do not. For instance, under Ontario's *Employment Standards Act*, holders of "political, religious or judicial office" are exempted from the statute, but this is not the case in all provinces and territories.[12]

Employment standards legislation deals with a range of employee rights and benefits, including hours of work, minimum wage, when overtime pay is required, pregnancy and parental leave, and the period of notice required for dismissal. While employees who are covered by employment standards legislation generally cannot waive their statutory protection, they can bargain for greater benefits. Furthermore, courts have held that employment standards legislation simply sets minimum protections; a court may decide that an employee is owed greater rights and benefits than those set out in the employment standards code.

Workers' compensation legislation

Employers also need to be aware of workers' compensation legislation. This legislation is based on the idea of an exchange: workers who are covered by workers' compensation legislation have an automatic right to compensation when they are injured in the course of their employment, without having to prove that the employer's negligence caused the injury. In exchange, the worker loses the right to sue his or her employer for work-related injuries. Employers who are covered by the legislation are required to contribute to the workers' compensation fund in their province or territory at an amount determined by the workers' compensation board. Church employers should consult with a lawyer to determine whether they fall within the legislation in their province or territory; for instance, under some legislation, an employer must have a certain minimum number of employees before the employer is bound by workers' compensation legislation.

An employee makes a claim by filing a form with the workers' compensation board. Compensation could include lost wages and money to compensate for permanent physical or mental impairment.

Many workers' compensation boards provide information brochures and maintain websites that could be a useful source of information for employers or employees in a church setting.

Occupational health and safety legislation

Under occupational health and safety legislation, employers, employees, contractors and others share a responsibility to keep the workplace safe and healthy. If work has, under occupational health and safety legislation, been determined to be unsafe, employees can refuse to do that work. Examples of unsafe activities include the following:

- allowing an employee or volunteer to use a very tall ladder, without a safety harness, in order to hang Christmas lights; or

- allowing an employee or volunteer who does not have the appropriate trade certification to fix the electrical system at the church.

An employer's failure to meet the occupational health and safety requirements in their province or territory could lead to charges and prosecution under the legislation. In extreme cases, employers can be charged under the *Criminal Code*, and a conviction could lead to imprisonment. Churches would be well-advised to have a risk assessment done of their work environments to ensure compliance with occupational health and safety legislation. You might find it useful to check with your church's insurance company to get names of experienced risk-assessment specialists in your area. Also, your church might consider inviting an occupational health and safety officer from the provincial or territorial government to review the church's policies and practices.

Depending on the number of employees, a church might be required to have an occupational health and safety plan or policy in place. Most provinces and territories maintain web-sites that provide basic information on occupational health and safety requirements, but it may also be necessary to consult with a lawyer to determine whether the requirement for an occupational health and safety plan applies to your congregation. Occupational health and safety policies are discussed in Chapter 5.

Workplace policies

Workplace policies established by the employer should be referred to in the employment contract, and it should be made clear that these policies form part of the contract. It should also be stated in the contract, and in the policies themselves, that a breach of the policy will lead to discipline, up to and including dismissal. If a church wants to be able to discipline an employee for breach of a policy, then it must be clear that the employee was informed of the policy; that the policy is reasonable and does not conflict with any terms agreed upon in the employment contract or with human rights legislation; and that the church has applied the policy consistently.

Church employers, whether a congregation or another entity within the church, should find out what employment-related policies are in place within the denomination and consider whether further policies are needed to fill any gaps. For instance, does your church have a policy on sexual harassment? On confidential information? On use of office technology? On privacy? These four areas are discussed briefly here; workplace policies are also discussed in Chapter 5.

Sexual harassment

A lawyer should be consulted in the development of a sexual harassment policy, and the policy should be reviewed regularly to ensure that it keeps pace with any changes in the law. Any sexual harassment policy must be applied consistently. The policy should explain what sexual harassment is, perhaps giving examples to clarify; state who the policy applies to; identify the person(s) to whom complaints of sexual harassment are to be made; and explain the procedure that will be followed when such a complaint is made. Employees and volunteers should be required to sign a form acknowledging that they are aware of the policy. Consideration should be given to whether training and discussion will be needed in order to implement the sexual harassment policy. Those within the church should be encouraged to think of such policies as implementing ideals of respect and concern for others.

An employer might also consider having a more general policy that includes other forms of harassment besides sexual harassment.

Confidential information

By the very nature of their work, clerics and others employed in church settings are entrusted with, or have access to, sensitive personal information that must be kept confidential. (Although this chapter focuses on employment law, it should be noted that church volunteers also need to maintain confidentiality in certain circumstances.) Workplace policies on confidentiality should be established. Any policy on confidentiality must define what information the policy covers. Clergy, as well as all other church employees and volunteers, must be made aware of the requirements for confidentiality, as set out in the policy. They must know when the law requires disclosure, even of confidential information, as for instance in the duty to report suspected child abuse. For more on this, see Chapter 18.

A congregation or other church employer may want certain information kept confidential even after a cleric or other employee moves on to a new call or a new position;

therefore, the employment contract should make it clear that the requirement of confidentiality extends beyond the end of the contract.

Use of office technology

What follows is general advice on policies regarding the use of office technology. These general suggestions should be modified to fit the particular situation. The workplace policy should include at least the following, with regard to the use of office computer, voice mail and e-mail:

- the employer owns everything – even personal data – created or stored on its computers;

- computers, voice mail and e-mail are to be used for business purposes only; and

- improper use of computers, voice mail or e-mail can lead to discipline, including termination.

While the definition of improper use should be open-ended, it is useful to give some specific examples of behaviour that will not be tolerated: for instance, downloading pornography from the Internet, or sending offensive or harassing messages. The policy should make it clear whether the employer intends to monitor how employees use office technology.[13]

Privacy

In the previous section, we noted that where employee use of office technology will be monitored, this should be stated in a written office policy. Monitoring of office use of technology is part of the broader question of privacy. To what extent does the law recognize employees as having privacy rights in the workplace?

Privacy has been defined in a variety of ways, including simply the "right to be left alone"[14] or, more formally, "the claim of individuals, groups or institutions to determine for themselves when, how, and to what extent information about them is communicated to others."[15] A few provinces have legislation that would apply in workplaces generally; in other provinces and territories, privacy issues in most workplaces are dealt with under the common law. Whether regulated by statute or the common law, the test is quite similar. Stated simply, each of us is entitled to the degree of privacy that could be reasonably expected in the particular context.

So, what does this mean for churches? As much as possible, employers should clarify in the employment contract the degree of monitoring that will occur, so that this will become part of what the employee can reasonably expect in the circumstances. For anything not covered in the employment contract, employers should ask themselves whether the proposed course of action is based on a legitimate workplace need for information and whether the degree of intrusion into the employee's affairs is proportionate to that need. It may be necessary to seek legal advice as to what is likely to be seen as reasonable in a particular context.

Performance evaluations

It is a good idea to have regular performance evaluations to allow an employer to identify the areas in which further training is needed, and to apprise employees of any improvements that may be required. Of equal importance, regular evaluations provide an opportunity to let good employees know that their performance is recognized and appreciated. Employees should be aware of how the performance evaluation will be conducted and how frequently.

If the performance evaluation shows that an employee needs to improve or change in some area, it is important that this information is communicated in a positive and non-derogatory manner, that the employee is given concrete and manageable goals to work toward, and that the employee is made aware of the consequences of not meeting these goals within a reasonable period.

Progressive discipline

Where an employment relationship exists, the law on progressive discipline applies.[16] If an employee acts in ways that he or she has the power to correct, an employer who wants the employee's behaviour to change must use progressive discipline. This means that, except in the most extreme situations, an employer cannot come down like a ton of bricks the first time that an employee makes a mistake, or even the first time that the employee engages in wrongdoing. In fact, even if it is the second or third or fourth time, the employer must still ensure that the seriousness of the discipline matches the seriousness of the problem. Thus, the concept of progressive discipline encompasses two concepts:

- lesser penalties for initial infractions, with the employee being informed of problems and given a timeframe within which to improve or change, before more serious disciplinary action is taken; and

- lesser penalties for more minor infractions.[17]

Depending on the seriousness of the error or misconduct and whether the employee has received any prior notice that a particular behaviour is not acceptable, sanctions could range from a verbal warning, to a more formal letter of reprimand, to suspension without pay for a set period of time. A letter of reprimand should refer to any previous warnings that the employee has been given regarding this behaviour; detail the current problem; explain how the employee's behaviour harms the church and why it needs to be corrected; state the sanction that will be imposed; and warn that, if the misconduct continues, the employee will be subject to further discipline, up to and including dismissal.

The above paragraphs refer to behaviour that can be corrected. Sometimes when an employee is not meeting expectations, it may not be clear whether the employee has it within his or her power to correct the situation. For instance, an employee who is frequently absent from work may simply be lackadaisical about the job, or may be suffering from an illness that makes it impossible to make it to work each day. If the impact on the workplace is sufficiently serious, the church should inform the employee in writing of the problem; request that the employee make all reasonable efforts to improve attendance; and warn that if he or she does not do so, the employment contract may be brought to an end. Different considerations may apply where the employee genuinely has an illness or disability that affects job performance. In that case, the employer should seek legal advice as to whether or how the employee must be accommodated; further, the employer should not take steps to discipline or terminate the employee without first consulting a lawyer.

Ending the employment relationship

When an employment relationship exists, the law on wrongful dismissal (sometimes called unjust dismissal) also applies. Unless an employment contract is for a specified term, an employee can only be dismissed for just cause or on being given proper notice or pay in lieu of notice.

Just cause

In order for there to be just cause, the courts will require that:

> ... an employee has been guilty of serious misconduct, habitual neglect of duty, incompetence, or conduct incompatible with his duties, or prejudicial to the employer's business, or ... [that] he has been guilty of willful disobedience to the employer's orders on a matter of substance ....[18]

As this quotation suggests, the courts interpret the concept of just cause quite stringently; in fact, people are often surprised at how badly an employee must behave in order to meet the threshold of just cause. Therefore, if an employer is considering dismissal for wrongdoing or misconduct, it is essential to get legal advice as to whether the employee's behaviour amounts to just cause. To justify dismissal, the employee's misconduct must be seen as so severe that it destroys the employment relationship. Examples in a church setting might include a blatant or Christian education worker who is convicted of child abuse; a cleric who is found by a court to have coerced an elderly parishioner into leaving the church all her money in her will; or a church secretary who has regularly, without any mitigating circumstances, stolen large sums from church funds.

When deciding whether a particular set of circumstances amounts to just cause, a court looks at all the facts of the case. For instance, is this the first time that the cleric or other employee has gone off the rails? Has the employee had an unblemished record until now? Is the employee under unusual stress (for instance, because of a child's illness or a disintegrating marriage) that might have caused him or her to act uncharacteristically? If there have been problems in the past, has progressive discipline been followed in an effort to correct the employee's behaviour?

If progressive discipline has been applied in the past, and if the behaviour of the employee is sufficiently serious to meet the test for just cause, then the employee may be dismissed without notice or pay in lieu of notice. However, when the circumstances do not amount to just cause, the employer can only dismiss the employee if the employee is given reasonable notice or pay in lieu of notice.

Reasonable notice

If an employer wishes to dismiss an employee but is not able to show just cause, the employee may still be dismissed if reasonable notice or pay in lieu of notice is given.[19] An exception exists in some employment standards legislation. This exception prohibits termination of long-time employees covered by that legislation unless there is just cause; in that context, termination with reasonable notice is not allowed.[20]

If an employer is planning to terminate an employee by giving reasonable notice, the employer may give the employee "working notice" (that is, the employee continues to work during the period of notice) or may pay the employee in lieu of notice. In either scenario, the employer must consider how much notice is required by law. Employment standards legislation (when it applies) sets a minimum notice period; however, courts have made it clear that this is only a minimum and that longer notice may sometimes be required. When the employment contract specifies a notice period, it must be adhered to.

Where a notice period is not specified in the contract, various factors must be considered in order to determine the appropriate length of notice. According to the Supreme Court of Canada, these factors include how long the employee has been working for this employer, his or her age and the chances of finding comparable employment. [21]

Wrongful dismissal

An employee who has been dismissed without just cause or appropriate notice or pay in lieu of notice may sue his or her employer for wrongful dismissal. (The other option would be to request judicial review of the decision to dismiss. For a discussion of judicial review, see Chapter 3.) Given the complexities of church organizations, an employee who intends to launch such an action should ensure that the appropriate entity within the church is named as employer.

Remedies for wrongful dismissal

If a court finds that an employee has been wrongfully dismissed, the most likely remedy is damages amounting to pay in lieu of the notice that the employee should have received. If there was "bad faith conduct in the manner of dismissal," the employee may be entitled to additional damages.[22] The amount of damages might also be increased if it were shown that the employee had been persuaded to leave a secure position in order to work for this employer.

As to whether reinstatement would be ordered rather than damages, there is some commentary in the cases to suggest that courts might be reluctant to reinstate a cleric. In *McCaw*, referred to above, the court required that Rev. McCaw be paid damages and that his name be replaced on presbytery and Conference rolls. On the issue of reinstatement, the court noted that:

> Mr. McCaw has specifically declined to ask for an order restoring him to his Pastoral Charge …. That saves this court from having to decide whether or not directing a minister be placed in a particular Pastoral Charge would amount to undue interference with the internal affairs of the church.[23]

In *Lindenburger v. United Church of Canada*, a cleric claimed that he had been coerced into resigning, and asked to be reinstated. The court stated:

> Even if I had thought that Mr. Lindenburger had been unfairly used in all the circumstances

of the case I would nevertheless be reluctant to exercise the court's discretion to grant the relief asked. It must be remembered that the dispute involves the internal affairs of the Church which unlike most other organizations is peculiarly concerned with the spiritual life of the members of the pastoral charge; to this fundamental role of the Church, mutual trust and confidence between the congregation and its Minister are essential. If they cannot work in harmony the spiritual life of the congregation will suffer.[24]

Thus, although the question is still open, it appears that courts will be more likely to award damages, rather than reinstatement, to a cleric who has been wrongfully dismissed.

Fair procedures

Procedural fairness is discussed in Chapter 3. The key point is that when a church committee, board or court is going to make a decision that would affect an individual's rights or interests, that individual is entitled to fair procedures. This would apply whether a cleric was found to be an employee or the holder of a spiritual office. Fair procedures require that the decision maker follow any procedural requirements set out in relevant legislation and in internal church rules. Decision makers must also meet the duty of fairness, which means that the individual affected by the decision is entitled to

- know the case against her or him;

- have an opportunity to respond; and

- have the decision made by an unbiased decision-making body.

Chapter 3 should be read by any church committee, board or court that is going to make employment-related decisions.

Conclusion

We opened this chapter with the old adage "An ounce of prevention is worth a pound a cure." If ever there was a subject to which that saying applies, it is to employment-related matters. Good hiring practices, clear-cut workplace policies, adherence to statutory obligations, an understanding of the law on discipline and dismissal, and a commitment to procedural fairness can go a long way to warding off employment difficulties. If difficulties do arise, it is important to get legal advice immediately.

Employment Law: Questions and Answers

Q. Who are employees in the church context?

A. Church employees clearly include administrative, secretarial and maintenance staff. The status of clergy is somewhat less clear. In certain contexts, clergy have been considered to be holders of a spiritual office rather than employees, while in other situations they have been characterized as employees.

Q. **Why would it matter whether a cleric is classified as an employee or a holder of a spiritual office?**

A: It could matter if one party to a dispute argues that an employment contract exists and that it has been breached. An employee and employer are bound by a contract of employment (even when it is not written down), and the terms of the contract may not be altered unilaterally by either party. Also, employees are entitled to certain benefits under employment-related legislation and have certain protections relating to discipline and dismissal. These same benefits and protections may not be available if the law classifies the cleric as the holder of a spiritual office rather than an employee. It may be necessary to get legal advice on whether a cleric is likely to be considered an employee in a particular context.

Q. **Is there any legislation that pertains to church employees?**

A. Yes, churches must be aware that general employment-related legislation applies to their employees. This includes legislation on employment standards, human rights, workers' compensation and occupational safety, among other matters.

Q. Is it a good idea to have a written contract of employment?

A. Yes, since this will make clear the terms of the employment relationship.

Q. Should a church develop policies pertaining to certain aspects of the employment relationship? If so, what policies should be considered?

A. Yes, it is wise for churches to develop workplace policies in relation to such matters as sexual harassment, confidentiality of information, health and safety, the use of church technology and privacy.

Q. What is meant by progressive discipline?

A. The concept of progressive discipline encompasses two concepts:

- lesser penalties for initial infractions, with the employee being informed of problems and given a timeframe within which to improve or change, before more serious disciplinary action is taken; and

- lesser penalties for more minor infractions.

Q. **Under what circumstances may a church dismiss an employee?**

A. When an employer has used progressive discipline, but the employee has continued to conduct himself or herself so badly as to meet the test for "just cause," then the employee may be dismissed without notice or pay in lieu of notice. However, it is important to realize that courts interpret just cause very stringently. To determine whether you have just cause to fire an employee, you should always seek legal advice. If the behaviour is not sufficiently egregious to meet the just cause test, then, in order to dismiss, the employer must give the employee reasonable notice or pay him or her in lieu of notice. Again, a lawyer should be consulted for assistance in determining what would amount to reasonable notice in a particular situation.

Notes

1   M. H. Ogilvie, "Christian Clergy and the Law of Employment: Office-holders, Employees or Outlaws" (1999) 3 *Journal of the Church Law Association of Canada* 2, p. 3.

2   Throughout this book, when we use the word *court*, we are referring to secular courts, unless we state explicitly that we are discussing church courts.

3   *McCaw v. United Church of Canada* (1991), 4 O.R. (3d) 481 (C.A.), [*McCaw*].

4   *Ibid.*, para. 24.

5   *Smith v. Worldwide Church of God* (1980), 39 N.S.R. (2d) 430 (S.C. (T.D.)).

6   *Ibid.*, para. 10.

7   *Ibid.*, para. 12.

8   *Ibid.*

9   For example, see the following, available on the denominations' web-sites: Anglican Church of Canada (www.anglican.ca): *Handbook of the General Synod of the Anglican Church of Canada*; Presbyterian Church in Canada (www.presbyterian.ca): *Book of Forms*; Roman Catholic Church (www.cccb.ca): *The Codes of Canon Law*; United Church of Canada (www.united-church.ca): *The United Church Manual*. Churches organized in the congregationalist model (see Chapter 1 for a discussion of different models of church structure) are unlikely to have binding terms and conditions for clerics established at the denominational level, but may have a congregational constitution that deals with these matters. See, for instance, a discussion of sample constitutions by the Baptist Convention of Ontario and Quebec, on the Convention's webpage (www.baptist.ca).

10 Diana Ginn and Malcolm Boyle, "Employment Law and Dentistry" in Jocelyn Downie et al., eds., *Dental Law in Canada* (Markham, Ont.: Butterworths, 2004) 113, p. 122. [*Ginn*].

11 One exception to the general rule that employees cannot waive rights and protections given by this kind of legislation is found in Ontario, where employees can contract out of some aspects of employment standards legislation. Geoffrey England and Roderick Wood, *Employment Law in Canada* (Markham, Ont.: LexisNexis Butterworths, 2005), section 8.43.1.

12   Ontario *Employment Standards Act, 2000*, S.O. 2000, c. 41, s. 3(5), #7.

13   The section on use of office technology is taken, with only minor changes, from *Ginn*, note 10, p. 124.

14   Samuel D. Warren and Louis D. Brandeis, "The Right to Privacy" (1890) 4 *Harvard Law Review* 193, p. 195.

15   Allan F. Westin, *Privacy and Freedom* (New York: Atheneum, 1968), p. 7.

16   *McCaw*, note 3, suggests that the concept of progressive discipline applies to clergy, even if the relationship is seen as analogous to (rather than expressly labelled as) an employment relationship.

17   *Ginn*, note 10, pp. 133–134.

18   *R. v. Arthurs, ex. P. Port Arthur Shipbuilding Co.* (1967), 62 D.L.R. (2d) 342 (Ont. C.A) 348; reversed on other grounds [1969] S.C.R. 85, cited in Geoffrey England, Innis Christie and Merran Christie, *Employment Law in Canada*, 3rd ed. (Markham, Ont.: Butterworths, 1998).

19   A 2006 *National Post* article suggests that some people are not aware of the option of terminating with reasonable notice or pay in lieu of notice. In "Employment Law: The True Story – employers have more rights than you think," Howard Levitt rebuts the "myth" that "excellent, loyal" employees cannot be fired, with the comment, "An employer can fire whomever it wants, even arbitrarily. It is entitled to make mistakes, as long as it pays appropriate severance." (*National Post*, February 8, 2006.) It should be noted that this statement applies to non-union settings.

20   See, for example, the Nova Scotia *Labour Standards Code*, R.S.N.S. 1989, c. 246. Section 71(1) provides that, in most cases, an employee covered by the Act who has been with the same employer for ten years or more may only be fired when there is just cause.

21   *Wallace v. United Grain Growers Ltd. (c.o.b. Public Press)*, [1997] 3 S.C.R. 701.

22   *Ibid.*, para. 88.

23   *McCaw*, note 3, para. 31.

24   *Lindenburger v. United Church of Canada* (1985), 17 C.C.E.L. 143 (Ont. Div. Ct.), para. 16, affirmed (1987), 17 C.C.E.L. 172 (C.A.).

16

Human Rights

Too small is our world to allow discrimination,
bigotry and intolerance to thrive in any corner of it ...
—Eliot Engel, United States congressman,
spoken in the U.S. House of Representatives,
April 22, 2004

The law on human rights tries to enshrine the important social ideal that individuals should be dealt with according to individual merit, rather than according to personal attributes such as race, gender or physical disability; it also tries to strike a balance between that ideal and other legitimate social goals. On the one hand, as a society we want to protect individuals from discrimination. On the other hand, Canadian society also recognizes individuals' (and, to some extent, institutions') freedom of choice. In this chapter, we look at how human rights legislation (sometimes referred to as human rights codes) tries to strike that balance.

We start with an overview of human rights legislation, setting out the kinds of discriminatory behaviour that are prohibited. We then consider how human rights law responds to the tension between human rights protection and other legitimate social goals. We do this by examining human rights provisions that allow employers to make choices that would otherwise be labelled discriminatory, so long as those choices reflect a *bona fide* occupational requirement. The chapter then sets out some practical steps to help churches and congregations review their practices to ensure compliance with human rights law. The chapter ends with an outline of the human rights complaints process.

Human rights legislation could affect various aspects of church life, particularly decisions relating to employment. Churches must ensure that they are informed about what the law requires of them in terms of human rights protection. We suggest that this chapter be read in conjunction with Chapters 3 and 15.

Protection of human rights

Role of human rights commissions and tribunals

Human rights codes establish human rights commissions to implement the provisions of the code, and provide for the appointment of tribunals to hear allegations of human rights violations. (Human rights tribunals are sometimes called boards of inquiry.)

While our focus in this chapter is on outlining the kinds of protections provided in human rights legislation and discussing what kinds of decisions might or might not be seen as violating these protections, it is important to note that dealing with allegations of human rights violations is not the only role of a human rights commission. Commissions are intended to be not only reactive (responding to complaints), but also to take positive steps to eradicate discrimination. Thus, the functions of a human rights commission may include such tasks as

- developing public information and educational programs on human rights;

- promoting understanding of and compliance with human rights legislation;

- conducting research on human rights issues or encouraging such research; and

- advising government departments or other organizations or individuals on human rights matters.

Any church or entity within a church that is interested in holding an information session on human rights matters should consider contacting the human rights commission in their province or territory. It is likely that the commission would be pleased to provide a speaker for such a session.

Exclusive jurisdiction

Human rights commissions and tribunals have exclusive jurisdiction over allegations that the human rights code has been breached. This means that a person who wishes to allege a violation of the code must follow the process provided, and make a complaint to the human rights commission. A complainant cannot bypass that process and start a lawsuit in the courts.[1] A step-by-step overview of the human rights complaint process is provided at the end of this chapter.

Some human rights codes provide rights of appeal, so that a party dissatisfied with the decision of a tribunal may appeal that decision to a court. When there is no right of appeal set out in the legislation, a party who wishes to challenge the decision of a human rights tribunal must apply to a court for judicial review. Judicial review is discussed in Chapter 3.

Discrimination

Every province and territory of Canada, as well as the federal government, has a human rights code that prohibits certain kinds of discriminatory behaviour. Some, but not all, define discrimination. For instance, Nova Scotia defines it as

> ... a distinction ... that has the effect of impos-
> ing burdens, obligations or disadvantages on an
> individual or a class of individuals not imposed
> upon others or which withholds or limits ac-
> cess to opportunities, benefits and advantages
> available to other individuals or classes of in-
> dividuals in society.[2]

Human rights legislation is directed at behaviour. The fact that someone holds discriminatory views does not mean that he or she has breached a human rights code. The question is whether he or she has acted on those views to distinguish between individuals in ways that are not permitted by the law on human rights. It is the behaviour (the kinds of distinctions we make in how we treat others), not the opinions, that matters. Since speech is an action, discriminatory speech might, depending on the context, violate human rights codes.

The emphasis on behaviour also means that good intentions are not enough to save discriminatory behaviour from a human rights challenge. Thus, it is not necessary to show that someone was acting from bad motives in order to show that discriminatory behaviour has occurred. For instance, an employer might decide not to hire women for hard labour or unpleasant tasks. This decision might be based on respect for women and a desire to protect them from such work. This decision would not have been motivated by a desire to harm women – just the opposite, in fact. Yet, the employer's decision, however well-intended, would have the consequence of limiting women's access to jobs and so would be a human rights violation.

Scope of human rights protection

Many personal decisions are not covered by human rights law. Personal choices such as whom we choose as our friends, whom we marry or how we raise our children are outside the reach of human rights legislation.

While the scope of human rights protection varies somewhat from one province or territory to the next, it is standard for human rights legislation to prohibit discrimination with regard to employment, housing and the provision of services. Some provinces and territories also prohibit discrimination in the making of contracts, the purchase and sale of property, membership in a professional association or trade union, and employment advertising.

Sexual harassment in the workplace is also prohibited in all provinces and territories. Sexual harassment is "any unwelcome comment or conduct of a sexual nature that may detrimentally affect the work environment or lead to adverse job related consequences for the victim of the harassment."[3] Some human rights codes also prohibit other kinds of harassment, including harassment in the workplace generally, or harassment in relation to housing.

Protected characteristics

Thus far, we have said that certain areas – such as employment, accommodation and the provision of services – may be regulated by human rights legislation. However, this does not mean that *every* distinction in these areas is a human rights violation. An employer can, of course, refuse to hire someone who does not have the core skills needed for a job; a landlord can refuse to rent an apartment to someone who likes to keep loaded guns in unlocked cupboards; and a bar owner can refuse to serve a patron who is already drunk and abusive.

Human rights law will come into play only when there is a link between the burden that is being imposed or the opportunity that is being withheld, and a protected personal characteristic. Each human rights code sets out a list of protected personal characteristics. This list typically includes the following:

- age;

- race, colour, ethnic, national or aboriginal origin;

- religion or creed;

- sex;

- sexual orientation;

- family or marital status;

- physical or mental disability; and

- political beliefs or activities.

Direct and indirect discrimination

Human rights legislation prohibits both direct and indirect discrimination. A refusal to hire or promote someone based on the applicant's religion, gender or ethnic background would be an example of direct discrimination. It is direct because the decision is based on a protected personal characteristic. It is important to ensure that employment decisions are made on valid grounds rationally connected to the requirements of the job, rather than on assumptions about people who have certain personal characteristics. For instance, when a congregation is hiring a youth worker, it is valid to look for someone who is able to relate well with teens and is energetic. It is not valid, however, simply to rule out anyone over a certain age or anyone with a physical disability, as this would amount to direct discrimination. Instead, the hiring committee must identify the core elements of the job and then give genuine consideration to each applicant's ability to perform those tasks.

Indirect discrimination refers to policies or practices that are not directly tied to a protected characteristic but that have the effect of limiting the opportunities of some groups more than others. For instance, an employment requirement that successful applicants must be at least six feet tall would affect women and members of some ethnic groups more than others. A school uniform requirement that prohibited all headgear would have a significantly different impact on some religious groups than others. At first glance, these policies would not seem to be covered by human rights legislation; after all, "height" and "the right to cover one's head" are not among the protected characteristics listed in any human rights code. But a more careful look at these policies makes it clear that they do in fact place greater burdens on certain groups, and those groups can be identified by characteristics that are protected – gender, ethnic background and religious belief. (As discussed below, the height requirement would be permitted if it was a *bona fide* occupational requirement.)

Here is an example from a church setting: suppose your congregation is hiring a new building custodian. The last custodian worked Saturday mornings to make sure that, after the week's activities, the church was clean and ready for services on Sunday. The hiring committee decides to make it a requirement of the job that the new custodian must also work a half-day on Saturday. On the face of it, this would not seem to fall afoul of human rights legislation. However, what if one of the applicants is a Seventh Day Adventist, whose religious beliefs prohibit him from working on Saturdays? Unless it is absolutely necessary that work be done on Saturday, this requirement is a form of indirect discrimination, since it keeps people of certain religions from having a chance at the job. The hiring committee must think about whether the job can reasonably be structured in such a way that applicants are not disadvantaged because of their religion. Perhaps this applicant is willing to work late on Friday, after all the week's activities are done and, in this way, ensure the building is ready for Sunday morning – or perhaps there are other solutions.

To ensure compliance with the law on human rights, employment practices and other decisions that might be regulated by human rights legislation should be reviewed by a lawyer who is knowledgeable in this area.

Exceptions: balancing human rights protections with other legitimate social goals

As noted in the introduction to this chapter, human rights legislation tries to balance the ideal of non-discrimination with other legitimate social goals. The starting position of all human rights codes in Canada is that when decisions are being made in areas such as employment, housing and access to services, individuals have the right not be discriminated against on the basis of race, religion, gender, sexual orientation or any of the other protected personal characteristics.

These rights are not absolute, however. Human rights codes also provide exceptions – that is, the codes set out limited circumstances in which certain decisions may be based on, or have an effect on, a protected characteristic. The breadth of these exceptions varies from one human rights code to another, so it is necessary to ensure that church practices are reviewed in light of the provisions applicable in your province or territory. We will explore exceptions to human rights protections by examining the concept of a *bona fide* (i.e. good faith) occupational requirement. (Sometimes the phrase *bona fide occupational qualification* is used instead of *requirement*; both mean the same thing.)

Bona fide occupational requirement

All human rights codes prohibit employers from making employment decisions based on a protected personal characteristic (direct discrimination) or having employment policies that adversely affect groups that can be identified by a protected characteristic (indirect discrimination). Such a decision or practice is permitted *only* if it can be shown to be a *bona fide* occupational requirement.

The meaning of *bona fide* occupational requirement has been reviewed in a number of cases. In the context of a human rights complaint that mandatory retirement for firefighters amounted to discrimination on the basis of age, the Supreme Court of Canada gave the following definition:

> To be a *bona fide* occupational qualification … a limitation, such as a mandatory retirement at a fixed age, must be imposed honestly, in good faith, and in the sincerely held belief that such limitation is imposed in the interests of the adequate performance of the work involved with all reasonable dispatch, safety and economy and not for ulterior or extraneous reasons aimed at objectives which could defeat the purpose of the Code. In addition it must be related in an objective sense to the performance of the employment concerned, in that it is reasonably necessary to assure the efficient and economical performance of the job ….[4]

This explanation from the Supreme Court of Canada identifies two parts to the *bona fide* occupational requirement test:

- The subjective element: did the employer impose the requirement in the honest, sincere and good faith belief that it is a necessary component of the job? and

- The objective element: is there a rational connection between the requirement and the "efficient and economical performance of the job"?

Let us apply this two-part approach to a church-run school with a policy that prohibits employees from living in common-law relationships. This policy is based on the religious beliefs of that particular church about the sanctity of marriage. If a school employee is dismissed because he or she is living in a common-law relationship, the employee might allege that the policy discriminated on the basis of marital status. Since marital status is a characteristic protected by human rights legislation, dismissal on that ground would be a human rights violation *unless* the church could show that it was a *bona fide* occupational requirement that employees refrain from living in common-law relationships. To meet the test, the church would have to show that:

- the policy was established and applied in good faith; and

- there is a rational connection between the requirement (not living in a common-law relationship) and the job (working at this particular school).

The subjective element

Turning first to the subjective element: was the church sincere in its belief that not living in a common-law relationship is a necessary part of the job? Or put another way, does the church sincerely believe that having students in contact with an employee living in a common-law relationship would be harmful to the students?

The church might be required to show that common-law relationships violated its core religious doctrines. The church would also need to show that the policy was applied consistently. This would reinforce the church's argument that the policy represents a core aspect of its beliefs, and is not simply used sporadically to target unpopular employees.

This issue of consistency played a significant role in the case of *Parks v. Christian Horizons*.[5] Christian Horizons was an "organization founded and run by primarily Evangelical Christian individuals and groups to provide deinstitutionalized care for the physically and mentally handicapped, in a Christian environment."[6] Christian Horizons refused to hire Ms. Parks because she was living in a common-law relationship. Ms. Parks made a human rights complaint, alleging that she had been discriminated against on the basis of marital status. Christian Horizons argued that it was justified in placing certain lifestyle restrictions – including the prohibition against common-law relationships – on its employees in order to provide a Christian environment for those within its care. In other words, Christian Horizons argued that prohibiting employees from living in common-law relationships was a *bona fide* occupational requirement.

The policy on common-law relationships had been applied only sporadically. The tribunal hearing Ms. Parks' complaint accepted that those running Christian Horizons genuinely believed that common-law relationships were wrong and genuinely saw some connection between an employee's personal relationships and the care provided in the homes. However, since the policy was applied inconsistently, the tribunal was not persuaded that the prohibition on common-law relationships was so vital to Christian Horizons as to meet the subjective part of the *bona fide* occupational requirement test. The tribunal stated that "for Christian Horizons to avoid … liability in this area, it must be consistent in the application of its policies concerning lifestyle requirements."[7]

The objective element

As noted above, in order to show that a *bona fide* occupation requirement exists, an employer must show not only that the requirement was established and applied in good faith, but also that it has a rational connection with the job. It was this second, objective part of the test that was at issue in the case of *Schroen v. Steinbach Bible College*.[8] Ms. Schroen, who worked as an accounting clerk at a college run by Mennonites, was fired when it was discovered that she was a Mormon. Ms. Schroen made a human rights complaint, arguing that she had been discriminated against on the basis of religion. The tribunal hearing the complaint accepted that being Mennonite was a *bona fide* occupational requirement for employees of Schroen Bible College. Even though Ms. Schroen was an accounting clerk, rather than a teacher, the tribunal accepted that:

> It was generally understood and a basic premise at SBC that all employees, be they teachers, staff, support staff, or executives would involve themselves with students and regularly attend Chapel prayer meetings, attend the school retreat held each year, have students at their

homes for group Bible study sessions, attend the
school cafeteria to have meals with students and
be available at anytime to discuss faith matters
with the students. In short, everyone employed
at SBC was expected to share in a faithful way
with students espousing the Christian faith, as
that was what SBC was about.[9]

Thus, the Schroen Bible College met the objective (as
well as the subjective) elements of the test for a *bona fide* occupational requirement.

Bona fide occupational requirement based on other grounds

It is possible that a church might also want to use the *bona
fide* exception on grounds other than its religious doctrine. In
the example given above of a congregation wanting a custodian
who will work on Saturdays, the congregation is not saying
that its religious doctrine requires Saturday work, but simply
that in order for the job to be done properly, work must be
done on Saturday. If the congregation can meet the subjective
and objective elements of the test, then working on Saturday
would be a *bona fide* requirement for that job, even though it
would rule out applicants whose religious beliefs did not allow them to work on Saturday. In order to rely on the *bona
fide* occupational requirement exemption, the church would
have to show both that the requirement to work on Saturday
was imposed in good faith and that the job could not be done
properly without Saturday work.

Any church or church-related organization that intends to argue that a particular employment policy reflects a *bona fide* occupational requirement should get legal advice before relying on the policy.

Steps to ensure human rights compliance

The human rights ideals of respect and non-discrimination resonate with Christianity's emphasis on justice. Therefore, churches and church-related organizations will want to adhere to human rights requirements. David Thwaites has developed a very helpful checklist that provides practical steps for churches to follow. He recommends the following:

- providing training on human rights issues for all those involved in church decision making;

- reviewing church policies and practices regularly, to ensure compliance with human rights legislation;

- keeping careful records of all employment matters, including job advertisements, interview questions and notes of interviews;

- developing policies and protocols for an appropriate response to complaints of discrimination within the church; and

- keeping up-to-date on developments in human rights law.[10]

Human rights complaint process

Although there may be some variations from one province or territory to the next, the typical human rights complaints process contains the following elements:

- A person (called the complainant) contacts the human rights commission and makes an allegation that another person or entity (called the respondent) has discriminated against him or her in a way that contravenes the human rights code in that province or territory;

- If it is clear on the facts that no violation has occurred – for instance, if the behaviour complained of clearly falls outside the scope of the code – the allegation is dismissed;

- If it appears that the behaviour complained of might be discrimination under the code, a commission employee (frequently called a complaints officer) makes further enquiries. This includes speaking with the respondent to get his or her version of events;

- When those enquiries reveal no reasonable grounds for believing that discrimination occurred, the officer dismisses the complaint. When the complaints officer concludes that there are reasonable grounds for believing that discrimination took place, the officer tries to effect a settlement between the parties;

- When a settlement cannot be reached, a tribunal is appointed to hear the matter. The person (or persons) appointed as a tribunal must be independent of the human rights commission. (See the discussion on bias in Chapter 3.);

- The tribunal holds a hearing into the complaint. This is an oral hearing, and both the complainant and respondent are entitled to fair procedures (see Chapter 3). Before the hearing, the respondent must be given sufficient detail of the complaint to know the case against him or her. During the hearing, both the complainant and the respondent must have an opportunity to make their case;

- At the hearing, the human rights commission takes the case forward on behalf of the complainant. Although a human rights hearing is not a criminal trial, an analogy may be helpful here. The human rights commission's lawyer acts as the prosecutor, while the tribunal is in effect the judge. The respondent may decide to represent himself or herself at the hearing, but is entitled to be represented by a lawyer;

- Even during the course of the hearing, there is an opportunity for the parties to come to a settlement; some human rights codes require that the tribunal approve any settlement reached at this stage;

- After the hearing is complete, the tribunal may either dismiss the complaint or find that a contravention of the code has occurred; and

- Most human rights legislation gives the tribunal a range of possible remedies that may be imposed once a contravention has been found, including the following:

- ordering that some form of compensation be paid to the complainant;

- requiring the respondent to apologize to the complainant (Depending on the circum-stances, the respondent might be required to make the apology public. For instance, if the contravention was employment-based, the employer might have to post the apology at the job site.);

- ordering the respondent to, as much as possible, place the complainant in the same position he or she would have been in had the contravention not occurred – for instance, reinstating a person who was wrongfully fired or accepting a student who was wrongfully denied access to a school;

- requiring the respondent to take some form of training aimed at increasing awareness of human rights issues or, in the case of an organization, requiring the respondent to make such training available to its members or employees; and

- requiring the respondent to take steps to ensure future compliance with the human rights code.

Conclusion

Human rights legislation reflects the ideal that all individuals should be treated with dignity, accorded equal respect and rights, and dealt with according to individual merit. Human rights codes try to strike a balance between protecting individuals from various kinds of discriminatory behaviour, while also recognizing other legitimate social goals. Churches must inform themselves about both the general human rights protections provided by the law and about the scope of applicable exceptions.

Human Rights: Questions and Answers

Q. What are human rights codes?

A. Human rights codes are statutes enacted by the provincial, territorial and federal governments. These codes set out the kinds of behaviour that will amount to discrimination in the eyes of the law.

Q. What is the principal aim of human rights legislation?

A. The aim of human rights legislation is to prohibit certain kinds of discriminatory behaviour in areas such as housing, employment, and services offered to the public.

Q. What is direct discrimination?

A. Direct discrimination occurs when someone is denied a benefit, or has a burden imposed upon him or her, because of a protected personal characteristic such as gender, race or religion; for example, when a person is not hired for a job because of religious affiliation.

Q. What is indirect discrimination?

A. A policy or practice that is not directly linked to a protected personal characteristic might still have a discriminatory effect. For example, a school uniform requirement banning the wearing of any form of headgear looks neutral, because it applies to everyone, but it places a greater burden on those whose religious beliefs require the wearing of headgear.

Q. Are there exceptions to the prohibition on discrimination?

A. Yes. Most human rights codes allow policies or requirements that would otherwise be discriminatory when it can be shown that there is a *bona fide* (i.e. good faith) justification for the policy or requirement. For instance, a church-run school might be able to require that employees not live in common-law relationships if it could be shown that this requirement had been imposed in good faith and was rationally connected to the job in question. The scope of the allowable exceptions can vary, so it important to have information on the exceptions allowed in your province or territory.

Notes

1   Throughout this book, when we use the word *court*, we are referring to secular courts, unless we state explicitly that we are discussing church courts.

2   Nova Scotia *Human Rights Act*, R.S.N.S. 1989, c. 214, s. 4.

3   Government of British Columbia, *Human Rights in the Workplace – Discrimination and Sexual Harassment Policy Directive 3.1* (www. bcpublicservice.ca). This source goes on to state:

> Examples of sexual harassment include, but are not limited to:
>
> • a person in authority asking an employee for sexual favours in return for being hired or receiving promotions or other employment benefits;
>
> • sexual advances with actual or implied work related consequences;
>
> • unwelcome remarks, questions, jokes or innuendo of a sexual nature including sexist comments or sexual invitations;
>
> • verbal abuse, intimidation or threats of a sexual nature;
>
> • leering, staring or making sexual gestures;
>
> • display of pornographic or other sexual materials;
>
> • offensive pictures, graffiti, cartoons or sayings;
>
> • unwanted physical contact such as touching, patting, pinching or hugging; and
>
> • physical assault of a sexual nature.

4   *Ontario (Human Rights Commission) v. Etobicoke*, [1982] 1 S.C.R. 202, para. 8.

5   *Parks v. Christian Horizons* (1992), 16 C.H.R.R. D/40 (Ont. Bd. Inq.).

6   *Ibid.*, para. 4.

7   *Ibid.*, para. 57.

8   *Schroen v. Steinbach Bible College* (1990), 35 C.H.R.R. D/1 (Man. B.A.).

9   *Ibid.*, para. 55.

10   David Thwaites, "Human Rights in Ontario – the Code's Impact on Churches and Charitable Organizations" in *Fit to Be Tithed: Risks and Rewards for Charities and Churches* (Toronto: Law Society of Upper Canada, 1994).

17

Privacy and Personal Information

I might have been a goldfish in a glass bowl
for all the privacy I got.
—Saki, pseudonym of H. H. Munro,
Scottish short-story writer and satirist,
1870–1916, *The Innocence of Reginald*

A cleric always knows or has access to various sorts of information. Some of this information is personal and confidential: for example, an employee's job performance evaluation or details about a family in crisis. Church employees and volunteers also often know or have access to personal and confidential information. The legal obligations that arise with respect to the collection, use and disclosure of such information are the subject of the next two chapters.

Privacy has been defined as "the claim of individuals, groups or institutions to determine for themselves when, how, and to what extent information about them is communicated to others."[1] This definition of privacy focuses on the right of individuals to control their personal information. We begin the chapter by noting a growing concern in our society over the use and misuse of personal information, and then discuss recent federal privacy legislation that addresses that concern.

Federal privacy legislation

Perhaps more than ever before, citizens, organizations and governments are concerned about privacy issues. Their concern – even, at times, alarm – has been prompted by the ability of new technologies such as computers and the Internet to gather, store and disseminate personal information.[2] The Australian Privacy Commissioner made the following relevant comments about personal information and privacy in a 1997 report:

> Information privacy concerns the handling of 'personal information', that is, information about a particular person or information that can be used to identify a particular person. The collection and use of personal information is essential to businesses, non-profit organizations, consumers and governments: it is a very valuable resource. But it differs from other resources in two ways. It can be shared and used by more than one person at the same time, and it can be used for an unlimited number of different purposes. These characteristics give rise to the fundamental ideas behind information

privacy: that organizations handling personal information have a responsibility to do so fairly, and that the subjects of personal information retain some rights in relation to the way it may be used (or collected or stored or disclosed) by others.[3]

A growing awareness in Canada of the need to control and limit the use of personal information led to the passage of the federal *Personal Information Protection and Electronic Documents Act* (PIPEDA),[4] which "ushered in a new era of privacy protection in Canada."[5] PIPEDA sets out rules to govern how organizations may collect, use and disclose personal information in a manner that respects the right of privacy of individuals.[6]

Personal information is defined in PIPEDA as "information about an identifiable individual."[7] This is an extremely expansive definition; the Privacy Commissioner of Canada has stated that it includes such things as age, name, identification numbers, income, ethnic origin, opinions, evaluations, comments, social status, disciplinary actions, and employee files.[8] It does not include the name, title or business address of an employee of an organization.

Application of PIPEDA

The first question to ask is whether PIPEDA applies to your church. PIPEDA states that it applies to every organization that collects, uses or discloses personal information in the course of commercial activities.[9] A threshold issue, therefore, is whether the church is handling personal information in a commercial context. If not, then the provisions and requirements of PIPEDA do not apply to the church. Commercial activity is defined at section 2 as:

> ... any particular transaction, act or conduct or any regular course of conduct that is of a commercial character, including the selling, bartering or leasing of donor, membership or other fundraising lists.[10]

The definition in section 2 is not particularly helpful, and there has been little case law defining the term *commercial activity*.[11] If commercial activity is defined as "for-profit activity," then it is unlikely that PIPEDA would apply to most churches. Even if a broader definition is used, such as "any activity involving an exchange of consideration [i.e. something of value], whether for profit or not,"[12] the activity of most churches would still fall outside the ambit of PIPEDA.

The Privacy Commissioner of Canada was asked to give direction on whether PIPEDA applied "to charities, non-profit organizations, associations and other similar organizations."[13] She stated:

> Most non-profits are not subject to the Act because they do not engage in commercial activities. This is typically the case with most charities, minor hockey associations, clubs, community groups and advocacy organizations. Collecting membership fees, organizing club activities, compiling a list of members' names and addresses, and mailing out newsletters are not considered commercial activities. Simi-

larly, fundraising is not a commercial activity. However, some clubs, for example many golf clubs and athletic clubs, may be engaged in commercial activities which are subject to the Act.[14]

The Privacy Commissioner also made clear, however, that "non-profit status does not automatically exempt an organization from the application of the Act."[15] In other words, PIPEDA will apply if and when a particular church handles personal information in the context of commercial activity. Even if a church concludes that it is not engaged in commercial activity and therefore is not subject to PIPEDA, it is still prudent and advisable to develop and implement a privacy policy that meets the standards set out in PIPEDA for at least two reasons. As one commentator has rightly noted, members of non-profit organizations such as a church expect the organizations to which they belong to respect and safeguard their right to privacy.[16] Second, a few provinces already have privacy legislation that is similar to PIPEDA and that does apply to churches whether or not they are engaged in commercial activity.[17] It appears that, in due course, all churches across Canada may therefore be required to comply with rules and principles similar to PIPEDA's regarding the collection, use and disclosure of personal information.

Complying with PIPEDA

PIPEDA contains a model code that "sets out the primary rules and obligations that organizations must adhere to in managing the personal information of individuals."[18] Following is an abridged recitation of the ten principles of the model code.[19]

Note that the word *shall* denotes mandatory requirements; the word *should* denotes recommended requirements.

Principle 1: Accountability

An organization is responsible for personal information under its control and shall designate an individual or individuals who are accountable for the organization's compliance with the following principles.

Principle 2: Identifying purposes

The purposes for which personal information is collected shall be identified by the organization at or before the time the information is collected.

Principle 3: Consent

The knowledge and consent of the individual are required for the collection, use or disclosure of personal information, except where inappropriate.

Principle 4: Limiting collection

The collection of personal information shall be limited to that which is necessary for the purposes identified by the organization. Information shall be collected by fair and lawful means.

Principle 5: Limiting use, disclosure and retention

Personal information shall not be used or disclosed for purposes other than those for which it was collected, except with the consent of the individual or as required by law. Personal information shall be retained only as long as necessary for the fulfillment of those purposes.

Principle 6: Accuracy

Personal information shall be as accurate, complete, and up-to-date as is necessary for the purposes for which it is to be used.

Principle 7: Safeguards

Personal information shall be protected by security safeguards appropriate to the sensitivity of the information.

The nature of the safeguards will vary depending on the sensitivity of the information that has been collected, the amount, distribution, and format of the information, and the method of storage. More sensitive information should be safeguarded by a higher level of protection.

Principle 8: Openness

An organization shall make readily available to individuals specific information about its policies and practices relating to the management of personal information.

Principle 9: Individual access

Upon request, an individual shall be informed of the existence, use, and disclosure of his or her personal information, and shall be given access to that information. An individual shall be able to challenge the accuracy and completeness of the information and have it amended as appropriate.

Principle 10: Challenging compliance

An individual shall be able to address a challenge concerning compliance with the above principles to the designated individual or individuals accountable for the organization's compliance.

Any organization that complies with the rules and obligations in the model code will be in compliance with PIPEDA. The provisions of the model code are eminently sensible and well thought out. Compliance should not be onerous or time-consuming. The model code strikes a good balance between every individual's right of privacy with respect to their personal information and the need of organizations to collect, use or disclose that information for appropriate purposes.

Conclusion

All church organizations should develop and implement a privacy policy that complies with the model code set out in the *Personal Information Protection and Electronics Documents Act* or with any applicable provincial or territorial privacy acts. Some have already done so.[20] Even if not subject to PIPEDA, churches should ensure that a policy is in place that will protect the personal information and privacy rights of church members.

Privacy and Personal Information: Questions and Answers

Q. How is the concept of privacy defined?

A. Privacy has been defined as "the claim of individuals, groups or institutions to determine for themselves when, how, and to what extent information about them is communicated to others."

Q. What has initiated the growing concern in Canada and elsewhere over privacy issues?

A. Concern has been prompted, at least in part, by the ability of new technologies to gather, store and disseminate personal information.

Q. What is the *Personal Information Protection and Electronic Documents Act* (PIPEDA)?

A. PIPEDA is a federal law that sets out rules to govern how organizations may collect, use and disclose personal information in a manner that respects the right of privacy of individuals.

Q. How is personal information defined in PIPEDA?

A. Personal information is defined in PIPEDA as "information about an identifiable individual."

Q. What sort of information does this definition include?

A. This definition is very expansive and inclusive. It includes such information as age, name, ID numbers, income, ethnic origin, opinions, evaluations, comments, social status, disciplinary actions and employee files. It does not include the name, title or business address of an employee of an organization.

Q. Does PIPEDA apply to a church?

A. It depends, but probably not. PIPEDA applies to every organization that collects, uses or discloses personal information in the course of commercial activities.

Q. How is commercial activity defined?

A. The definition is unclear. A broad definition, such as any activity in which things of value are exchanged, would not describe the activity of many churches, and therefore these churches would not be obliged to comply with PIPEDA.

Q. **Should a church comply with PIPEDA even when not legally obligated to do so because the church is not engaged in commercial activity?**

A. Yes, for at least two reasons. Church members expect churches to respect their privacy rights, and provincial legislation that is similar to PIPEDA and that applies to churches exists in a few provinces and may someday be the law in every province and territory.

Q. **What is the model code contained in PIPEDA?**

A. The model code "sets out the primary rules and obligations that organizations must adhere to in managing the personal information of individuals." Any organization that complies with the rules and obligations in the model code will be in compliance with PIPEDA.

Notes

1   Allan F. Westin, *Privacy and Freedom* (New York: Atheneum, 1968), p. 7, cited in Colin H. H. McNairn and Alexander K. Scott, *Privacy Law in Canada* (Markham, Ont.: Butterworths, 2001), p. 11.

2   See Barbara McIsaac et al., *The Law of Privacy in Canada* (Toronto: Carswell, 2000), p. 1-2 [*Law of Privacy in Canada*].

3   Privacy Commissioner of Australia, *Information Privacy in Australia: A National Scheme for Fair Information Practices in the Private Sector* (1997) (www2.austlii.edu.au), cited in *Law of Privacy in Canada*, note 2, pp. 1-2 – 1-3.

4   *Personal Information Protection and Electronic Documents Act*, S.C. 2000, c. 5 [*PIPEDA*].

5   *Law of Privacy in Canada*, note 2, p. 4-3.

6   *PIPEDA*, note 4, s. 3.

7   *Ibid.*, s. 2(1).

8   Office of the Privacy Commissioner, *Your Privacy Responsibilities – A Guide for Businesses and Organizations* (www.privcom.gc.ca).

9   *PIPEDA*, note 4, s. 4(1) (a).

10   *Ibid.*, s. 2.

11   *Privacy Law in the Private Sector: An Annotation of the Legislation in Canada* (Aurora, Ont.: Canada Law Book, 2002), pp. PIP-7 – PIP-8.1 [*Privacy Law in the Private Sector*].

12   *Ibid.*, p. PIP-8.1.

13   Office of the Privacy Commissioner of Canada, *The Application of the Personal Information Protection and Electronics Documents Act (PIPEDA) to Charitable and Non-Profit Organizations* (www.privcom.gc.ca).

14   *Ibid.*, para. 4.

15   *Ibid.*, para. 5.

16   U. Shen Goh, *Privacy Legislation Increasingly Applied to Charitable and Non-Profit Organizations* (2005) (www.carters.ca).

17   British Columbia, Alberta and Quebec have passed privacy legislation similar to PIPEDA. Ontario is expected to do so soon.

18   *Privacy Law in the Private Sector*, note 11, p. PIP-157.

19   *PIPEDA*, note 4, schedule 1. The entire model code can be viewed at http://laws.justice.gc.ca.

20   See, for example, the websites of the Baptist (www.baptist.ca), Lutheran (www.lutheranchurch.ca), Presbyterian (www.presbyterian.ca) and United (www.united-church.ca) churches.

18

Confidentiality

Confide: A synonym of the word "trust";
meaning to put into one's trust, keeping, or confidence.
—Black's Law Dictionary

Clergy have an ethical, professional and legal duty not to divulge confidential information disclosed to them, except with the consent of the person or as required by law. Confidential information is "a statement made under circumstances showing that the speaker intended the statement only for the ears of the person addressed" or in circumstances in which it was intended and understood that the communication would be kept secret.[1] Disclosing confidential information may result in a cleric's loss of standing within the community, censure by the governing church body or a lawsuit by the person whose confidences were breached.

This chapter sets out some important aspects of the law related to confidentiality. We begin with a discussion of the duty of confidentiality and the sort of claims that might be made against someone who breaches a confidence. Next is practical advice about preventing the disclosure of confidential information. The chapter concludes with a description of two situations in which the law imposes a duty to disclose confidential information.

Duty of confidentiality

Clergy, and other professionals such as doctors, lawyers and social workers, receive confidential information and give advice as part of their work. The duty of confidentiality, however, is not limited to or defined by a professional relationship. It is broader in scope. Courts have said that a duty of confidentiality "arises when confidential information comes to the knowledge of a person (the confidant) in circumstances where he has notice, or is held to have agreed, that the information is confidential ...."[2]

Principles of fairness and good-faith dealing form the underlying rationale or basis for the protection courts afford to confidential information. Courts have concluded that it runs contrary to the duty to act in good faith to allow someone to use information gained in confidence for improper purposes.[3]

A person whose confidences have been disclosed could, depending on the facts, sue for breach of confidence, breach of fiduciary duty, invasion of privacy, or negligence.

Breach of confidence and breach of fiduciary duty

To succeed in an action for breach of confidence a plaintiff must establish three things: "that the information conveyed was confidential, that it was communicated in confidence, and that it was misused by the party to whom it was communicated."[4]

Closely related, and often intertwined with breach of confidence, is a claim for breach of fiduciary duty. A fiduciary is a person who has a duty to act solely for the benefit of another, the beneficiary. One duty of a fiduciary is not to use confidential information to benefit himself or herself or a third party, or to disadvantage the beneficiary (see Chapter 13).

A claim for both breach of confidence and breach of fiduciary duty was made in *Deiwick v. Frid*.[5] (See Chapter 13 for a description of the facts of this case.) The court found that Rev. Frid was in breach of his fiduciary duty to Ms. Deiwick, concluding that "when the plaintiff and her husband sought counseling [from Rev. Frid] in relation to their marriage problems, Frid was in a fiduciary relationship with the plaintiff. Also, that when he entered into a sexual relationship with the plaintiff he was in breach of his fiduciary duty."[6]

The court also concluded that Rev. Frid misused confidential information learned during the counselling sessions and therefore had breached a confidence.

> While it may be that Frid did not contribute to the marriage breakdown, he learned that the marriage was breaking down. He was in a position of trust and confidence and the plaintiff was vulnerable to him. The evidence supports the

inference that there was a breach of confidence
in the sense that the defendant used confidential information to foster a sexual relationship
with the plaintiff for his own purposes. [7]

Damages of $20,000 were awarded to Ms. Deiwick for
emotional and mental stress, and anxiety. The court concluded
that "I have no difficulty in finding the defendant liable to the
plaintiff in damages for breach of fiduciary duty where there
was also a breach of confidence."[8]

Invasion of privacy

Misuse of confidential information could also be an invasion
of privacy; confidential information is often personal and
private. Several provinces have enacted privacy acts that give
a person a right to sue when his or her privacy is intentionally
violated.[9] In addition, some courts have recognized a common-
law tort of invasion of privacy that protects substantial and
unreasonable interference with a person's privacy.[10] In an
American case, a pastor divulged confidential information
about a family that he learned in the course of counselling.
A Montana court affirmed that an action for unreasonable
intrusion on the privacy of another could be maintained.[11]

Negligence

Failure to keep a confidence may also lead to an action in
negligence. A hospital was sued for negligence by a patient
when confidential information about her medical condition
was posted at her workplace.[12] As a result, she suffered mental
anguish. Exactly how the information got from the hospital to
the plaintiff's workplace was unknown. The court ruled that

the hospital had a duty of care to maintain the confidentiality of her medical records, and that carelessness by the hospital in controlling access to the information caused the situation and the resulting harm suffered by the plaintiff, who was awarded $5,000 in damages.

Complying with the law on confidentiality

The law can be summed up accurately in a nutshell: Confidential information must not be disclosed, except with the consent of the person or as required by law. It is of obvious importance to identify what information is confidential. Accomplishing this can be as simple as a cleric asking whether the information is conveyed in confidence. Of course, in certain situations, such as clergy counselling or the confessional, the confidentiality of the communication is presumed. Committees should turn their minds to determining what part, if any, of their discussions and deliberations are confidential and ensure that their policy is known to all concerned. The general rule is that board directors must keep confidential all matters discussed at meetings of the church's governing body (see Chapter 2).

Church, clergy, directors, employees and volunteers should take steps to safeguard confidential information. Church directors have a positive duty to ensure that appropriate measures are in place. Confidential information should be kept under lock and key. Access to computer files containing confidential information should be restricted. Confidential files should not be left on desktops or on computer screens where they can be seen by passersby. Confidential information should be kept only as long as is necessary and then shredded.

Disclosure required by law

The law mandates the disclosure of confidential information in certain situations. The legal duty to disclose takes precedence over any church policy or professional code of conduct.

Statutory duty to report. A duty is imposed under child welfare statutes in every province and territory – for example, in Ontario under the *Child and Family Services Act* – to report immediately, to the appropriate government authority, information about child abuse.[13] It is important to underscore that the statutory duty to report child abuse overrides the duty of confidentiality and any claim of privilege.

Similarly, there are adult welfare statutes, such as the *Adult Protection Act* in Nova Scotia and Prince Edward Island, which impose a duty to report to appropriate authorities when an adult is in need of protection.[14]

Clergy and others receiving information that is the concern of such statutes should familiarize themselves with these and any other relevant statutory disclosure requirements. When disclosure of confidential information is mandated by a statute, only disclose the information required to be disclosed and no more.

Public safety exception. The Supreme Court of Canada has stated that, in certain situations, claims of privilege or confidentiality must give way to paramount concerns for public safety.[15] In a case involving a psychiatrist who sought to disclose confidential and privileged information about a patient who revealed to the psychiatrist that he planned to kill prostitutes, the court concluded that disclosure of such information was permitted if three conditions were met: 1) an imminent risk; 2) of serious bodily harm or death; 3) to an identifiable person or group. Although the court did not indicate whether disclosure was mandatory or permissive, it seems certain that in such circumstances, disclosure and warning to appropriate authorities would be mandatory.

A church or cleric involved in a lawsuit or subject to a court order may be compelled to disclose confidential information. These situations are discussed at Chapter 14.

Conclusion

Those entrusted with confidential information must take all reasonable steps and safeguards to avoid its disclosure. Furthermore, they must be familiar with a competing and overriding duty to disclose this information to appropriate authorities when required to do so by law. Difficult ethical issues can arise in this area. For example, persons may struggle with a perceived or actual conflict between their duty of confidentiality and their duty of disclosure. Determining when the duty of disclosure arises may be complex, and knowing what information to disclose and what not to disclose may be quite vexing. It is of obvious importance for churches to develop policies and procedures around these issues, and to seek legal advice when questions arise.

Confidentiality: Questions and Answers

Q. What is confidential information?

A. Confidential information is "a statement made under circumstances showing that the speaker intended the statement only for the ears of the person addressed" or in circumstances in which it was intended and understood that the communication would be kept secret.

Q. When does a duty of confidentiality arise?

A. A duty of confidentiality "arises when confidential information comes to the knowledge of a person (the confidant) in circumstances where he has notice, or is held to have agreed, that the information is confidential ...."

Q. What are the possible consequences of a breach of confidentiality?

A. A person disclosing confidential information may suffer a loss of standing within the community, censure by the governing church body or a lawsuit by the person whose confidences were breached.

Q. **Are there situations in which the law requires the disclosure of confidential information?**

A. Yes. A duty is imposed under child welfare statutes in every province and territory to report information about child abuse. There is also a requirement to disclose confidential information when there is an imminent risk of bodily harm to a person or group. In addition, confidential information often must be disclosed in the context of a lawsuit (see Chapter 14).

Notes

1   *Black's Law Dictionary*, 5th ed., *s.v.* "confidential communication."

2   A.G. *v. Guardian Newspapers (No.2)*, [1990] 1 A.C. 109, p. 281.

3   John Sopinka et al., *Law of Evidence in Canada*, 2nd ed. (Toronto: Butterworths, 1999), p. 718.

4   *Lac Minerals Ltd. v. International Corona Resources Ltd.*, [1989] 2 S.C.R. 574, para. 129.

5   *Deiwick v. Frid*, [1991] O.J. No. 1803 (Ct. J. (Gen. Div.)) (QL).

6   *Ibid.*, para. 61.

7   *Ibid.*, para. 86.

8   *Ibid.*

9   British Columbia *Privacy Act*, R.S.B.C. 1996, c. 373; Manitoba *The Privacy Act*, C.C.S.M., c. P125; Newfoundland *Privacy Act*, R.S.N.L. 1990, c. P-22; Saskatchewan *The Privacy Act*, R.S.S. 1978, c. P-24.

10   *Roth v. Roth* (1991), 4 O.R. (3d) 740 (Gen. Div.); *Saccone v. Orr* (1981), 34 O.R. 2d 317 (Co. Ct.); *Lipiec v. Borsa* (1996), 31 C.C.L.T. 2d 294 (Ont. Gen. Div.). The law is unsettled and unclear in this area. It is difficult to predict whether a particular court would recognize a common-law tort of invasion of privacy. There may be an emerging consensus by the courts that liability issues around invasion of privacy are best left to the legislatures: federal, provincial and territorial.

11   *Hester v. Barnett*, 723 S.W.2d 544 (Montana, 1987).

12   *Peters-Brown v. Regina District Health Board* (1995), 136 Sask. R. 126 (Q.B.).

13   Ontario *Child and Family Services Act*, R.S.O. 1990, c. C.11.

14   Nova Scotia *Adult Protection Act*, R.S.N.S. 1989, c. 2; Prince Edward Island *Adult Protection Act*, R.S.P.E.I. 1988, c. A-5.

15   *Smith v. Jones*, [1999] 1 S.C.R. 455.

Part IV:

Property

Every church owns some property, whether land and buildings (what lawyers call real property) or items such as money, furniture and Bibles (what lawyers call personal property). Some churches may also use property that they do not own (for instance, a congregation that has no church building but worships at the local school), while some churches may own property that others use (for instance, local community groups may rent space in the church hall on evenings and weekends). The ownership or use of property carries with it both rights and obligations, and it is a review of some of these rights and obligations that forms the core of Part IV.

Chapter 19 introduces a number of legal concepts related to property, then focuses on legal restrictions or requirements that might affect how a church can deal with its property. This chapter also introduces the law on a variety of other property-related issues, including trespass, undue influence, liability for debts, and copyright.

Two torts of particular relevance in the context of property issues are dealt with in the final two chapters. Chapter 20 discusses the concept of occupiers' liability: the extent to which occupiers (defined as those who have control over land) are held liable when someone is injured on their land. Activities that substantially interfere with someone's right to use and enjoy his or her property constitute the tort of nuisance and are discussed in Chapter 21.

19

Church Property

Property has its duties as well as its rights.
—Thomas Drummond, Scottish engineer, 1797–1840,
Letter to the Tipperary Magistrates

As noted in the introduction to this Part, most churches own some property, and some churches own quite a bit of property. This property could be money, land, buildings, pews, tables and chairs, books, baptismal fonts, choir gowns, the dishes, pots and pans in the church kitchen … the list could go on and on. Church property may be owned by an individual congregation, by a multi-point pastoral charge or by the denomination itself. Sometimes church property is owned by a corporation, and sometimes it is owned by the members of an unincorporated association. (See Chapter 1 for more on corporations and unincorporated associations.) Some church property will have been given as a gift, whether through regular offerings, a contribution for a specific purpose, or a bequest in a will. Other property will have been purchased – although the money used for the purchase may have come from gifts.

Whatever the factual variations, there are certain property issues that are likely to arise at some point in the life of the church. The purpose of this chapter is to give an introduction to several of these key issues. We start with a brief overview of what is meant by property rights and obligations. We then address the following: legal restrictions that might be placed on how churches can deal with their property; trespass and disputes over the right to use church property; undue influence; liability for debts; and issues relating to copyright.

Property rights and obligations

Property rights include ownership, possession and use; the right to exclude others from possession and use; and the right to transfer ownership or possession. However, these rights are not unlimited. They are accompanied by obligations and limitations. For instance, if I own a car, I can use it but I am not allowed to drive my car over the speed limit or lend it to an underage or unlicensed driver.[1] Furthermore, if I use my property in ways that harm others, then, depending on the facts, I may be subject to the sanctions of the criminal law, or the civil law, or both. Thus, if a drunk driver causes an accident, he or she might be charged with the criminal offence of driving "while under the influence" or might be sued in negligence by the person who was harmed. (For a discussion of negligence, see Chapter 11.)

Ownership of the car also means that I decide whether or not to let others use it. If others interfere with my property rights (i.e. use my car without permission), either or both of the criminal or civil law might be called into play. Someone who takes my car without my permission might be charged criminally with theft. I might also sue him or her in the civil courts[2] for interfering with my property rights.

Property rights also include the ability to transfer all or some of those rights to others. (As is explored later in this chapter, sometimes there may be steps that have to be taken to ensure that such a transfer is valid.) If I transfer all my rights over the car to you, you now own the car, and you now have the right to possess it, use it and exclude others from using it. Once the car is transferred to you, I no longer have any property rights with regard to it. On the other hand, if instead of selling my car to you, I simply rent or lend it to you, I have retained the right of ownership, but, for the term of the rental or loan, you now have the right to possess and use the car.

Church property: limits on decision making

Some of the property issues that a church confronts will be no different than those that arise in a non-church context. Thus, if a congregation decides to rent the church parking lot to a nearby bank for use on weekdays, the key issues involved in creating an enforceable contract will be similar to those encountered by any other entity entering into a commercial contract of this nature. In other situations, the fact that church property is involved may require that particular considerations be taken into account. For instance, there may be limits on the kinds of decisions that can be made regarding church property, or particular approvals may be required in order to make certain kinds of property-related decisions. These limitations or requirements might be found in a variety of sources, including the following.

Legislation dealing generally with religious and other charitable bodies

Most of the provinces and territories have legislation that deals with property held by religious institutions. In several provinces or territories, the relevant legislation is called the *Religious Societies' Land Act*; other titles include the *Religious Communities and Societies Act*, the *Religious Organizations' Land Act*, and the *Trustee (Church Property) Act*.

Such legislation generally sets out the purposes for which religious organizations may hold land; provides for the appointment of trustees; and requires congregational approval before land can be bought, sold, mortgaged or (in some cases) leased. Provisions vary somewhat from one province or territory to the next, so it is important to be familiar with the Act that applies to your congregation.

If property is dealt with in ways that contravene this legislation, and the matter is challenged in court, the unauthorized dealing will be set aside as invalid. Thus, in *Harder v. Lindgren et al.*,[3] a congregation failed to give notice of a congregational meeting as required by the provisions of the Alberta *Religious Societies' Land Act*. As a result, a sale of church property that had been approved at the congregational meeting was set aside. (For more cases illustrating the need to follow proper procedures in church decision making, see Chapter 3.)

Special legislation relating specifically to a particular church

There may be legislation relating specifically to your congregation or denomination that sets out requirements for dealing with property. For instance, the legislation incorporating the Roman Catholic Diocese of St. Boniface provides that the archbishop must seek advice from two members of the clergy in order to sell, mortgage or lease land held by the church.[4] *The United Church of Canada Act* stipulates that Presbytery must give its consent to a congregation's request to sell or mortgage church land or buildings.[5]

Documents of incorporation

When a congregation or other entity has been incorporated by way of documents of incorporation, these documents may deal with property matters. (For a discussion of the different methods by which a corporation may be formed, see Chapter 1.) For example, the model constitution for incorporation of congregations approved by the Evangelical Lutheran Church stipulates that the trustees cannot acquire, lease, mortgage or dispose of church property unless authorized to do so by a majority vote of members and adherents present at a properly called congregational meeting.

Internal church rules

Many denominations have developed handbooks or manuals dealing with property, and any individuals or committees within the church who are empowered to make property-related decisions should be familiar with the relevant rules established by their denomination. Examples include:

- Anglican Church of Canada: *Handbook of the General Synod of the Anglican Church of Canada*;

- Presbyterian Church in Canada: *Book of Forms*;

- Roman Catholic Church: *The Codes of Canon Law*; and

- United Church of Canada: *The Manual*.

Churches whose structure is congregationalist (see Chapter 1 on different models of church structure) are less likely to have denomination-wide requirements for dealing with property, although of course individual congregations may devise such rules.

Trusts doctrine

Property may be held by way of a trust, and when that is the case, there may be limitations on how the property can be used. Trusts and the legal duties of trustees are discussed more fully in Chapter 1; we focus here on the kinds of requirements that might be expressed in the document creating the trust, or read into a trust relationship by a court.

A trust exists when one person (or a group of people) hold property for the benefit of others. The person in whose name the property is held is called the trustee. The people who are entitled to benefit from the property are called the beneficiaries. Although the trustee holds title to the property, it is a very particular type of ownership: the trustee must use the property not for his or her own benefit, but for the benefit of the beneficiaries. In some congregations, trustees are appointed to manage the church property for the benefit of the congregation. Since the trustees are themselves members of the congregation, they will receive the same benefits as any other member, but they must not deal with the property in ways intended to give themselves greater personal benefit.

The basic rules of trust law are that the trustee must deal with the property so that it benefits the beneficiary, not the trustee, and must be aware of, and strictly adhere to, any terms or conditions set out in the trust. The only possible exceptions would be if the terms could no longer be followed (for instance, because all the beneficiaries had died); if the terms of the trust were so repugnant as to be, in the judgment of a court, contrary to public policy (for instance, if the terms of the trust required the trustee to discriminate on the grounds of race); or if all the beneficiaries agreed to a change of the trust terms. If a church-related trust appeared to fall into one of these exceptions, the congregation should get legal advice; it might even be necessary to make an application to court, asking the judge to rule on the issue.

To determine whether there are terms and conditions on how trust property may be used, the first step is to look at the document by which the property was acquired. If the document explicitly states that the property is to be used for certain purposes or not to be used for other purposes, this is referred to as an express trust, because the limitations on use are expressly set out. Depending on the clarity of the terms of the express trust, legal assistance might be needed in interpreting them. For instance, a member of the congregation might leave money to the congregation in his or her will to be used "for Christian camping." Clearly, this money cannot be used for anything other than Christian camping, but questions might still arise as to whether this requires the congregation to run its own church camp, or whether the money could be used to send children in the congregation to other church-run camps. The key point to remember, however, is that any express terms and conditions set out in the trust document must be obeyed. Suppose someone sold land to a church on the following terms: "To X congregation for so long as it remains faithful to the doctrine of the Free Church of Scotland." Disputes might arise at some future time as to exactly what was encompassed by "the doctrine of the Free Church of Scotland," but if the congregation decided to join the Moravian Church, this term would clearly be breached.

When there are no such express trust terms or conditions, sometimes courts find that there is an implied trust. Thus, in some cases in which disputes have arisen about use or ownership of church property, courts have read in the condition that the particular property in question "is held in trust for those members adhering to … the original doctrine, polity and practices of the church."[6]

If a dispute arose within a congregation about the use of church property and one group argued that the other group's proposed use violated the "original doctrine, polity and practices of the church," the court would require evidence as to exactly what those original doctrines and practices were. Depending on whether detailed records were kept, it may be difficult to provide clear evidence on that point.

This is illustrated in the case of *Chong et al. v. Lee et al.*[7] A disagreement arose between members of a congregation who favoured baptism by total immersion and those who favoured baptism by sprinkling of water. The majority (who preferred baptism by immersion) wished to tear down existing church buildings and build a larger church with facilities for baptism by immersion. A minority of the congregation sought an injunction preventing those who believed in baptism by immersion from using or possessing church property. The minority argued that the original doctrine of the church only allowed baptism by sprinkling; however, they were not able to prove this. The court held that neither the written constitution of this congregation, nor any evidence of a long-established practice, indicated that the church had a defined doctrine as to the mode of baptism. Therefore, there was no implied trust that the church buildings could only be used by those who practised baptism by sprinkling. Similarly, in *Balkou et al. v. Gouleff et al.* the court rejected the argument that property belonging to a Russian Orthodox congregation was bound by an implied trust that prevented any contact with communism.[8] However, if a court does accept that certain church property is affected by implied trust terms, those terms cannot be breached.

Trespass and disputes over the use of church property

When an individual is behaving in a disruptive way on church property, the question may arise as to whether the congregation can ask him or her to leave. If the individual is not a member of the congregation, then he or she can be asked to leave by the congregation and can be denied further admittance. If the individual refuses to leave, or comes back later, he or she would be trespassing. (One limitation on this should be noted. A church would be precluded from refusing entry to a person on the basis of a personal characteristic, such as race, gender or country of origin, that is protected under human rights legislation. Human rights issues are dealt with in Chapter 16.)

The law of trespass protects possession as well as ownership. Thus, a congregation that rented, rather than owned, its premises would be in possession of the premises, and could deny access in just the same way as a congregation that owned its own building. Most provinces and territories have legislation that sets out the offence of trespass. For example, the Nova Scotia *Protection of Property Act* states:

> Every person who, without legal justification
> … remains on premises after being directed to
> leave by the occupier of the premises or a person
> authorized by the occupier is guilty of an offence
> and is liable on summary conviction to a fine of
> not more than five hundred dollars.[9]

As this section makes clear, it is first necessary that the person be requested to leave. This request can be verbal or written. Where a sign has been posted requesting trespassers to keep off, or making it clear that certain activities are prohibited on the premises, then, in effect, the request has been made ahead of time. Signs must be clearly posted, however, and if there are several access routes onto the property, the signs must be visible from each of those routes. A person who is asked to leave must be given reasonable time to do so. If he or she refuses to go, and the congregation is determined that the trespasser cannot stay, the wisest course is to call the police, rather than for members of the congregation to attempt to eject the trespasser. While the courts have recognized that some force may be used to protect one's property, it is difficult to know ahead of time what a court will find to have been reasonable in a particular context. Furthermore, any confrontation between a member of the congregation and a trespasser could lead to either or both being injured – obviously something to be avoided.

Property disputes within a congregation

The question of who is or is not entitled to enter or use church property becomes more complicated when the individual or group to whom access is being denied is part of the congregation. Certainly, when any individual – even a member or adherent – is threatening physical harm to others, the police should be notified. It is possible, however, that the attempt to deny access might arise out of a division within the congregation that has deepened to the point that one or more factions exist, and each faction is claiming that it, and only it, is entitled to enter, use and make decisions about church property.

If one group within a congregation sued another group over use of or access to church property, then the court might take one of several approaches:

- The dispute might be decided on the basis of ownership as determined by relevant legislation. In the wake of the decision of the United Church's General Council to allow the ordination of individuals who are gay or lesbian, three United Church congregations in Ontario voted to separate from the national church. In order to prevent the separating congregations from taking church property with them, the United Church applied to a court for a declaration that, when a congregation leaves the United Church of Canada, ownership reverts to the United Church of Canada. The court agreed, based on the Trusts of Model Deed which is an appendix to the *United Church of Canada Act*.[10] According to the Model Deed, church property is held by trustees for the benefit of the individual congregation on the condition that the congregation continues as part of the United Church of Canada; if, however, that condition is breached, the trustees then hold the property for the benefit of the United Church of Canada.[11]

- The dispute might be decided through an examination of the document by which the church acquired the property in question. As discussed above, a court might find that an express or implied trust existed, requiring that the property be used in a particular way. In that case, if one group's proposed use of the land fit within the terms of the trust while the other's did not, the court would probably award the land to the first group.

- It is also possible that a court might find some other solution to a property-related dispute between two factions; for instance, it might rule that neither group has the right to oust the other.[12] Or, if a higher body within the church structure had ruled on the dispute, the court might decline to intervene. (For further discussion of the degree to which courts are willing to intervene in church decisions, see Chapter 3.)

Undue influence

Individuals can indicate in their will who they wish to leave their property to when they die. (Property that is left by will is called a bequest.) Congregations or other entities within a church may on occasion be left a bequest. In order to be valid, any bequest in a will must truly represent the wishes of the person making the will (the testator), and the testator must not have been coerced into making a bequest. A will can be challenged in the courts on the grounds of undue influence; that is, on the grounds that the testator was pressured to make a particular bequest. If it were shown that a bequest to a church had been made because of undue influence by the cleric or another person, the court would invalidate the bequest.

The concept of undue influence has been described as follows:

> To constitute undue influence in the eyes of the law, there must be coercion. The burden of proof of undue influence is on the attackers of the will to prove that the mind of the testator was overborne by the influence exerted by another person or persons such that there was no voluntary approval of the contents of the will …. Essentially, the testator must have been put in such a position that if he could speak he would say, "This is not my wish, but I must do it." A testamentary disposition will not be set aside on the ground of undue influence unless it is established on a balance of probabilities that the influence imposed by some other person

or persons on the deceased was so great and overpowering that the document reflects the will of the former and not that of the deceased testator. Further, it is not sufficient to simply establish that the benefiting party had the power to coerce the testator, it must be shown that the overbearing power was actually exercised and because of its exercise the will was made.[13]

It is important, therefore, from both an ethical and a legal standpoint, that those working within the church be aware of the law on undue influence and be very careful not to coerce or pressure someone into making a will in favour of the church. If a church member is considering making a bequest to their church, that member should have independent legal advice (that is, advice from their own lawyer), so that there is no room for later allegations of undue influence.

Liability for debts

Congregations or other entities within a church may take on any number of obligations to pay money, including a mortgage on church property, the salary of the cleric or office staff, paying a carpenter for repairs made to the church roof, or paying employment insurance for any employees. These financial obligations are simply part of the everyday life of most congregations, and so long as resources exceed or at least match expenditures, all is well. However, when a congregation does not have sufficient funds to satisfy all its debts, the question arises as to whether individuals within the church (for instance, the members of the board, council or other authorized decision-making body within the congregation) might be held personally liable.

When the congregation is not incorporated, then the board members are personally liable for contractual obligations (for instance, the contract of employment entered into with the cleric or the contract to repair the roof entered into with the carpenter). It is even possible that other members of an unincorporated congregation could be held liable to pay the church's contractual debts, if those members were involved in the decision to enter into the contract. Where a church is incorporated, the corporation is a legal entity, separate from the members of the church. In that case, it is the corporation, not the officers and directors, who are responsible for paying contractual debts incurred by the corporation. (See Chapters 1 and 2.)

When an obligation to pay arises under a statute (for instance, the requirement to remit Employment Insurance and Canada Pension Plan payments to the Canada Revenue Agency), then that statute will set out who would be held liable if payments are not properly made. (See Chapter 15 for a discussion of employers' statutory obligations.)

Congregations and other entities within the church that enter into contracts or that have statutory obligations to pay money should consider obtaining insurance that would indemnify board members and other decision makers. The need for such insurance should be discussed with the congregation's legal advisor. (Insurance is discussed in Chapter 5.)

Copyright

The focus in this chapter thus far has been on property owned by the church. Congregations also need to be careful not to infringe the property rights of others, including rights of copyright. The *Copyright Act* of Canada provides copyright protection for original works, including original music, original text (for instance, the words of hymns) and original artwork. Copyright is defined as the "exclusive right to produce or re-produce (copy), to perform in public or to publish an original literary or artistic work."[14] Thus, copyright, which the law classifies as a kind of property right, protects against unauthor-ized copying, and copying is defined quite broadly to include making photocopies, putting on a play, showing a movie, etc. Generally, copyright protection exists for the life of the author, composer or artist, and for 50 years after his or her death.

Copyright is an area of the law frequently more honoured in the breach than the observance. Most of us would never dream of taking our neighbour's car and using it without his or her permission, but this is, in effect, what we are doing if we make unauthorized copies of another's work. It may be easy to fall into thinking that "it's no big deal" to make photocop-ies of a particular song for the choir, to copy a script for the Sunday school pageant, or to show a movie for a church movie night. However, anytime a congregation is planning to do one of these things, it should check whether the song, script or movie is under copyright protection. If the material is under copyright protection, then, in order to use it legitimately, the congregation must do one of the following:

- get permission from the holder of the copyright (this may or may not be the original author or artist; for instance, an author of a book may have transferred copyright to the publisher); or

- obtain a licence through organizations such as LicenSing.[15]

Conclusion

All churches own or use property, and so property-related issues will inevitably crop up. This chapter introduces some of these issues, including: the kinds of requirements that might exist for making valid decisions regarding church property; trespass and disputes over the right to use church property; undue influence; liability for church debts; and copyright issues. Where property issues do arise, it may be necessary to get advice from knowledgeable persons, including (depending on what information is needed) informed members of the congregation, other levels within the church organization, or a lawyer.

Church Property: Questions and Answers

Q. What is a property right?

A. The term *property right* includes ownership, possession and use, as well as the right to exclude others from possession or use of the property in question. Sometimes one person will hold all the rights with regard to a particular thing or piece of land, but it is also possible to have the rights divided among several people. For instance, if I own a house and rent it to you, we both have property rights in the house – I have the right of ownership, while you have the rights of possession and use.

Q. What sort of things do churches have property rights in?

A. Churches have property rights in real property, including the church buildings and the property they are situated on, as well as personal property, including things like hymnals, prayer books, and vestments.

Q. What does it mean to say that property may be held by way of a trust?

A. A trustee holds property for the benefit of someone else, known as the beneficiary. In the church context, it is fairly common for a congregation to appoint trustees to hold church property for the benefit of the congregation. The trustees have a duty to use or dispose of the property not for their own benefit but for the benefit of the congregation.

Q. Are there restrictions on how church property can be used?

A. Beyond the general rules that apply to all those who own or use property, there may be further restrictions on the use of particular church property. Such restrictions might be found in legislation dealing with landholding by religious organizations, in legislation relating to a specific congregation or denomination, in the articles of incorporation (if the church is incorporated), in internal rules or by-laws of the church, or in a trust document (if the property in question is held by way of a trust).

Q. Can a congregation keep a trespasser off church property?

A. Yes, the law of trespass allows those who are in possession of land or buildings to restrict others' access (so long as this is not being done on discriminatory grounds).

Q. Is it wrong for people within a church to persuade some-one to leave property to the church in a will?

A. If this persuasion takes the form of undue influence over the person making the will, then the bequest of property will be invalidated if challenged in a court.

Q. How can a church avoid infringing copyright?

A. When churches photocopy music or other material, or show a movie, etc., they need to consider the issue of copyright. To avoid copyright infringement, churches should make sure that the work is not protected by copyright. If it is protected by copyright, they should get permission from the copyright holder to use it. Another option is to obtain a license that allows use of the material in a legitimate fashion.

Notes

1   This example involving a car comes from materials used in teaching first-year Property Law at Dalhousie Law School: Jeremy Waldron, *The Right to Private Property* (New York: Clarendon Press, 1988), pp. 26–31.

2   Throughout this book, when we use the word *court*, we are referring to a secular court, unless we state expressly that we are discussing a church court.

3   *Harder v. Lindgren et al.*, [1950] 1 W.W.R.. 833 (Alta. S.C.).

4   *La Corporation Archiespiscopale Catholique Romaine de Sainte-Boniface Incorporation Act*, R.S.M. 1990, c. 44, s. 2(1).

5   *United Church of Canada Act*, S.C. 1924, c. 100, Schedule A, "Polity," s. 6.

6   M. H. Ogilvie, "Church Property Disputes: Some Organizing Principles" (1992) 42 *University of Toronto Law Journal* 377, p. 381.

7   *Chong v. Lee* (1981), 29 B.C.L.R. 13 (S.C.).

8   *Balkou et al v. Gouleff et al.* (1989), 68 O.R. (2d) 574 (C.A.).

9   *Protection of Property Act*, R.S.N.S. 1989, c. 363, s. 4.

10 *United Church of Canada Act*, note 5.

11 Our thanks to Ms. Cynthia Gunn, legal counsel for the United Church of Canada, for her illuminating explanation of the Model Deed. (Correspondence between D. Ginn and C. Gunn, by e-mail, December 7, 2004).

12 Alvin J. Esau, "The Judicial Resolution of Church Property Disputes," (2003) 40 *Alberta Law Review* 767.

13 *Boghici Estate v. Benke* (2005), 13 E.T.R. (3d) 295 (Ont. Sup. Ct. J.), para. 26.

14 *Duhaime's Online Legal Dictionary*, *s.v.* "copyright" (www.duhaime.org).

15 The United Church of Canada's online *Copyright Guide for Congregations* (www.united-church.ca) provides the following information about licensing organizations for church music:

> An alternative to seeking permission from individual copyright holders every time you need to use copyrighted

music is to obtain an annual license from a licensing agency. If you find you frequently need to use copyrighted music or worship material, you may want to consider going this route. For an annual fee, usually based on the size of congregation, a congregation can use a wide range of copyrighted material. The congregation periodically reports the items it uses to the licensing agency. There is no universal licensing scheme that would cover all of the items you want to use, however, so you will need to understand the scope of any license you purchase and the range of needs of your congregation before signing a contract.

Before buying a license, you need to understand the specific limitations as to material covered by it, permitted uses, and record-keeping required. LicenSing (www.join-hands.com, and follow the links under "Church Music"), an international collective representing a broad range of mainstream Christian worship music, and Christian Copyright Licensing International (CCLI, www.ccli.com), focusing on more popular music, are widely used in Canada by congregations that frequently wish to use copyrighted material. The coverage offered by CCLI, while extensive and mainstream, does not include the hymns owned by some major publishers, and United Church of Canada congregations will find a significant number of items from *Voices United* are not covered.

20

Occupiers' Liability

Wisely and slow; they stumble that run fast.
—William Shakespeare, English poet and playwright,
1564–1616, *Romeo and Juliet*

Churches must take positive action to make their premises reasonably safe. Lawsuits for slip-and-fall type injuries on church property are one of the most common claims brought against a church. People slipping on ice in a church parking lot, falling from a stepladder while decorating a Christmas tree or tripping on the ragged edge of a carpet are examples of typical claims. Anyone injured on church property, whether by a fall or in some other way, including volunteers helping to clean up, church members worshipping at a Sunday morning service or someone attending a yoga class on a weeknight, are possible plaintiffs. This chapter first sets out the law of occupiers' liability and then describes three illustrative cases.

411

Statutes

The law in this area is governed in most provinces by legislation called the *Occupiers' Liability Act*. The various statutes are similar in important respects, and even in those provinces and territories without a statute the law is basically the same. The law on occupiers' liability is now almost indistinguishable from the tort of negligence, in that both expect and demand the same standard of reasonable care.

The Supreme Court of Canada described the goals of the Ontario *Occupiers' Liability Act* in the following way:

> The goals of the Act are to promote, and indeed, require where circumstances warrant, positive action on the part of the occupiers to make their premises reasonably safe.[1]

An occupier is defined as anyone who has control over land, including anyone renting property as well as owners who are in possession and control of their property.

An occupier is required to take reasonable care for the safety of anyone coming on their premises, including trespassers, although a few provinces limit or reduce the care owed to trespassers.[2] Injuries are often the result of a fall, but the statute applies to any sort of injury or loss suffered by a person while on the premises. Premises could include a cemetery, a summer camp, a parking lot, a work site, as well as the steps leading up to the church building and the church building itself. The injury could occur anytime someone is on church premises, for whatever reason, whether a church-related event or not. An occupier can also be responsible for damage caused to property brought on the premises, for example damage caused to a motor vehicle.

Basic principles

If someone is injured while on church property, the essential inquiry will be whether or not the church took reasonable care for the safety of that person or their property. That duty does not change, but the factors which are relevant to an assessment of what constitutes reasonable care will necessarily be very specific to each fact situation – thus the oft-repeated proviso, "such care as in all the circumstances of the case is reasonable."

In a typical slip-and-fall case, the sorts of factors courts consider include "weather, time of year, the size of the parking area, the cost of preventive measures, the quality of the footwear worn by [the plaintiff], the length of the pathway and the fact that these were rural and residential premises."[3]

The following is a summary of the relevant principles of occupiers' liability set out by the Newfoundland and Labrador Court of Appeal:

> 1. There is a positive obligation upon occupiers to ensure that those who come onto their properties are reasonably safe.
>
> 2. The onus is on the plaintiff to prove on a balance of probabilities that the defendant failed to meet the standard of reasonable care – the fact of the injury in and of itself does not create the presumption of negligence – the

plaintiff must point to some act or failure to act on the part of the defendant which resulted in her injury.

3. When faced with [what appears to be sufficient evidence] of negligence, the occupier can generally [succeed] by establishing he has a regular regime of inspection, maintenance and monitoring sufficient to achieve a reasonable balance between what is practical in the circumstances and what is commensurate with reasonably perceived potential risk to those lawfully on the property. An occupier's conduct in this regard is to be judged not by the results of his efforts (i.e. whether or not the plaintiff was injured) but by the efforts themselves.

4. The occupier is not a guarantor or insurer of the safety of the persons coming on his premises. [Numerous courts have stated that] there was no duty to completely clear sidewalks of snow in a Winnipeg winter, and that frozen patches were inevitable, notwithstanding that the occupier took reasonable care to make the property reasonably safe.[4]

This is a helpful summary of the basic principles. Occupiers are expected to make their property reasonably safe. Anyone injured on church property must prove that the injury occurred because of a church's failure to do so. An occupier does not guarantee the safety of someone coming on its premises; even when reasonable care is taken, people still suffer harm sometimes. When injuries do occur on church premises, a court will require evidence that the church had a regime of inspection, maintenance and monitoring in place commensurate to the risks. With such a system in place, a church will likely be absolved of liability.

Illustrative cases

A review of three recent cases helps to elucidate the approach courts take when judging this type of lawsuit.

In one case, the plaintiff, Mrs. Gallant, was a member of a community group that was loosely associated with the church but not a formal part of the church program. Some members of the group were parishioners of the church, although Mrs. Gallant was not. The group met in the basement of the church. One of the group members had a key to the church, and so no church staff needed to be present on the night of the group meetings. On a November night, Mrs. Gallant fell on ice when walking on an asphalt pathway toward the door to the church basement.

On the day Mrs. Gallant fell, the weather was not unusual for that time of year. It was about minus seven degrees Celsius. The previous day, thirteen centimetres of snow had fallen and been cleared by a contractor, hired by the church. The contractor did not put down sand or salt. Only a fraction of a centimetre of snow had fallen the day of the incident. One of the church priests was responsible for monitoring the safety of the parking lot and pathway and applying sand when necessary. The priest did not apply sand, even though it was apparent that the parking lot and driveway were slippery. The failure to do so was not reasonable in the circumstances, and the court found the church liable for the injuries suffered by Mrs. Gallant.

In another case, Mrs. Stacey, the plaintiff, accompanied by her sister-in-law, entered a church cemetery with the goal of visiting various graves.[5] Both women were familiar with the cemetery, having visited it many times over several decades. To visit the graves, they walked along the pathways of the cemetery. When approaching one gravesite, they were surprised to find that a stone stairway that had been there for more than 30 years was gone. In its place was a grassy slope of about 30 degrees. Instead of using another staircase a short distance away, the two women decided to walk down the slope because it was the shortest route to where they were going and they saw other people doing so. Mrs. Stacey fell walking down the slope and broke her ankle. The court dismissed her claim against the church, concluding that the church did not do anything unreasonable. The judge stated:

> In acting as she did, she took a route which was not sanctioned or intended for such usage by [the church] and which, in my view, cannot be said to have been within the [the church's] reasonable contemplation. Surely, it is not reasonable to expect that the cemetery authorities should anticipate that patrons would not use the paths provided and thus be required to, in effect, create new paths randomly simply on the expectation that persons using the premises were prepared to take chances with their own safety.[6]

Finally, in a third case, Mr. Haydu, the plaintiff, lost the tips of two of his fingers preparing for a bazaar at his church.[7] The day before the bazaar, several church members met at the church to get ready. The preparations included making sausages. The church members ground the meat and then made the sausages. The meat grinder had a "horizontal oblong shape with a funnel on the top side of it." It was attached to the kitchen table with two clamps. Mr. Haydu had used the meat grinder several times previously and was therefore knowledgeable about its operation. After grinding more than 200 pounds of meat, the meat grinder began to vibrate and move on the table. Mr. Haydu reached out to steady it by grabbing the funnel. Two of his fingers went into the funnel and were severed by the rotating mechanism.

The church was found not liable. Even though there were safer meat grinders, it was not a breach of any duty under the *Occupiers' Liability Act* for the church to use the one it did. In other words, it was reasonable to use the machine it did. The judge concluded that the accident was caused by the carelessness of the plaintiff, not by anything unreasonable the church had done or failed to do. The judge stated that:

> The duty on the occupier is to take that care that in all the circumstances was reasonable. Based on the previous experience of the other members of the congregation when using this or a similar meat grinder and based on the experience of the Plaintiff, there was nothing to indicate that this grinder was unsafe. It was certainly clear to the Plaintiff (as he indicated in his testimony that it was), that the meat

grinder had to be used with caution. The evidence fell far short, in my view, of proving that the occupier had failed to take all reasonable steps to ensure that the premises were safe.[8]

These three cases are good illustrations of the law. An occupier is not legally responsible for any and all harm that befalls people who come on its premises. In order for liability to be imposed, it must be proven that the loss was caused because the occupier failed to take reasonable care.

Conclusion

Claims by people injured by falling or other misadventures on church property are one of the most common types of lawsuit a church will face. An occupier is under a duty to take reasonable care for the safety of people coming on the property. As the Newfoundland and Labrador Court of Appeal has said, "a regular regime of inspection, maintenance and monitoring"[9] appropriate to the risks of the situation is what the courts expect.

Occupiers' Liability: Questions and Answers

Q. What is an occupier?

A. An occupier is a person or organization that has control over land. Land includes a cemetery, a summer camp, a parking lot and a work site, as well as the steps leading up to the church building and the building itself.

Q. What are goals of the *Occupiers' Liability Act*?

A. The goals of the *Act* are to ensure that occupiers of land take the appropriate steps to make their property reasonably safe.

Q. What can a church do to protect itself against this type of liability?

A. When someone is injured while on church property, the essential inquiry is whether or not the church took reasonable care for the safety of that person. If the court concludes that reasonable steps were taken, then the church would not be held liable. An occupier should be able to demonstrate that he or she has a regular regime of inspection, maintenance and monitoring commensurate with the risk involved.

Q. Can the church be held liable for an injury on their property when the harm occurred during non-church activity?

A. Yes. A church is responsible for harm that occurs on its property that could have been avoided through reasonable care on its part.

Q. Is an occupier responsible for any and all injuries that occur?

A. No. An occupier does not guarantee the safety of everyone coming onto the premises. If someone suffers a loss, the occupier will not be liable if reasonable care was taken for the person's safety.

Notes

1   *Waldick v. Malcolm*, [1991] 2 S.C.R. 456, para. 45 [*Waldick*].

2   For example, Ontario *Occupiers' Liability Act*, R.S.O. 1990, c. O.2, s. 4(3); Prince Edward Island *Occupiers' Liability Act*, R.S.P.E.I. 1988, c. O-2, s. 4(3).

3   *Waldick*, note 1, para. 32.

4   *Gallant v. Roman Catholic Episcopal Corp. for Labrador* (2001), 200 Nfld. & P.E.I.R. 105 (Nfld. C.A.), para. 27 [*Gallant*].

5   *Stacey v. Anglican Church of Canada (Diocese Synod of Eastern Newfoundland and Labrador)* (1999), 182 Nfld. & P.E.I.R. 1 (Nfld. C.A).

6   *Ibid.*, para. 37.

7   *Haydu v. Calvin Presbyterian Church Vancouver*, (1991) CanLII 499 (B.C.S.C.) (CanLII).

8   *Ibid.*, para. 46.

9   *Gallant*, note 4, para. 27.

21

Nuisance

*A nuisance may be merely a right thing in the wrong place,
like a pig in the parlor instead of the barnyard.*
—Justice George Sutherland,
United States Supreme Court,
Euclid v. Ambler Co. (1926)

The old saying that "a man's home is his castle" is a misleading exaggeration, because the law has always exerted control over what a person may do on his or her own property. In the modern world, many of the important restrictions are found in zoning and building statutes. For centuries, the tort of nuisance has also placed limits on how land can be used. This chapter briefly describes the salient features of nuisance and concludes with three illustrative cases.

Defining nuisance

A nuisance is defined as a substantial interference with the use and enjoyment of land. The plaintiff in a nuisance action is claiming that something a neighbour is doing substantially interferes with the plaintiff's use and enjoyment of his or her property. Typical examples of what may be considered a nuisance are loud noise, smoke and pollution. A successful plaintiff could be awarded damages or an injunction, which is a court order prohibiting the offensive activity. The courts try to find the correct balance between the right of a person "to do what he likes with his own [property] and the right of his neighbour not to be interfered with."[1]

To determine whether the interference is substantial, courts consider the type, severity and duration of the interference and the character of the neighbourhood (hence the pig in the parlour quip). Also relevant is whether the defendant's conduct has any social utility. A plaintiff with unusual sensitivities will not be protected.

The Supreme Court of Canada explained the role of the courts in claims of nuisance:

> The courts are thus called upon to select among the claims for interference with property and exclude those based on the prompting of excessive "delicacy and fastidiousness" .... The courts attempt to circumscribe the ambit of nuisance by looking to the nature of the locality in question and asking whether the ordinary and reasonable resident of that locality would view

the disturbance as a substantial interference
with the enjoyment of land.[2]

A plaintiff does not need to prove that the interference
was done intentionally or negligently. The court focuses on
the interference itself, rather than on how or why the interference occurred. The inquiry is directed toward whether the
interference can properly be described as substantial. A person
can be found liable for nuisance, therefore, even when he or
she took all reasonable steps to prevent it and did not intend
for any harm to occur. By way of contrast, a defendant sued
for negligence will not be held liable for the harm he or she
caused if reasonable care was taken.

Illustrative cases

A review of three cases may help to elucidate the approach
courts take when judging this type of claim.

In the first case, George Friis, the plaintiff, bought a home
in Halifax in 1961.[3] A retaining wall extended approximately
sixteen metres along the rear of his property and bordered
the property owned by his neighbour, the Roman Catholic
Episcopal Corporation. In 1963–64, St. Agnes Church was
built on the neighbouring property. Blasting was done during
construction, and a bulldozer moved earth near the retaining
wall. In the spring of 1964, Mr. Friis noticed that the retaining
wall had tipped a bit, and it continued to tip a bit more each
year until it fell over in 1973.

Mr. Friis sued the Roman Catholic Episcopal Corporation in nuisance, claiming that the construction of St. Agnes
Church in the early 1960s had caused the wall to tip and fall.

The overarching legal issue was whether the Episcopal Corporation had done something on its property that substantially interfered with the right of Mr. Friis to enjoy his property. If someone engaged in construction caused a neighbour's wall to collapse, that would certainly be a nuisance. However, Mr. Friis was unsuccessful in his claim because the court was not convinced that the blasting and bulldozing, some ten years before, had actually caused the wall to tip and eventually fall.

In another lawsuit, the neighbours of a church in New York State were bothered by the loud ringing of church bells, contending that the volume of the ringing affected one neighbour, a boy who had a neurological disorder, and another neighbour whose migraine headaches were aggravated by the ringing.[4] The neighbours claimed that the church bells were a nuisance. The court rejected the claim, concluding that the noise from the bells would not bother a person of normal sensitivity in the same circumstances. To constitute a substantial interference, the sound from the bells would have had to be loud enough to bother the average person. The law of nuisance, in both Canada and the United States, affords no protection to persons of abnormal or heightened sensitivities.

In a third case, members of a church in British Columbia were involved in a long-running and bitter dispute over the theological doctrine of baptism.[5] The church was divided, with the majority supporting the pastor. The minority group had taken to carrying signs in front of the church with messages attacking the pastor. They also videotaped persons entering and leaving the church. The church sought an injunction to prevent this activity, alleging that these activities were a nuisance, i.e. a substantial interference with their right to use and enjoy the church property.

As in every claim of nuisance, the court in this case had to balance the competing rights of neighbours, to strike the appropriate balance between the right of the minority group to protest in various ways on neighbouring property and the right of the plaintiff church to use and enjoy its property. Courts will only find in a plaintiff's favour when the interference is substantial. The court found that the signs were a nuisance because "they undoubtedly seriously interfere with the right of the majority of members to the enjoyment of attending the church and worshiping there."[6] An injunction was granted to prevent the minority group from carrying signs within sight of the church.

Conclusion

A church always has neighbours living or working on land nearby. When the church does something on its property that substantially interferes with the right of someone else to use and enjoy his or her land, the church could be sued for nuisance. Conversely, a church might make a claim in nuisance against a neighbour who is making it difficult for the church to use and enjoy its property. The tort of nuisance is one way the law helps to ensure that an appropriate balance is struck between the right of one person to do what he or she likes with his or her property and the right of the neighbours not to be interfered with.

Nuisance: Questions and Answers

Q. What is a nuisance?

A. A nuisance is defined in law as a substantial interference with the use and enjoyment of land.

Q. What is the nature of a plaintiff's claim?

A. A plaintiff in a nuisance action is claiming that something a neighbour is doing substantially interferes with the plaintiff's use and enjoyment of his or her property.

Q. What are typical examples of something that could be a nuisance?

A. Typical examples of what may be considered a nuisance include loud noise, smoke and pollution.

Q. Can a defendant in a nuisance lawsuit avoid liability by showing that the nuisance was not caused intentionally or negligently?

A. No. The court focuses on the interference itself, rather than how or why the interference occurred.

Q. **What are the possible legal consequences of creating a nuisance?**

A. A successful plaintiff in a nuisance claim could be awarded damages or an injunction, which is a court order prohibiting the offensive activity.

Notes

1   *Sedleigh-Denfield v. O'Callaghan*, [1940] A.C. 880, p. 903.

2   *Tock v. St. John's Metropolitan Area Board*, [1989] 2 S.C.R. 1181, para. 64.

3   *Friis v. Roman Catholic Episcopal Corp.* (1976), 22 N.S.R. (2d) 390 (S.C.(T.D.)).

4   *Impellizerri v. Jamesville Federated Church*, 428 N.Y.S. 2d. 550 (S.C.).

5   *Christ Church of China v. Lee*, [1986] B.C.J. No. 2685 (S.C.) (QL).

6   *Ibid.*, para. 19.

Part V:

Canadian Law Background

Part V is made up of Chapter 22, on the sources of Canadian law, and Chapter 23, the conclusion to the book.

Chapter 22 provides an overview of the three main sources of Canadian law:

- the Constitution (the supreme law of Canada);

- legislation (all statutes passed by federal, provincial and territorial legislatures, as well as all regulations passed by federal, provincial and territorial cabinets); and

- the common law (law that has developed through judicial decisions).

Chapter 23 makes explicit a theme that runs throughout this book: acting in accordance with the secular law is an important, but achievable, goal. Those involved in the affairs of the church are not expected to display the wisdom of Solomon. They are simply expected to be reasonable, careful and diligent when dealing with church matters.

22

Sources of
Canadian Law

Whereas Canada is founded upon principles that recognize
the supremacy of God and the rule of law.
—Canadian Charter of Rights and Freedoms, preamble

This chapter provides a brief overview of the main sources of law in Canada: the Constitution, legislation and the common law. It is placed at the end of the book on the assumption that many readers will want to dive straight into the topics that most interest them, and then read this chapter if further background is needed. On the other hand, some readers may decide to read this chapter first, as a foundation for the discussion in other chapters.

The Constitution

A constitution is the "system of fundamental laws and principles that prescribes the nature, functions, and limits of a government."[1] The Constitution of Canada is not found in any one document. Canadian constitutional principles flow from a variety of sources, the most significant of which are the *Constitution Act, 1867* (as the *British North America Act* was renamed in 1982) and the *Constitution Act, 1982*, which includes the *Canadian Charter of Rights and Freedoms*.[2] The Constitution is the supreme law of Canada.

Three consequences flow from the supremacy of the Constitution:

- Canada is a federal state. In federalism, the power to pass laws is divided between a central authority and other units. In Canada, these other units are called provinces. Sections 91 and 92 of the *Constitution Act, 1867* allocate legislative authority (i.e. jurisdiction) between the federal and provincial legislatures. Because the Constitution is supreme, the federal and provincial legislatures may not simply pass any law that they wish (or any law that they think would meet with voter approval). The federal legislature is permitted to pass legislation only within its sphere of jurisdiction, and may not encroach on provincial jurisdiction. Provincial legislatures are similarly limited to legislating within provincial jurisdiction. (Although we often speak of provinces and territories as though they were the same, in constitutional terms they are not. True, the legislatures of the three territories exercise many of the same powers as do provincial legislatures; however, provinces have inherent jurisdiction, while territories do not. In other words, provinces are allowed to legislate in certain areas because the Constitution says that they can, not because some other level of government has decided to allow it. The territories, on the other hand, do not have any such inherent powers – instead, they have only whatever jurisdiction is delegated to them by the federal government.);

- The supremacy of the Constitution also means that legislation must not violate the rights and privileges that have constitutional protection under the *Canadian Charter of Rights and Freedoms*. The *Charter*, which became part of the Canadian Constitution in 1982, starts with the preamble quoted at the beginning of this chapter; states that the rights and freedoms guaranteed in it are "subject only to such reasonable limits pre-scribed by law as can be demonstrably justified in a free and democratic society"; and then sets out a series of rights and freedoms.[3] These include freedom of speech and religion; protection from unreasonable search and seizure and from arbitrary detention and imprisonment; equality rights; and minority language rights.

The *Charter* applies to government action – that is, legislation and government policies. The basic prem-ise of the *Canadian Charter of Rights and Freedoms* is that the rights set out in it may not be abrogated by federal, provincial or territorial statutes or by govern-ment policy. Because the Constitution is the supreme law of Canada, any law (unless shielded by use of the notwithstanding clause) that is inconsistent with the *Charter* is, to the extent of that inconsistency, void.[4] The *Charter* does not apply to individuals and groups of individuals operating in their private capacity. Churches are not "government" and so are not bound by the *Charter;*

• Because the Constitution is the supreme law, it cannot be easily changed. This differentiates the Constitution from other laws. When a new federal government comes to power, it has the legal authority to amend or repeal any existing federal legislation. The same holds true for provincial and territorial governments; each can amend or repeal the laws of their own province or territory. It is a far more significant – and difficult – proposition to amend the Constitution. A leading scholar explains what is required to amend the Constitution:

> The general rule is that a matter that directly affects federal/provincial relations can be amended by consent of the federal government and two-thirds of the provinces, provided those provinces constituting two-thirds contain 50 per cent of the population of Canada. There are special amendment procedures relating to special matters which require unanimity for amendment.[5]

To summarize, then, the supremacy of the Constitution means that federal and provincial legislatures can only pass legislation on the topics constitutionally allocated to them, legislation cannot violate the *Charter of Rights and Freedoms,* and rigorous requirements have to be met in order to amend the Constitution.

Legislation

The term *legislation* includes

- acts or statutes (the terms *act* and *statute* are synonymous) passed by a federal, provincial or territorial legislature; and

- regulations passed by a federal, provincial or territorial cabinet.[6]

In deciding what legislation to pass, governments may be constrained or prompted by myriad political considerations. In legal terms, however, the two key constitutional constraints are those set out above: one level of government may not pass legislation that falls within the jurisdiction of the other level of government, and legislation must be consistent with the *Charter of Rights and Freedoms*.

The last 50 years have seen a proliferation of statute law in Canada. Therefore, the first question to ask regarding any legal issues is "Is there a statute on this? And, if so, what does it say?" It may also be necessary to know how a court[7] or a board or tribunal has interpreted the statute; however, when a statute exists, the ultimate source of the law is the statute itself. For example, the criminal law of Canada is set out in a federal statute, the *Criminal Code of Canada*. To determine what actions constitute criminal behaviour, and what defences might be raised to a criminal charge, we must look to the *Criminal Code*. Thus, the *Criminal Code* provides that anyone whose actions show a "wanton or reckless disregard for the lives or safety of other persons" has committed the offence of criminal negligence.[8] Although there are many cases in which judges interpret whether a particular action, in a particular context, shows wanton disregard for others, the offence itself is set out in a statute – the *Criminal Code*.

An entity such as a church is subject to a wide range of legislation, including legislation directed solely at the church in question (for instance, a statute incorporating a congregation or diocese); legislation that relates to a number of churches or similar organizations (for instance, statutes dealing with land holding by religious and other charitable institutions – see Chapter 19); and legislation directed at society generally (for instance, human rights codes – see Chapter 16).

The common law

Despite the recent proliferation of statutes, not all areas of law are dealt with by legislation. Examples include a great deal of the law of negligence, certain aspects of property law, and much of the law on judicial review (that is, the law on when a court will review the decision of a church board, committee or court – see Chapter 3). The law in these areas is found primarily in decisions made by judges. The law that originates in these judicial decisions is referred to as the common law. Thus, if we say that the basic law on negligence is found in the common law, this means that there is no *Negligence Act* that sets out the principles that courts will apply to determine whether A is liable to B for harm caused by A's carelessness. Instead, these principles are found in decisions made by the courts.

A legislature may decide to legislate in an area that, until then, has been governed by the common law. The legislation might reflect the principles developed by judges, or it might change the common law. Legislation trumps the common law; if there is a conflict between the legislation and the common law, the legislation will prevail.

The term *common law* can have different meanings, depending on what the concept is being contrasted with. As set out above, common law can be used as a contrast to legislation. In this context, the term indicates that we are talking about an area of law that is not set out in a statute. However, common law can also be used to contrast common-law jurisdictions to civil-law jurisdictions. All the provinces and territories in Canada, except Quebec, are considered to be common-law jurisdictions, despite the fact that each of those provinces and territories has a great deal of statute law. These provinces and territories inherited the common-law tradition from Britain – a legal system based historically on judge-made law, rather than on having all law set out in codes or statutes, as is done in civil-law jurisdictions. Quebec is a civil-law jurisdiction, having inherited from France the civil-law system, based on the Napoleonic Code.[9]

The term *civil law* can also mean various things, depending on the context. While the term may be used to distinguish Quebec from the other provinces and territories, civil law can also be used to mean "not criminal law." The civil law deals with disputes between individuals over matters relating to torts, contracts and property. If a person causes harm to another through, for instance, a breach of contract, this dispute would be dealt with through the civil law; the person who was harmed would sue the person alleged to have caused the harm. As noted above, the *Criminal Code* sets out the criminal offences with which a person may be charged. Such a charge would lead to criminal proceedings by the Crown against the accused. Sometimes the same set of facts may give rise to both a criminal charge and civil proceedings. For instance, if a drunk driver caused a car accident, he or she might be charged with a criminal offence. The driver might also be sued for damages, in a civil action, by anyone who was harmed in the accident.

In this book, we look at the common-law jurisdictions of Canada. Further, our focus is on the civil law in those provinces; that is, we do not, except in the occasional general comment or endnote, touch on criminal-law matters.

Conclusion

The law of Canada is found in the Canadian Constitution, legislation and the common law. The Constitution allocates law-making authority between the federal and provincial legislatures, and sets out certain fundamental rights and freedoms that governments cannot violate. In today's world, a great deal of law is set out in statutes passed by federal, provincial or territorial legislatures; however, there are still areas of law where this is not the case, where the relevant law is found primarily in the common law – that is, in decisions made by judges.

Sources of Canadian Law:
Questions and Answers

Q. What are the three main sources of Canadian law?

A. The three main sources of Canadian law are the Constitution, legislation and the common law.

Q. What is the supreme law of Canada?

A. The Constitution is the supreme law of Canada.

Q. What does it mean to say that the Constitution is supreme?

A. First, federal and provincial legislatures may not simply pass any law that they want to. Laws must adhere to constitutional principles, such as the division of legislative powers between the federal and provincial legislatures, and must not violate the fundamental rights and freedoms protected in the Constitution. Also, the Constitution cannot easily be changed. There is a much more demanding formula for constitutional amendment than for the amendment of any other kind of law.

Q. What is the place of the *Canadian Charter of Rights and Freedoms* within the Constitution?

A. The *Charter* is part of the Constitution of Canada and applies to government action only. The purpose of the *Charter* is to ensure that legislation and government policies respect and uphold fundamental rights and freedoms of Canadians.

Q. What is meant by the term *legislation*?

A. The term *legislation* includes all of the statutes passed by the federal, provincial or territorial legislatures, as well as all regulations passed by the federal, territorial or provincial cabinets.

Q. What is meant by the term *common law*?

A. The common law is the body of law that is created by judicial decisions. It is sometimes described as judge-made law. The common-law system was inherited from Britain by all the Canadian provinces and territories, except Quebec. This can be contrasted to the civil system that Quebec inherited from France. Civil law is centred on a code of law, while the common law stems from judicial decisions.

Q. What happens if there is a conflict between a statute and the common law?

A. If there is conflict between the common law and a statute, the statute will prevail.

Notes

1.   *The American Heritage Dictionary of the English Language*, 4ᵗʰ ed., *s.v.* "constitution."

2.   P. Macklem et al., *Canadian Constitutional Law*, 2ⁿᵈ ed. (Toronto: Emond Montgomery, 1997) p. 5. *Constitution Act, 1867* (U.K.), 30 and 31 Vict., c. 3, reprinted in R.S.C. 1985, App. II, No. 5. *Constitution Act, 1982*, being Schedule B to the *Canada Act 1982* (U.K.), 1982, c. 11.

3.   *Canadian Charter of Rights and Freedoms*, Part I of the *Constitution Act, 1982*, note 2.

4.   Section 33 of the *Constitution Act, 1982* does permit Parliament or a provincial legislature to expressly declare that an Act shall operate notwithstanding certain sections of the *Charter*; however, there has been almost no use of this notwithstanding clause, except in Quebec. Quebec has added a notwithstanding clause to each of its statutes.

5.   Gerald G. Gall, *The Canadian Legal System*, 2ⁿᵈ ed. (Toronto: Carswell Legal Publications, 1983), p. 81.

6.   Regulations are sometimes called subordinate legislation to distinguish them from statutes. A statute must be passed, or amended or repealed in Parliament (if it is a federal statute) or in a provincial or territorial legislature – that is, the statute is debated and voted upon by the elected representatives. Regulations do not go through this process; instead, they can be passed (or amended or repealed) by a Minister of a government department or by Cabinet as a whole. However, no regulations can be passed unless the authority to do so is set out in a statute – it is this that makes regulations subordinate. For instance, a motor vehicle statute might say that a person wishing to register his or her car must pay the prescribed fee. The statute would then state that the provincial Cabinet has the authority to pass regulations setting the fee for car registrations.

7.   Throughout this book, when we use the word *court*, we are referring to secular courts, unless we explicitly state that we are discussing church courts.

8.   *Criminal Code*, R.S.C. 1985, c. C-46, s. 219.

9   Civil law has been defined as

> Law inspired by old Roman Law, the primary feature of
> which was that laws were written into a collection; codi-
> fied, and not determined, as is common law, by judges.
> The principle of civil law is to provide all citizens with
> an accessible and written collection of the laws which
> apply to them and which judges must follow.

Duhaime's Online Legal Dictionary, s.v. "civil law" (www.duhaime.org).

23

Conclusion

Tort law does not require the wisdom of Solomon.
All it requires is that people act reasonably in the circumstances.
—Justice John Major, Supreme Court of Canada,
Stewart v. Pettie (1995)

Acting reasonably in the circumstances is the law's most fundamental and pervasive requirement. Liability is rarely visited on a person or church that acts reasonably and uses common sense to order its affairs.

The requirement to act reasonably is obvious in tort law: make sure the church steps are in good repair so that a visitor does not fall and hurt himself or herself; be sure to provide appropriate training and supervision of staff; watch the young children closely; avoid a defamation suit by minding what you say. Reason and common sense are called for in other areas, too: ensure fair process at discipline hearings; find out about and meet statutory obligations; fulfill your duties as a board director by attending meetings and asking questions; put in place and adhere to appropriate policies and procedures; learn effective ways to resolve disputes; write out good questions before the job interview; respect the law of copyright; take care not to disclose confidential information; establish a good system of record keeping; and so on. There *is* wisdom required here, but it is of a practical, common-sense sort – the wisdom of the reasonable person, not the wisdom of Solomon.

The reasonable person knows when expert help is needed, whether it be the expertise of an electrician or a lawyer. There are many aspects of church business in which a lawyer should always be involved. No one, for example, should buy or sell property or take on significant contractual obligations without the assistance of a lawyer. A call to a lawyer before any decisions are made or any steps taken can help avoid stumbling into a quagmire of problems.

Canadian citizens are not expected to be experts in the law. But you do not have to be an expert to know what the law requires of you and how to respond. The aim and goal of the secular law is to avoid causing harm and to ensure a safe and healthy society. Each church, therefore, guided by committed and careful leaders, must assess the church environment to identify risks of harm and bad practices. Risks can be reduced or eliminated, and best practices learned and followed. With thoughtful preparation, diligent work and ongoing commitment, the demands of the law will be met.

Glossary

Alternative dispute resolution (ADR) – An umbrella term that encompasses a variety of processes, including negotiation, mediation and arbitration. The aim of these processes is to resolve disputes efficiently without resorting to adversarial forms of resolution (such as litigation) that can be costly and demoralizing for those involved.

Action – See *lawsuit*.

Case law – The reported decisions of the courts. See *common law*.

Cause of action – The facts necessary to give a person the legal right to sue.

Civil law – (1) Non-criminal law. If a person causes harm to another in a non-criminal area of law (e.g. tort or contract), the matter will be dealt with through the civil law. The person harmed would sue the person alleged to have caused the harm. This is different from criminal law, in which the Crown initiates criminal proceedings for the commission of an offence in the *Criminal Code*. (2) The legal system of Quebec that is based on the French civil-law tradition. In a civil-law system, all law is set out in codes or statutes.

Common law – (1) An area of law that is not codified into statute. The principles of common law are found in various court cases in which judges state, restate and refine the law, and apply it to new situations. (2) The legal system of Canadian provincial and territorial jurisdictions that have inherited the common-law tradition from England. All provinces and territories in Canada, except for Quebec, are common-law jurisdictions.

Contributory negligence – A partial defence to the tort of negligence. It is careless behaviour by a plaintiff that contributed to the loss he or she suffered.

Corporation – An artificial "person" under the law, created by the incorporation of an organization or group. For all legal purposes (e.g. paying taxes, entering into contracts, assuming liability) the corporation is a person.

Damage – Loss, harm or injury caused by the wrongdoing of another.

Damages – Monetary compensation awarded to a successful plaintiff for loss, harm or injury he or she sustained because of another's wrongdoing. A plaintiff receives damages for the damage caused by a wrongdoer.

Defamation – Words that harm the reputation of another.

Director – A person who sits on the governing board of an organization, elected or appointed to manage the affairs of the organization, sometimes called a trustee or board member.

Discovery – The stage of a lawsuit after a defence is filed when each party gathers information about the other side.

Duty – A legal obligation to conform to a standard of behaviour or action.

Duty of fairness – Also called natural justice. It is an obligation of procedural fairness. A person whose interests may be affected by a decision of a church committee, board or court has a right to know the case against him or her, to have an opportunity to respond and to have the matter decided by an unbiased decision maker.

Equity – (1) Justice or fairness. (2) A body of rules or principles that developed as an alternative to the inflexibility of the common law and that allow a court to do what is fair or just in a particular situation.

Fiduciary – A fiduciary is a person who has power to affect the interests of a vulnerable person and has a duty to act solely for the benefit of that person (the beneficiary). The fiduciary has a duty of loyalty to the beneficiary, must avoid conflicts of interest and is prohibited from profiting at the expense of the beneficiary.

Human rights codes – Statutes enacted by provincial, territorial and federal governments that set out what kinds of behaviour will amount to discrimination in the eyes of the law.

Injunction – A court order prohibiting a person from doing a particular act.

Judicial review – A superior court's examination of the conduct of a lower court, board, tribunal or church court to ensure compliance with the law.

Jurisdiction – (1) The power or authority of a court to hear a case. (2) The geographical area in which a court has power or authority.

Lawsuit – A proceeding in a civil court, usually between two private citizens, also called an action, suit, cause or claim.

Legislation – All acts or statutes passed by the federal, provincial and territorial legislatures.

Liable – To be responsible for or obligated by law.

Negligence – A tort comprised of four basic elements: duty, standard of care, causation and damage. The purpose of the tort of negligence is to prevent careless behaviour that causes harm and to provide compensation for those injured by careless behaviour.

Nuisance – A tort consisting of an unreasonable interference with the use and enjoyment of land. Typical examples include loud noise, smoke and pollution.

Occupiers' liability – The law relating to the liability of a person or organization that has control over land (i.e. an occupier).

Officer – A director of an organization's governing board, elected or appointed to a particular position or role, such as president or treasurer.

Privilege – (1) The legal right to refuse to disclose information to a court. (2) In the tort of defamation, a privilege is an exemption from liability, i.e. a defence.

Remedy – The means employed by the courts to enforce a right or redress an injury. The most common remedy is an award of damages (i.e. money).

Restorative justice – A method of responding to wrongdoing that reflects accountability and healing, rather than retribution and punishment.

Small claims court – A court designed to provide a quick and inexpensive forum in which to resolve disputes involving relatively small amounts of money.

Tort – A civil wrong, aside from breach of contract, for which a court will award damages (i.e. money).

Trust – A way to hold property. A trust exists when one person (or a group) holds property for the benefit of others.

Unincorporated association – An organization of people who are seen by the law as having entered into an agreement for a common purpose. Because the organization has not incorporated, the association is not a separate legal entity and therefore cannot hold property, enter into a contract or bring a lawsuit in its own name.

Vicarious liability – A legal doctrine that holds one person (individual or corporation) responsible for the misconduct of another, based on the relationship between them.

Waiver – Intentionally giving up a right, such as the right to sue.

How to Find a Case

Throughout the book, reference to case law has appeared with proper legal citation. Citation rules have developed to give readers of legal writing all the information they need to find a case in printed volumes or online. To those unfamiliar with legal citation, however, it can appear to be little more than a jumble of letters and numbers. This section will explain the components of legal citation and give direction on how to go about locating court decisions in print and online.

Printed reports

We will use the following case as our example: *Brown v. Doe* (1980), 23 B.C.L.R. 34 (S.C.).

A citation has four main components:

1. The name of the case;

2. The year of the decision (or report);

3. The specific volume and page of the report; and

4.   The jurisdiction and/or court level (if needed).

Law reports collect judicial decisions by a particular court or group of courts, or decisions within the same area of law. These reports are usually first printed in temporary paperback volumes and then bound in hardcover volumes by year or volume number. Law reports may be either official (published by a government entity) or unofficial (published by a private publisher). When citing case law, preference is given to official reports.

Brown v. Doe is the name of the case or the "style of cause." The parties' names appear as *Plaintiff v. Defendant*, or, if the case is an appeal, the names appear in the order of *Appellant v. Respondent*.

The name is followed by the year of the decision in parentheses: (1980) in our example. Sometimes the year of the report is given in brackets, e.g. [1952], if the report is organized by year of publication rather than as a numbered series. (The Supreme Court Reporter is an example of a report organized by year.)

Next appears the volume number of the report: volume 23 in our example. The abbreviated name of the report follows the volume number: B.C.L.R. A list of the abbreviations for common official and unofficial reports is set out below.

Some reports are divided into series. If so, then the series number appears next in parentheses: (5th) or (3rd), for example. The series number, if any, is followed by the first page number of the decision in the report (page 34 in the above example).

Lastly, the jurisdiction and court level is given in parentheses if this information is not evident from the name of the report. In the above example, the report is the British Columbia Law Reports, so the jurisdiction (British Columbia) is evident. The court level is not evident, so it is indicated in parentheses as S.C., i.e. Supreme Court.

If you have access to a law library, most of the case law in the book can be found in bound reports, arranged by volume number or year. In order to find our example, we would first locate the British Columbia Law Reports. On page 34 of volume 23 we would find *Brown v. Doe*.

Many cases (especially those that are important from a legal perspective) appear in multiple reports. So, if the library you are using does not have the report that the case is cited to, consult other reports that cover the same jurisdiction, court level, or area of law.

Online databases

Another kind of citation appears occasionally in the book: neutral citation. When compiling the reports, the editors must be selective. As a result, not all cases can be found in printed reports. We have used neutral citations when the case is unavailable in printed reporters – that is, when the case is available only in online databases. A neutral citation looks like this:

Hong v. Young Kwang Presbyterian Church of Vancouver, 2002 BCSC 1503.

The court assigns the neutral citation, so it is permanent and independent of electronic databases or printed reporters. The citation consists of the year of the decision (2002), the court identifier (BCSC) and the number of the decision (1503). This is enough information to find the case in either of the electronic databases discussed below, which can be searched by case name, year, jurisdiction and court level. A list of court abbreviations is provided below.

However, not all cases are given neutral citations by the court. A few cases mentioned in the book are not available in printed reports and have not been given neutral citations. For these cases, we have given the citation to an electronic database where the case can be found. Preference has been given to the database on the website of the Canadian Legal Information Institute (www.canlii.org) because it is available for anyone to use, free of charge. CanLII is a non-profit organization that seeks to make primary sources of Canadian law available online. The site contains case law for the various jurisdictions and court levels in Canada. The site can be searched in a variety of ways, including by jurisdiction, case name, date, area of law, and court level. Coverage varies from jurisdiction to jurisdiction, but, for the most part, CanLII has case law only from the last ten to fifteen years. CanLII also contains federal, provincial and territorial statutes.

If the case is not available on the CanLII website, we have given the citation to Lexus Nexus Quicklaw (www.lexisnexis. ca). Quicklaw is a commercial online database with more coverage than CanLII. It offers comprehensive coverage of case law and statutes from Canada, the United States, the United

Kingdom and around the world. A subscription fee is required to get access to Quicklaw.

The citations to online databases are in a format somewhat similar to the citations to printed reporters, but they have abbreviations at the end ("CanLII" or "QL") to indicate that they are citations to electronic databases. Citations to electronic databases look like this:

McGarrigle v. Canadian Interuniversity Sport, 2003 CanLII 17862 (Ont. S.C.) (CanLII).

Deiwick v. Frid, [1991] O.J. No. 1803 (Ct. J. (Gen. Div.)) (QL).

Each consists of the name of the case followed by the year of the decision. Next comes the name of the electronic report and the reference number that the electronic database has given the case. The court jurisdiction and level is given followed by the electronic database's abbreviated name. By using the name of the case, the year, jurisdiction and reference number, the case can be found in the indicated electronic database.

Case law reports

Below are names of reports (with abbreviations used in citation) that can be found in bound volumes in law libraries.

A.	Atlantic Reporter (U.S.)
A.C.	Law Reports, Appeal Cases (U.K.)
All E.R.	All England Law Reports (U.K.)
A.L.R.	American Law Reports (U.S.)

Alta. L.R.	Alberta Law Reports
B.C.L.R.	British Columbia Law Reports
C.B. (N.S.)	Common Bench Reports (New Series) (U.K.)
C.C.E.L.	Canadian Cases on Employment Law
C.C.L.T.	Canadian Cases on the Law of Torts
C.H.R.R.	Canadian Human Rights Reporter
D.L.R.	Dominion Law Reports
E.T.R.	Estates and Trusts Reports
N.B.R.	New Brunswick Reports
N.E.	Northeastern Reporter (U.S.)
Nfld. & P.E.I.R.	Newfoundland and Prince Edward Island Reports
N.S.R.	Nova Scotia Reports
N.Y.S.	New York Supplement (U.S.)
O.A.R.	Ontario Appeal Reports
O.L.R.	Ontario Law Reports
O.R.	Ontario Reports
Q.B.	Queen's Bench Reports (U.K.)
Sask. R.	Saskatchewan Reports
S.C.R.	Supreme Court Reports

W.L.R.   Weekly Law Reports (U.K.)

W.W.R.   Western Weekly Reports

Courts and tribunals

The abbreviations for courts and tribunals consist of the jurisdiction (federal, provincial or territorial) and the court or tribunal level. In citations, if the jurisdiction and/or court level is apparent from the report, this information will not be repeated at the end of the citation.

The jurisdiction abbreviations are generally straightforward. They are:

Alta.   Alberta

B.C.   British Columbia

C. or Can.   Canada

Man.   Manitoba

N.B.   New Brunswick

Nfld.   Newfoundland (before 2002)

N.L.   Newfoundland and Labrador

N.W.T.   Northwest Territories

N.S.   Nova Scotia

Nu.   Nunavut

Ont.   Ontario

P.E.I.   Prince Edward Island

Qc.	Quebec
Sask.	Saskatchewan
Y.	Yukon

The abbreviation for the jurisdiction is then combined with the abbreviation of the court level.

C.A.	Court of Appeal
Co. Ct.	County Court
Ct. J. (Gen. Div.)	Court of Justice, General Division
Div. Ct.	Divisional Court
H.C.J.	High Court of Justice
H.L.	House of Lords (U.K.)
Q.B.	Court of Queen's Bench
S.C.	Supreme Court
S.C. (A.D.)	Supreme Court, Appellate Division
S.C. (T.D.)	Supreme Court, Trial Division
S.C.C.	Supreme Court of Canada
Sup. Ct. J.	Superior Court of Justice

Selected Bibliography

Administrative

Sara Blake, *Administrative Law in Canada* (Markham, Ont.: LexisNexis Butterworths, 2006).

David P. Jones, *Principles of Administrative Law* (Scarborough, Ont.: Thomson Carswell, 2004).

David J. Mullan, *Administrative Law* (Toronto: Irwin Law, 2001).

Alternative dispute resolution

Roger Fisher and William Ury, *Getting to Yes: Negotiating Agreement Without Giving In*, 2nd ed. by Bruce Patton (Boston: Houghton Mifflin Company, 1991).

Andrew J. Pirie, *Alternative Dispute Resolution: Skills, Science and the Law* (Toronto: Irwin Law, 2000).

Contract

G. H. L. Fridman, *The Law of Contract in Canada* (Scarborough, Ont.: Carswell, 1999).

S.M. Waddams, *The Law of Contracts* (Aurora, Ont.: Canada Law Book, 2005).

Corporate

Christopher C. Nicholls, *Corporate Law* (Toronto: Emond Montgomery, 2005).

Dictionary

John Yogis, *Canadian Law Dictionary*, 5th ed. (Hauppauge, N.Y.: Barron's Educational Series, 2003).

Employment

Geoffrey England and Roderick Wood, *Employment Law in Canada* (Markham, Ont.: LexisNexis Butterworths, 2005).

Insurance

Craig Brown et al., *Insurance Law in Canada* (Scarborough, Ont.: Thomson Carswell, 2002), 2 vols.

Legal system

Gerald G. Gall, *The Canadian Legal System*, 5th ed. (Toronto: Thomson Carswell, 2004).

Non-profit organizations

Donald J. Bourgeois, *The Law of Charitable and Not-for-profit Organizations*, 3rd ed. (Markham, Ont.: Butterworths, 2002).

Peter Broder et al., *Primer for Directors of Not-for-Profit Corporations (Rights, Duties and Practices)* (Industry Canada, 2002) (http://strategis.ic.gc.ca).

Nuisance

Beth Bilson, *The Canadian Law of Nuisance* (Toronto: Butterworths, 1991).

Privacy

Barbara McIsaac et al., *The Law of Privacy in Canada* (Toronto: Carswell, 2000), 2 vols.

Property

Bruce Ziff, *Principles of Property Law*, 4th ed. (Scarborough, Ont.: Thomson Carswell, 2006).

Religious institutions

M. H. Ogilvie, *Religious Institutions and the Law in Canada* (Toronto: Irwin Law, 2003).

Risk management

Linda Graff, *Better Safe… Risk Management in Volunteer Programs & Community Service* (Dundas, Ont.: Linda Graff and Associates Inc., 2003).

Torts

Lewis Klar, *Tort Law*, 3rd ed. (Toronto: Thomson Carswell, 2003).

Allen M. Linden, *Canadian Tort Law*, 7th ed. (Markham, Ont.: Butterworths, 2001).

Trusts

Mark R. Gillen and Faye Woodman, eds., *The Law of Trusts: A Contextual Approach* (Toronto: Emond Montgomery, 2000).

Donovan W. M. Waters, ed., *Waters' Law of Trusts in Canada* (Toronto: Thomson Carswell, 2005).

Index